LAND IN TRANSITION

LAND IN TRANSITION
Reform and Poverty in Rural Vietnam

Martin Ravallion

Dominique van de Walle

A copublication of Palgrave Macmillan and the World Bank

© 2008 The International Bank for Reconstruction and Development / The World Bank
1818 H Street, NW
Washington, DC 20433
Telephone: 202-473-1000
Internet: www.worldbank.org
E-mail: feedback@worldbank.org

All rights reserved

1 2 3 4 11 10 09 08

A copublication of The World Bank and Palgrave Macmillan.

Palgrave Macmillan
Houndmills, Basingstoke, Hampshire RG21 6XS and 175 Fifth Avenue,
New York, NY 10010
Companies and representatives throughout the world

Palgrave Macmillan is the global academic imprint of the Palgrave Macmillan division of St. Martin's Press, LLC and of Palgrave Macmillan Ltd.

Macmillan® is a registered trademark in the United States, United Kingdom, and other countries.
Palgrave® is a registered trademark in the European Union and other countries.

This volume is a product of the staff of the International Bank for Reconstruction and Development / The World Bank. The findings, interpretations, and conclusions expressed in this volume do not necessarily reflect the views of the Executive Directors of The World Bank or the governments they represent.

The World Bank does not guarantee the accuracy of the data included in this work. The boundaries, colors, denominations, and other information shown on any map in this work do not imply any judgement on the part of The World Bank concerning the legal status of any territory or the endorsement or acceptance of such boundaries.

Rights and Permissions
The material in this publication is copyrighted. Copying and/or transmitting portions or all of this work without permission may be a violation of applicable law. The International Bank for Reconstruction and Development / The World Bank encourages dissemination of its work and will normally grant permission to reproduce portions of the work promptly.

For permission to photocopy or reprint any part of this work, please send a request with complete information to the Copyright Clearance Center Inc., 222 Rosewood Drive, Danvers, MA 01923, USA; telephone: 978-750-8400; fax: 978-750-4470; Internet: www.copyright.com.

All other queries on rights and licenses, including subsidiary rights, should be addressed to the Office of the Publisher, The World Bank, 1818 H Street, NW, Washington, DC 20433, USA; fax: 202-522-2422; e-mail: pubrights@worldbank.org.

ISBN: 978-0-8213-7274-6 (softcover) and 978-0-8213-7275-3 (hardcover)
eISBN: 978-0-8213-7276-0
DOI: 10.1596/978-0-8213-7274-6 (softcover) and 10.1596/978-0-8213-7275-3 (hardcover)

Library of Congress Cataloging-in-Publication Data
Ravallion, Martin.
  Land in transition : reform and poverty in rural Vietnam / Martin Ravallion and Dominique van de Walle.
      p. cm.
   Includes bibliographical references and index.
   ISBN 978-0-8213-7274-6—ISBN 978-0-8213-7276-0 (electronic)
   1. Land reform—Vietnam. 2. Vietnam—Economic policy—1975– 3. Vietnam—Economic conditions—1975– I. Van de Walle, Dominique. II. Title.
   HD890.5.Z63R38 2008
   333.3'1597—dc22
                                                                            2007048485

Contents

Preface		*ix*
About the Authors		*xi*
Abbreviations		*xii*
1	**Introduction**	**1**
	The Issues	2
	Guide to the Book	7
	Notes	11
2	**The Historical Context and Policy Debates**	**13**
	Decollectivization	16
	Creating a Market	20
	Debates	23
	Regional Differences	30
	Conclusions	34
	Notes	35
3	**Data and Summary Statistics**	**37**
	The Vietnam Living Standards and Household Living Standards Surveys	37
	The Initial Land Allocation	39
	The 1993–98 Household Panel: Land Reallocations	48
	Overall Comparisons of Poverty and Landlessness, 1993–2004	53
	A Pseudo-Panel Based on Age Cohorts for 1993–2004	59
	Lessons from the 2004 Land Module	60
	Community-Assessed and Self-Assessed Welfare	62
	Data from the Survey of Impacts of Rural Roads in Vietnam	64
	Annex 3A: Irrigated-Land Equivalents	66
	Annex 3B: Means of Key Variables by Age Cohort, 1993 and 2004	70
	Notes	72
4	**Welfare Impacts of Privatizing Land-Use Rights**	**75**
	Models of the Actual and Counterfactual Land Allocations	76

v

	Empirical Implementation	78
	Regressions for Consumption and Allocated Land	81
	Welfare Comparisons	90
	Conclusions	97
	Annex: Theoretical Model	97
	Notes	99
5	**Land Reallocation after the Introduction of a Land Market**	**101**
	Gainers and Losers from the Initial Administrative Allocation	103
	Modeling the Postreform Land Reallocation	105
	Results	108
	Conclusions	119
	Notes	120
6	**Rising Landlessness: A Sign of Success or Failure?**	**121**
	Land Markets, Occupational Choice, and Welfare	122
	Incidence and Sources of Rising Landlessness	125
	Rising Landlessness and Urbanization: Evidence from the Pseudo-Panel	140
	Poverty-Increasing Landlessness?	142
	Conclusions	148
	Annex 6A: Model of Occupational Choice with and without a Land Market	149
	Annex 6B: Data for Decomposition of the Change in Aggregate Landlessness	155
	Notes	156
7	**Access to Credit for the Landless Poor**	**159**
	Land and Credit	159
	Land and Participation in Antipoverty Programs	162
	Why Are the Landless Poor Being Missed for Targeted Credit?	167
	Conclusions	172
	Notes	173
8	**Conclusions**	**175**
	References	183
	Index	193

Figures

3.1	Frequency Distributions of Consumption, 1993 and 2004	40
3.2	Lorenz Curves for Annual and Perennial Cropland in Rural Vietnam, 1993 and 2004	58

3.3	Households Classified as Poor by the Commune, 1999 and 2003	63
3.4	Self-Assessed Increases in Living Standards, 1999–2004	65
4.1	Distribution of Consumption Losses Relative to the Efficient Allocation	93
5.1	Proportionate Land Reallocations from 1993 to 1998 against the Proportionate Land Deficit (Efficient Minus Actual) in 1993	109
5.2	Proportionate Land Reallocations from 1993 to 1998 Relative to the 1993 Efficiency Loss, Stratified by Quintile of 1993 Household Consumption per Person	110
6.1	Landlessness and Consumption per Person in Rural Vietnam, 1993 and 2004	126
6.2	Noncultivating Households Compared with Landless Households, 1993 and 2004	128
6.3	Landlessness and Consumption per Person for Ethnic Minorities, 1993 and 2004	129
6.4	Landlessness and Consumption in Rural Areas of the Two Deltas, 1993 and 2004	130
6.5	Land and Living Standards for Those with Land, 1993 and 2004	131
6.6	Share of Annual Cropland That Is Irrigated, 1998 and 2004	132
6.7	Land-Quality Gradients as Assessed by Commune Authorities, 1998 and 2004	132
6.8	Incidence of Market-Based Land Transactions, 1994–2004	133
6.9	Incidence of Land Selling, 1997 and 2003	134
6.10	Incidence of Land Buying	134
6.11	Sources of Land in Rural Vietnam, 2004	135
6.12	Incidence of Land Titles Based on the Vietnam Household Living Standards Survey, 2004	135
6.13	Incidence of Land Titles Based on the Survey of Impacts of Rural Roads in Vietnam, 1997 and 2003	136
6.14	Wage Earners by Household Consumption per Person, 1993 and 2004	137
6.15	Wage Earners by Household Consumption per Person in the Two Deltas, 1993 and 2004	138
6.16	Landlessness Rates by National Age Cohorts, 1993 and 2004	141
6.17	Changes in Landlessness Rate and Urbanization Rate, 1993–2004	142
6A.1	Functions Used in the Theoretical Analysis $(g_1(A_0) = g_0(A_0))$	152

7.1	Perceived Credit Constraint, 1993 and 2003	160
7.2	Formal Credit Use by Consumption, 1993 and 2004	162
7.3	Use of Informal Credit Sources, 1993 and 2004	163
7.4	Participation in Targeted Antipoverty Programs, 2004	165
7.5	Incidence of Participation in Antipoverty Programs in Rural Mekong Delta, 2004	166
7.6	Knowledge about the Antipoverty Programs, 2004	169
7.7	Impacts of the Antipoverty Programs on Community-Assessed and Subjective Welfare, 2004	171
7.8	Impacts of Antipoverty Programs, by Land Status	172

Tables

3.1	Variable Definitions and Descriptive Statistics, 1993	45
3.2	Variable Definitions and Summary Statistics, 1993–98	49
3.3	Poverty, Inequality, and Landholding Status in Rural Vietnam	54
3.4	Poverty, Inequality, and Landholding Status, by Region	56
3A.1	Determinants of Farm Profits	68
3B.1	Means of Key Variables by Age Cohort, 1993 and 2004	70
4.1	Reduced-Form Regressions for Consumption	82
4.2	Determinants of Consumption	84
4.3	Actual Land Allocations Compared to Consumption-Efficient Allocations	87
4.4	Mean Consumption, Inequality, and Poverty under Alternative Land Allocations	91
4.5	Mean Consumption, Inequality, and Poverty with Mobility between Communes	96
5.1	Proportionate Gain in Allocated Annual Agricultural Land, 1993–98	112
5.2	Effects of Adding Controls on the Partial Adjustment Coefficients	113
5.3	Determinants of Changes in Allocated Annual Agricultural Land	114
5.4	Disposal of Allocated Land	118
6.1	Decomposition of the Change in Aggregate Landlessness, 1993–2004	139
6.2	Pseudo-Panel Data Regressions for the Changes in Landlessness and Urbanization as Functions of 1993 Characteristics	143
6.3	Panel Data Regressions for Change in Log Consumption per Person, 1993–98	148
6B.1	Data for Decomposition of the Change in Aggregate Landlessness	155

Preface

No thoughtful observer can fail to be struck by the size and potential welfare significance of the legal reforms and other institutional changes that are required to transform a control economy into a market economy. The stakes are particularly high when it is an economy in which the bulk of the population lives in extreme poverty. One motivation for us in undertaking this research was to understand the impacts on living standards of the dramatic economic changes that have been going on in rural Vietnam. Vietnam has arguably gone further and faster than any other developing socialist economy in implementing market-based reforms to the key rural institutions determining how the main nonlabor asset of the poor, agricultural land, is allocated across households. Have these reforms promoted greater efficiency? If so, did the efficiency gains come at a cost to equity? On balance, was poverty reduced? We hope that this book will help answer these questions.

There was another motivation for us: a desire to do something better from a methodological point of view than what is typically on offer for assessing the poverty impacts of economywide changes, including structural reforms. One can hardly be happy with "impact assessments" that rely on either anecdotes from observer accounts of uncertain veracity or highly aggregated "off-the-shelf" economic models of uncertain empirical relevance to the specific setting. Finding something credible between these extremes is not easy. We believe, however, that much more can be learned about economywide reforms from the careful analysis of household surveys, especially when that analysis is guided by both economic theory and knowledge of the historical and social contexts. That is what we hope to demonstrate in this book.

In writing *Land in Transition*, we have assumed familiarity with economics, but we have also tried to make the exposition more accessible than the typical journal articles in economics. In particular, we provide extra detail on the steps taken in the analysis, and we relegate more technically demanding material to annexes. The book draws on material from some of our more academic papers on these topics—notably Ravallion and van de Walle

(2004, 2006, 2008)—but it goes well beyond those papers in a number of areas and aims to provide a unified treatment of the topic.

We have benefited from the help of many people and institutions. The book was largely written at the World Bank, where the collegiate and stimulating intellectual environment of the Bank's research department has been invaluable, as in all our work. We got the idea for this project during an enjoyable and productive visit at the Department of Economics, University of Toulouse. For useful discussions and comments on our previous papers on the subject, our thanks go to George Akerlof, Haroon Akram-Lodhi, Bob Baulch, Quang Binh, Klaus Deininger, Quy-Toan Do, Jean-Yves Duclos, Eric Edmonds, Gershon Feder, Andrew Foster, Emanuela Galasso, Paul Glewwe, Karla Hoff, Luc Duc Khai, Jean-Jacques Laffont, Mai Lan Lam, David Levine, Michael Lipton, Alice Mesnard, Dilip Mookherjee, Rinku Murgai, Pham Quang Nam, Pham Thi Lan, Martin Rama, Vijayendra Rao, Dinh Duc Sinh, William Smith, Rob Swinkels, Johan Swinnen, Tomomi Tanaka, Carrie Turk, Chris Udry, and participants at presentations at the Vietnam Academy of Social Sciences, the National Economics University (Hanoi), the University of Massachusetts, DELTA Paris, Laval University, the University of California–Berkeley, the McArthur Foundation Research Network on Inequality, the University of Michigan, Michigan State University, Yale University, the University of Minnesota, the University of Melbourne, and the World Bank.

The publisher's anonymous referees made many useful comments on the manuscript. The able research assistance of Hai Anh Dang, Tomomi Tanaka, and Silvia Redaelli is also gratefully acknowledged. Important acknowledgments go to the World Bank's Research Committee and the Bank's Poverty and Social Impact Analysis initiative; without their support, this volume would not exist. However, we alone take responsibility for the views expressed here, which need not reflect those of the World Bank or any affiliated organization.

Martin Ravallion
Dominique van de Walle

About the Authors

Martin Ravallion is director of the World Bank's Development Research Group. He holds an MSc and a PhD in economics from the London School of Economics and has taught economics at a number of universities. He has held various positions in the Bank since joining the staff in 1988. His main research interests over the past 25 years have concerned poverty and the policies for fighting it. He has advised numerous governments and international agencies on this topic, and he has written extensively on this and other subjects in economics, including three books and over 170 papers in scholarly journals and edited volumes. He currently serves on the editorial boards of 10 economics journals, is a senior fellow of the Bureau for Research in Economic Analysis of Development, a founding council member of the Society for the Study of Economic Inequality, and he serves on the advisory board of the International Poverty Reduction Center in China.

Dominique van de Walle is a lead economist in the World Bank's Gender and Development Group. She holds an MSc in economics from the London School of Economics and a PhD in economics from the Australian National University, and began her career at the Bank as a member of the core team that produced the 1990 *World Development Report: Poverty.* Her research interests are in the general area of poverty and public policy and public expenditures. She has worked in numerous countries including Argentina, Hungary, Laos, Morocco, Tunisia, Vietnam, Yemen, and Zimbabwe. The bulk of her recent research has been on Vietnam covering poverty, rural development, infrastructure and poverty (rural roads and irrigation), impact evaluation, and safety nets.

Abbreviations

CBG	credit-borrowing group
D	dong (Vietnamese currency)
DD	difference-in-difference
GSO	General Statistical Office
HEPR	Hunger Eradication and Poverty Reduction (Program)
ITB	indicator-targeting bias
LSMS	Living Standards Measurement Study
LTT	Land-to-the-Tiller (program)
LTU	long-term-use (land)
LUC	land-use certificate
MLD	mean log deviation
NGO	nongovernmental organization
NLF	National Liberation Front
OLS	ordinary least squares
PILE	poverty-increasing landlessness effect
SIRRV	Survey of Impacts of Rural Roads in Vietnam
SOE	state-owned enterprise
VHLSS	Vietnam Household Living Standards Survey
VLSS	Vietnam Living Standards Survey
VPU	Vietnam Peasant Union

1

Introduction

The policy reforms called for in the transition from a socialist command economy to a developing market economy bring both opportunities and risks to a country's citizens. In poor economies, the initial focus of reform efforts is naturally the rural sector, which is where one finds the bulk of the population and almost all the poor. Economic development will typically entail moving many rural households out of farming into more remunerative (urban and rural) nonfarm activities. Reforms that shift the rural economy from the relatively rigid, control-based farming institutions found under socialist agriculture to a more flexible, market-based model in which production incentives are strong can thus play an important role in the process of economic growth.[1] However, such reforms present a major challenge to policy makers, who are concerned that they will generate socially unacceptable inequalities in land and other dimensions relevant to people's living standards.

The two largest transition economies of East Asia, China and Vietnam, undertook truly major institutional reforms to their rural economies in the 1980s and 1990s. Both countries saw rapid poverty reduction in the wake of those reforms. In Vietnam, the poverty rate fell from 57 percent to 20 percent over the period 1993 to 2004 (World Bank 2005).[2] In China, the poverty rate fell from 53 percent in 1981 (only shortly after reforms began) to 22 percent in 1991 and 8 percent in 2001 (Ravallion and Chen 2007). Rural economic growth has been the main driving force in poverty reduction in both countries.[3] Of course, simply observing that poverty incidence fell following reforms does not tell us that those reforms were the reason. Many other things were happening at the same time in both economies. The role agrarian reforms played in the success of these countries against poverty remains far from clear.

This book studies how the changes in land institutions and land allocation required for Vietnam's agrarian transition affected people's living standards—notably that of the country's rural poor. *Living standards* means household command over commodities, as measured by consumption. (The terms *welfare* and *living standards* are used interchangeably.) The rest of this chapter first reviews the specific issues at stake and then provides an overview of the book's contents.

The Issues

In less than one lifetime, China and Vietnam radically reformed their rural economies, first collectivizing agriculture and then decollectivizing it. This book is concerned with the welfare impacts of Vietnam's rural land reforms from decollectivization on, although it comments at times on similarities and dissimilarities with China.

After Vietnam's victory against the French in the War of Independence in 1954, land reform and redistribution figured prominently in the agendas of Vietnam's leaders in both the North and the South. North Vietnam initially redistributed agricultural land in what appears to have been (according to the historical record) a relatively equitable manner across households. But this situation of a relatively equitable "family farm economy" did not last long. The collectivization of farming came in the late 1950s in the country's North. Multiple land reform and redistribution programs were also pursued in the South, often at cross-purposes, both prepartition and postpartition, as well as during the war with the United States. The end result appears to have been uneven geographically within the South, with tenants and poor farmers gaining in some localities and large landlords maintaining the upper hand in others. At the country's reunification in 1975, some redistribution of large landholdings was implemented before attempts were made to also collectivize the South. Yet only 11 years later and three decades after collectivization began in the North, Vietnamese policy makers had come to the view that, by and large, collectivized farming was inefficient, and so the pendulum swung back to family farming.

The switch from a socialist control economy to a regulated market economy officially began with the *Doi Moi* (renovation) program of 1986.[4] Two years later, the government introduced the 1988 Land Law, which mandated the breakup of the agricultural collectives—nearly 10 years after China's decollectivization.[5] It was the first major step in agrarian reform, namely, to transfer decision-making powers over farm inputs and outputs to households and to free up input and output markets.

This entailed what was surely one of the most radical land reforms in modern times. The bulk (80 to 85 percent) of the country's agricultural land area was scheduled for effective privatization over a relatively short period. Initially, the collectives and local cadres still set production quotas and allocated land across households for fixed periods; households were not free to transfer, exchange, or sell their allocated land, but they did become the residual claimants on all output in excess of the contracted quotas. Those farmers with a surplus were free to sell their output at market prices. This reform was similar to China's "household responsibility system" introduced in the late 1970s.[6] Soon after, however, Vietnam took the further step of abandoning the production quotas (in 1989, a number of years before China took this step) and allowing a private market in agricultural output. In a matter of only a few years, Vietnam had gone from a highly controlled collective-farming system to the type of free-market economy in farm outputs found in nonsocialist economies.

While much has been written about these agrarian reforms in both China and Vietnam, the literature tells very little about the welfare distributional impacts of these truly major economic changes. In the case of China, Fan (1991) and Lin (1992) have argued that by linking rewards to effort and thus improving farmers' incentives, China's decollectivization significantly enhanced agricultural productivity. However, as for Vietnam, the literature for China has not assessed the welfare distributional outcomes of the assignment of land-use rights at decollectivization. Could higher efficiency gains have been achieved with some other allocation? What would the implications have been for equity?

Subsequent poverty reduction depended crucially on the success of this first stage of agrarian reform. A highly unequal postreform allocation of land assets would have risked jeopardizing prospects of higher agricultural outputs for key crops (where scale economies in marketing and distribution are minimal, such as rice), and it would also have meant that the growth that did occur had less impact on poverty than it could have. Naturally, when the poor have a small share of the aggregate land available, they tend to have a small share in the aggregate output gains over time.[7] At the other extreme, a highly equal allocation—that ignores the differing productive capabilities of households—might well have jeopardized economic efficiency to the point of famine. With its food shortages and low productivity, Vietnam under collectivization is itself a telling example of the huge social costs that excessive emphasis on equality can bring.

The classic economic arguments in favor of redistributive land reform in market economies are based on the proposition that market imperfections entail that large farms use too little labor relative to capital, while the reverse is true for small farms.[8] In a market economy setting, the resistance of rural landlords with large holdings is the main impediment to achieving efficiency-enhancing redistributive land reforms.

This model is clearly not applicable to either China or Vietnam at the time of their decollectivization. In their case, the role of the landlords was essentially played by the local cadres who ran the collectives and stood to lose from the reform. The central governments of both countries had little choice but to decentralize the process of decollectivization and land allocation to households, assigning responsibility to the commune level. The center could not control the local commune authorities, who were (naturally) much better informed about local conditions. With high costs of acquiring the information needed to control land assignment locally—recognizing that local agents may well have little sympathy for the center's aims—the center faced an accountability problem in this decentralized reform.[9] Malarney (1997: 900) describes well the problem faced by the reformers:

> [G]iven the institutional dominance of the Communist Party, local politicians with party backgrounds, which is to say all, are compelled by the party to be impartial and committed to official policies; yet, as politicians drawn from local kin and community, they are also pressured to nurture interpersonal relations, selectively avoid official dictates, and use their positions to bring advantages to kin and/or co-residents.

The cooperation of local cadres was thus essential if the reform was to succeed. In principle, the outcomes from this decentralized reform could range from an equitable allocation of land (at least within communes) to a highly inequitable allocation that favored the cadres and their friends and families.

It is now well known that agricultural productivity increased appreciably on switching back to the family farm model. After decades of decline, or at best stagnation, food-grain availability per capita started to rise on a persistent trend after 1988 (see, for example, Akram-Lodhi 2004, 2005: figure 1). Breaking up the collectives and returning to family farming quickly put an end to Vietnam's food crisis. However, given the poor incentives for production in the collective system, it is likely that almost any assignment of land would have increased aggregate output. Indeed, outcomes under the collectives are not a particularly interesting counterfactual for judging the performance of Vietnam's decollectivization. Instead, we ask: Did this reform bring Vietnam closer to the equitable allocation of land across households that had been aimed for under the redistributive land reforms introduced immediately after the War of Independence? If so, did this allocation come at a large cost to aggregate efficiency when judged relative to a competitive market in land?

Agrarian policies in China and Vietnam diverged from the late 1980s. Decollectivization had not initially been accompanied by the introduction of a free market in land in either country. Indeed, in China, the cadres and collectives have largely retained their powers in setting quotas and allocating (and reallocating) land.[10] There have been concerns about the efficiency costs of China's nonmarket land allocation (see, for example, Brümmer, Glauben, and Lu 2006; Carter and Estrin 2001; Jacoby, Li, and Rozelle 2002; Li, Rozelle, and Brandt 1998). While freeing up land markets is expected to promote economic efficiency, policy makers have worried that it would undo socialism by re-creating a rural proletariat—a class of poor rural workers. This concern has inhibited liberalizing agricultural land markets in China, despite the likely efficiency gains.

By contrast, Vietnam embarked on this seemingly risky second stage of land reform and established de facto private ownership of agricultural land. Five years after the first set of reforms in 1988—whereby agriculture in Vietnam was decollectivized, land was allocated to households by administrative means, and output markets were liberalized—legal reforms were undertaken to support the emergence of a land market. The 1993 Land Law introduced official land titles and permitted land transactions for the first time since communist rule began. Land remained the property of the state, but usage rights could be legally transferred, exchanged, mortgaged, and inherited. A further (much debated) resolution in 1998 removed restrictions on the size of landholdings and on the hiring of agricultural labor.

Economic efficiency was clearly the primary objective of these reforms. Without a market mechanism to guide the land allocation process at the time of decollectivization, inefficiencies in the allocation of land could be expected, with some households having too much land relative to an efficient allocation and some having too little. In response to those inefficiencies, the second stage of Vietnam's agrarian transition entailed reforming land laws to create the institutional framework for a free market in agricultural land-use rights. Having removed legal obstacles to buying and selling land-use rights, the government expected that land would be reallocated to eliminate the initial inefficiencies in the administrative assignment achieved at decollectivization.

Freeing up agricultural land markets was a risky reform. The outcomes are far from obvious on a priori grounds. Land was clearly not the only input for which the market was missing or imperfect. As a stylized fact, other factor markets were still poorly developed, which was likely to limit the efficiency gains from freeing up land transactions alone. Pervasive market failures fueled by imperfect information and high transaction costs could well have stalled the process of efficiency-enhancing land reallocations during the transition. And there have been concerns about the possibilities of rising inequity in the wake of these reforms. Since these reforms, there have been signs of sharply rising rural landlessness, which have fueled much debate about the wisdom of Vietnam's reforms.

The outcomes of this second stage of land reform in Vietnam are clearly of interest to China. Although China has not followed Vietnam in liberalizing the exchange of agricultural land-use rights, the issue has been much debated within China at the highest levels of policy making.[11] As in Vietnam, proponents of a greater reliance on markets in rural land allocation hope that land will then be reallocated to more efficient users and that inefficient farmers will switch to (rural or urban) nonfarm activities. And, as in Vietnam, there are concerns in China that local officials and elites will subvert the process and that the gains from a market will be unfairly distributed among farmers, with some becoming, in due course, landless and impoverished.

The local state has continued to play an active role during the agrarian transition in Vietnam after the legal changes needed to allow a free market in land-use rights. It is an open question whether the continuing exercise of communal control over land has been synergistic with the new market forces or opposed to them. Possibly the local political economy operated to encourage otherwise sluggish land reallocation to more efficient users.[12] Or it may have worked against an efficient agrarian transition, given risk-market failures and limitations on the set of redistributive instruments. Resistance to the transition on the part of local cadres may then be interpreted as a form of social protection, recognizing the welfare risks that a free market in land entails. Or one might argue that the frictions to the agrarian transition stemming from the local political economy worked against both greater equity and efficiency; while socialism may have left ingrained preferences for distributive justice, the new possibilities for capture by budding local elites—well connected to the local state authorities—presumably would not have gone unnoticed.

Assessing the welfare impacts of such an economywide reform is never going to be easy. The first step is to be clear on the objective against which success is to be judged. We take the primary objective of the reforms in this setting to be raising absolute levels of living, as reflected in command over commodities. When an assumption is needed about what trade-offs are allowed between welfare gains at different initial levels of living, we assume that highest weight is given to gains for the poorest, as reflected (for example) in a standard measure of absolute poverty.[13] Note that this characterization of the objectives of policy does not attach a value to equity independent of the measured level of poverty, but a reform's impacts on poverty will depend on both its efficiency and its equity impacts. In essence, the impact on poverty defines the equity-efficiency trade-off one is willing to accept. While the impact on the absolute levels of living of the poor is taken to be the main measure of success, we also acknowledge the heterogeneity in impacts of these reforms, which can have both losers and gainers at any given level of preintervention welfare.

But how is performance against that objective to be assessed? One does not have the enormous informational advantage of being able to observe nonparticipants in the reform at the same time as one observes participants. The lack of a comparison group means that one must rely more heavily on economic theory to infer the counterfactual of what the economy would have looked like without the institutional changes of interest and to assess which types of households are likely to gain and which are likely to lose. While we have little choice but to use methods of analysis that make many assumptions about how the economy works, we want the assumptions made to be explicit and tailored to the specifics of the setting. We offer a set of methods for this purpose, drawing on the tool kit of theories and empirical methods of modern economics. By providing a set of tools and case studies in their application, we hope that this book will help stimulate future efforts in the counterfactual analysis of the poverty impacts of economywide reforms and structural changes.

Guide to the Book

Chapter 2 begins with an overview of the historical context for our study and a review of the ongoing debates on land markets in Vietnam and elsewhere in East Asia. Chapter 3 then discusses our data, primarily drawn from four nationally representative household surveys spanning the period 1993 to 2004. That chapter also provides some key summary statistics, calculated using those data, on the changes in poverty, inequality, and landlessness over time, which we return to often later in the volume.

Turning to the reforms, chapter 4 offers an assessment of the welfare distributional outcomes, from both an efficiency and an equity perspective, of the assignment of land-use rights achieved by Vietnam's decollectivization following the 1988 Land Law. We model the actual allocation of land at decollectivization using a theoretical model that is capable of encompassing a potentially wide spectrum of objectives for local administrators, ranging from benevolent egalitarianism to a corrupt self-interest. We then use a micro model of farm-household consumption conditional on the land allocation to simulate the impacts of alternative counterfactual allocations, holding other factors, such as the agricultural terms of trade and the joint distribution of nonland endowments such as human capital, constant.

We use two counterfactuals. One is an equal allocation of (quality-adjusted) land per capita; this is of interest as one possible "equity" benchmark for assessing the actual allocation. The other counterfactual is the allocation that would have maximized the commune's aggregate consumption, as would have been achieved by a competitive market-based privatization under ideal conditions. This is our efficiency benchmark. We do not claim that a competitive market was a feasible option at the time in Vietnam. Indeed, agricultural land markets were virtually nonexistent. Other markets (notably for credit) and institutions (for property rights enforcement) were probably not functioning well enough to ensure an efficient market-based privatization of land. However, a reasonably close approximation to the market allocation might still have been in reach by nonmarket means. Very little mobility of households had been allowed up to this time; so people may have been well enough informed within each village to know if one family attached an appreciably higher value to extra land than another, even though a market did not exist. The competitive market allocation is then an interesting benchmark. Comparing this with the actual allocation allows us to estimate the implicit value that was placed on efficiency versus distributional goals in the initial allocation of the collectives' land to households. We can also characterize the specific distributional outcomes of the realized land allocation; possibly efficiency was sacrificed, but the poor would have been better off if it had not been.

Chapter 4 shows that the first stage of Vietnam's agrarian reform was done in a relatively equitable way—giving everyone within the commune roughly the same irrigated-land equivalent on average. Thus, we show that Vietnam started its reform period with the kind of egalitarian land reform often advocated for developing countries.[14] Of course, many sources of inequality remained. Despite land's being relatively equitably distributed within most communes, there were communes in which it was not distributed equitably. Furthermore, there was no mechanism for redistribution *between* communes; there was little geographic mobility within rural areas (although this appears to have increased over time, notably in the South). Inequalities remained in other (nonland) dimensions. Access to farm capital was probably more unequally distributed than land or labor inputs. Inefficiencies also remained. We show that after decollectivization, some households ended up with more land than they would have had in a competitive market allocation, while others had less.

Next, chapter 5 assesses whether the subsequent reallocations of annual agricultural land-use rights redressed the inefficiencies of the initial administrative allocation of land resulting from the 1988 Land Law. Using a panel of farm households spanning the change in land laws and controlling for other nonmarket factors bearing on land allocation, we see to what extent inefficiencies in the initial allocation, as measured in chapter 4, can explain the land reallocations that occurred following the 1993 Land Law.

We find signs of a land reallocation process toward the efficient solution, with those households that had too much land (relative to the efficient solution) decreasing their holdings over time, while those with too little land subsequently increased their holdings. However, we also show that this process has been slow, eliminating only about one-third of the inefficiencies in the initial administrative allocations over five years. We find no evidence that nonmarket forces stemming from the local political economy worked systematically against market forces. Rather, the market process appears to be inherently a slow one.

Next we turn to the "equity" side of the story. We ask whether, on starting from a relatively equitable allocation of land-use rights, the forces of the market economy and the local political economy interacted with inequalities in other (nonland) dimensions to make the rural economy more inequitable over time. Did the introduction of a land market hurt the poor and result in higher inequality? The distributional outcomes in a dynamic economy are impossible to predict on a priori grounds. In a development context, some critiques of the case for market-friendly agrarian reforms have asserted that class differentiation and large inequalities will inevitably reemerge, even after a radical redistributive land reform.[15] That is clearly too strong a claim to be widely accepted on a priori grounds. However, the key point is that a return to high inequality cannot be ruled out. Indeed, we know from evolutionary game theory that even in relatively simple bargaining models, inefficient and inequitable equilibria can sometimes arise over time, starting from an equal initial allocation.[16] The concerns raised in Vietnam in the debates over liberalizing land markets (as reviewed in chapter 2) should be taken seriously.

What then happened in the case of Vietnam? To address this question, chapter 6 turns its main focus to the controversy over rising landlessness. The chapter tries to throw new light on the questions that lie at the heart of the current concerns about rising landlessness in rural Vietnam. Is the country heading toward a South Asian style of rural development in which there is a large and unusually poor landless class? Or are farmers simply selling their land to pursue more rewarding activities? In short, does rising rural landlessness in the wake of market-oriented reforms signal an emerging new poverty concern for Vietnam, or is it simply a by-product of the process of poverty reduction? Is rising rural landlessness retarding the country's progress against poverty?

Chapter 6 first uses a simple theoretical model of occupational choice to see how we might expect both landlessness and poverty to be affected by introducing a land market. The model predicts that landlessness will rise, and class differentiation will reemerge, but the process may well be poverty reducing. The chapter then turns to various empirical methods for investigating the evolving relationship between landlessness, urbanization, and living standards and relevant aspects of how participation in labor and credit markets has changed. Finally, the chapter studies the role played by rising landlessness in reducing poverty.

The main conclusion of chapter 6 is that rising rural landlessness in the wake of these major agrarian reforms is on the whole a positive force in the country's progress against absolute poverty. However, the process entails both gainers and losers, including among the poor.

Chapter 7 turns to an exploration of how access to formal credit (primarily through public or quasi-public institutions) and to the government's antipoverty programs is linked with access to land assets in Vietnam's current policy setting. We show that there has been rising formal credit usage over time, though largely through a displacement of informal credit. The expansion in credit has had a strong economic gradient and has largely bypassed the landless poor. We present evidence that this is also the case for the main antipoverty programs. We argue that public policies in credit provision and social protection have not adapted as well as they might to the changes in Vietnam's rural economy.

Chapter 8 concludes by drawing out the main lessons from this case study of one country's efforts to fight poverty using market-oriented agrarian reforms. Here we also try to draw out some implications for current policy debates in China and elsewhere.

Notes

1. For a fine overview of the agrarian reforms found in transition economies (in both East Asia, and Eastern Europe and the former Soviet Union) and what is known about their effects on growth, see Rozelle and Swinnen (2004).

2. It is not possible to measure poverty on any comparable basis before 1993.

3. See Ravallion and Chen (2007) for China and World Bank (2004) for Vietnam.

4. However, signs that the leadership was openly questioning collectivized farming have been traced back to the Sixth Plenum of the Fourth Party Congress in 1979 (Kerkvliet 2006).

5. From the early 1980s, limited contract farming was allowed in Vietnam, whereby individual households were contracted to supply specific outputs to the collectives. However, this approach was more an attempt to enhance the efficiency of the collectives than a return to the family farm model (Akram-Lodhi 2004).

6. The collectives had been stronger in China, where (unlike in Vietnam) family farming of any sort had been more heavily suppressed (Kerkvliet and Selden 1998; Wiegersma 1988).

7. Evidence on this point for income inequality (rather than land inequality) can be found in Ravallion (1997).

8. Good expositions of this argument can be found in Binswanger, Deininger, and Feder (1995) and Griffin, Khan, and Ickowitz (2002).

9. This problem echoes concerns in recent literature and policy discussion about the "capture" of decentralized programs by local elites (Bardhan and Mookherjee 2000; Galasso and Ravallion 2005).

10. The history of China's (rural and urban) land policies is reviewed in Ho and Lin (2003). Childress (2004) provides an overview of the means by which agricultural land is leased or bought across selected countries in East Asia, including China and Vietnam.

11. See, for example, the reports from high-level meetings of the Communist Party found in *The Economist* (2006), McGregor and Kynge (2002), and Yardley (2006).

12. In the context of rural China, Benjamin and Brandt (2002) argue that administrative land reallocations served an efficiency role given other market failures.

13. By *absolute poverty*, we mean that the real value of the poverty line is fixed across people and space. For further discussion of these concepts and how they are implemented in practice, see Ravallion (1994).

14. See, for example, the discussion of redistributive agrarian reforms in Griffin, Khan, and Ickowitz (2002).

15. See, for example, Byres's (2004) critique of Griffin, Khan, and Ickowitz (2002).

16. See, for example, the model of how a class structure can emerge in a multiperson bargaining model starting from equality in Axtell, Epstein, and Young (2001).

2

The Historical Context and Policy Debates

Land issues have long been center stage in policy debates in Vietnam. The latter half of the 20th century had seen numerous efforts at land reform. During the War of Independence (1945–54), the anticolonial resistance movement—the Viet Minh—had transferred to farmers with small or medium holdings the large tracts of land that had been controlled by the French or the Vietnamese landlords who supported the French. In the North, this policy effectively dispossessed most landlords. After victory against the French, there were further redistributive land reforms and campaigns to forcibly remove rich peasants from positions of power in an effort to alter rural production relations. Then, around 1957, collectivized farming was introduced, following the Chinese model. This was seen by its advocates at the time as the final step in redressing and preventing a reappearance of the pervasive rural inequalities and class divisions that had plagued Vietnam since its colonization by the French (Wiegersma 1988).

Prior to 1954, the Viet Minh had also made progress in redistributing land from large landowners and colonials to tenants in the areas it controlled in the South. After the French defeat, consecutive U.S.-supported governments also put a premium on land issues but pursued policies that dovetailed with the interests of large landlords rather than those of tenants or small farmers (Callison 1983). At the same time, the resistance movement led by the National Liberation Front (NLF) drew considerable strength and support through its land-rent reductions and redistributions of land to the landless and poor farmers in areas under its control. The realization that the NLF's land policy was a key source of its popularity with the rural population eventually led the United States to instigate a major

Land-to-the-Tiller (LTT) program (Callison 1983; Wiegersma 1988). The LTT program was implemented by the Saigon government late in the war. The law governing the program aimed to provide cultivators with ownership rights through land titling and to put strict limits on the size of landholdings; all land held in excess of 20 hectares was to be distributed to tenant farmers.[1] The degree to which the program achieved its objectives varied by location, depending on the landlords' power to circumvent the law. For example, implementation appears to have been far more successful in places where the NLF (or earlier, the Viet Minh) had wielded power and already dispossessed landlords. Also, the LTT program focused on tenant farmers, leaving the numerous landless laborers no better off. This last-ditch effort to win the hearts and minds of the South's rural population failed to have much impact on the course of the war. Soon after, following the U.S. withdrawal and the country's reunification in 1975, tenancy was banned, and remaining large tracts of land were redistributed. One observer estimates that this effort reduced landlessness from as much as 20 percent in 1968 to 6 percent of southern peasants by 1978 (T. S. Nguyen 1990, quoted in Kerkvliet 2006). A campaign to collectivize the South followed but was largely unsuccessful because of intense resistance on the part of farmers.

Under the cooperatives set up in the North, land was farmed by production brigades of 40 to 100 people and run by brigade heads, who entered contracts for supplying outputs to the cooperative, assigned the work across the brigade members, and collected their work reports. Performance was measured by days of work, which were nonvoluntary (with brigade members expected to work 200 to 250 days per year). Payment was in units of output (such as paddy), according to individual labor contribution. In the South, after reunification, a push was made to organize farmers into "collectives" as a first step toward full-blown cooperatives (Pingali and Xuan 1992). Under this system in the South, households continued to cultivate privately on land assigned to them temporarily, while tools were shared and inputs and outputs managed collectively.

However, as in China in the 1970s, collectivized agriculture—whether in the form of strict "cooperatives" as in the North or "collectives" as in the South—had become very unpopular in Vietnam by the 1980s. The evident inefficiency of all these forms of collectivized farming was the main reason. Overall agricultural growth rates had been quite high in the first five years or so of collectivization, although the attribution to the collectives is unclear. By the early 1980s, it seems to have been widely believed that most (though certainly not all) of the cooperatives and collectives were inefficient, because of pervasive incentive problems.[2] Collectivization in all its forms was widely seen to be a failure, echoing complaints about the inefficiencies of this form of farming going back decades (T. Q. Tran 2001; Wiegersma 1988).

While the North's cooperatives may have made some sense in a country at war (by providing an assured food supply to the army and some security for soldiers' families), they made much less sense to the rural population after reunification of the country in 1975.[3] The rural population had started to actively and widely resist the collective system, which made collective farming even less efficient; as a prominent observer of Vietnamese society has put it, "villagers' everyday politics gnawed the underpinnings of the collectives until they collapsed. Rural households, for the most part, wanted to farm separately" (Kerkvliet 2006: 285). In large parts of the country, the peasants had stopped farming the collective lands altogether. Instead, farm households focused their efforts and resources on their small amount of privately owned land, often augmented with land appropriated from the collective. Private land plots—in theory equal to 5 percent of the cooperative's cultivable land per capita, though often more—had been allocated to members at the beginning of collectivization for growing vegetables and other produce not available through the cooperatives. By all accounts, in the 1970s output per unit area on this land was much higher than on the collective land. In certain areas, the local authorities even surreptitiously experimented with different production systems—the so-called sneaky contracts. The collective farming system was imploding from within. Swinnen and Rozelle (2006) describe a very similar process at work prior to decollectivization in China.

Many of Vietnam's rulers and urban elites were also unhappy with collectivized farming in the late 1970s, given that the low yields were putting a strain on food availability, notably to the cities. Food shortages were common in the late 1970s and in the 1980s. But the government simultaneously faced a multitude of other pressures. The U.S. war had been costly and destructive, and it left many bereaved, injured, and displaced persons. In its wake, other tribulations aligned with the dreadful economic situation of the late 1970s to shake the leadership and force a reassessment of policy. The centrally planned industrial sector was also performing poorly. A deterioration of relations with China led to an end of Chinese food aid in the summer of 1978. Vietnam attacked Cambodia in January 1979, and the West then ceased its food aid. A few months later, Vietnam was at war with China. During this tumultuous period, the more doctrinaire old guard of the Communist Party was gradually losing ground to younger, more pragmatic, pro-market reformers among the party, often coming from the South. Hints of a rethinking of agricultural policy are found in party documents as early as 1979 (Kerkvliet 2006). In the early 1980s, a number of policy adjustments were introduced to collective agriculture, including Contract 100, which replaced the work contract with a household-specific production-quota contract. Vo Van Kiet, a pro-market-reform southerner and successful ex–party leader of Ho Chi Minh City, was promoted to head of the State Planning Commission in 1982. And in 1986, the Sixth Party Congress announced the retirement of the old leaders and their replacement with a number of well-known reformers who favored greater reliance on markets. *Doi Moi* and a series of far-reaching reforms soon followed.

Decollectivization

Under Vietnam's 1988 Land Law and its implementation directive, Resolution 10, the households that had previously farmed land as members of large cooperatives and collectives were granted individual long-term-use rights over land.[4] Land was to remain the property of the state, reverting to the authorities when a household moved or stopped farming.[5] After the 1988 Land Law, the decollectivization process was rapid and was largely complete by 1990 (V. L. Ngo 1993).

How was the vast amount of agricultural land that had been farmed collectively to be allocated across individual households? Resolution 10 made a number of recommendations. The commune authorities were instructed to take into account the household's labor force as well as its historical claims to land prior to collectivization. Certain limits were stipulated on how much land could go to any one household.[6] However, while the new law extended some guidelines, it left local cadres with considerable power over land allocation and the conditions of contracts. The center's directives were disseminated by Provincial Peoples' Committees, which in turn relied on the local authorities, allowing them wide berth in adapting the guidelines to local conditions, priorities, and customs.

Under the political system of central authority combined with decentralized local autonomy introduced by the Vietnamese communists, villagers were organized and trained to partake in local decision making and self-government. Opportunities for political promotion and access to power and status were ostensibly open to all, and this helped build support for the revolution at the grassroots level (St John 1980). Cadres were intended to be those among the villagers who had risen to positions of authority through merit.

However, despite preferences favoring the poorest peasants and repeated attempts at repressing the "middle-peasant class," the latter often dominated among local officials and the party (Wiegersma 1988). Although seemingly class-blind, the system allowed certain individuals to maintain their economic and social status and their clout and others to develop it through the political process:

> The middle peasants initially showed less interest in collectivization than did the poor peasants but the middle peasants were eventually able to work within the new structure in ways which tended to preserve their positions and status. If they achieved positions of leadership in the collective, they received extra shares of collective returns and they could best preserve their family economy interest by being aware of collective policies and the "contracting out" of some collective responsibilities such as rice-drying. (Wiegersma 1988: 152–53)

Thus, those who were making the decisions locally concerning land and other productive input allocations were often the same cadres who had positions of relative privilege as the managers of the cooperatives and relatively high living standards under the collective mode of agricultural production (Selden 1993; Sikor and Truong 2000). The reform threatened to undermine their power and privilege. One could expect the pursuit of quite different objectives on their part in implementing the central directives.

There was a real risk that the benefits of reform would be captured by self-interested local cadres, potentially undermining the center's aims. Anecdotal evidence suggests abuse of local power, against the center's interests. Gabriel Kolko (1997: 92) claims that "from its inception, the land redistribution was marred by conflict, ambiguity and corruption. Cadres in many villages immediately began to distribute the best land to their families and relatives, and abuse was rife." There were a great many public disputes at the time, stemming from (among other things) conflicting historical claims over land, disputes over village and commune boundaries, and complaints about corrupt party cadres (Kolko 1997; V. T. Nguyen 1992; Pingali and Xuan 1992). Peasants in the thousands wrote petitions to the central government with land grievances. In the South alone, 59,505 petitions concerning land disputes were registered between January and August 1988 by the Party Central Committee's Agricultural Commission (T. Q. Tran 2005); by 1990, 200,000 written complaints had been submitted (Kolko 1997). It has also been argued that those with the weakest prior claims on plots did poorly in the land allocation. For example, Vinh Long Ngo (1993) argues that war veterans and demobilized soldiers were short-changed in the land allocations and were overrepresented as protagonists in disputes.

It is unimaginable that such an enormous land reform was corruption free. However, the interpretation of the existing qualitative evidence on this issue is unclear. Cases of extreme abuse of power by local elites were visible when they boiled up in local protests—Vietnam's "hot spots" (Beresford 1993, Kolko 1997, and T. Q. Tran 2005 all cite examples)—and often taken to urban centers. For example, Beresford (1993) relates the case of demonstrations in Ho Chi Minh City by farmers accusing cadres of abuse and malfeasance—namely, appropriating most of the land for themselves and even demolishing collectively built irrigation systems. The resolution of the demonstrations required intervention by the Party Secretariat. The fact that local protests were possible can also be interpreted as evidence that there were constraints on the local abuse of power.

The possibility for bias in the qualitative-historical account cannot be ignored; the cases of abuse may well have been uncommon but far more visible. Objective village-level assessments were rare. In the only village study we know of to address this issue, Tanaka (2001) describes the elaborate efforts of the "land allocation committee" in a North Vietnamese village to equalize land allocation. Such efforts are unlikely to have attracted much publicity at the time. While one would not want to generalize from a single village study, it is no less hazardous to infer from the available evidence that capture by local elites was the norm.

There were some constraints on the power of the cadres. Article 54 of the Land Law threatens punishment for officials found to abuse their power in the allocation process. Enforcement is, of course, another matter. There were other means of constraint. The very fact that local elites had to live in their communities—interacting with others in daily activities—would presumably constrain excessive abuses of power. Kerkvliet (2006) notes the strong preference for equitable outcomes voiced by farmers in the North. More organized farmers' actions also helped. As already described, farmers' resistance to the collective system had been common in the 1980s, and this resistance is believed to have been a factor motivating the center's decollectivization reforms (Beresford 1985, 1993; Kerkvliet 1995, 2006; Selden 1993). With the support of the new band of reformers in the central leadership, the Vietnam Peasant Union (VPU) was created in 1988 with the explicit aim of giving farmers a stronger voice in reform policies and—implicitly at least—promoting the center's reforms locally. As with past farmers' unions, it seems that the VPU was eventually captured by local elites; Wurfel

(1993: 32) argues that by 1990, the VPU had been "tamed by local party cadre, who had interests to protect." But for a critical period, the VPU appears to have acted as a counterweight to cadres that may have otherwise been tempted to manipulate the reforms to their advantage (Wurfel 1993). During the reform period, the center also gave greater freedom to the press. The press subsequently carried much criticism of the bureaucracy, again helping the reform process (Wiegersma 1988; Wurfel 1993).

The reform movement was clearly driven by more than the center's concerns about the welfare of farmers. The inefficiencies of the collective farming system constrained the resources available to the center for its industrialization plans and created food shortages in urban areas during a period rife with problems (Beresford 1993; Kerkvliet 1995). Arguably, the reforms were possible only through an implicit coalition between the farmers and the newly installed reformers at the center—a coalition that clearly aimed to constrain the power of local cadres to capture the process.

History provided reference points in deciding how the land should be allocated. As noted, collectivization came soon after the completion of land-reform programs that had gone a long way toward redressing the high inequality of landownership under French colonial rule (Beresford 1985; Pingali and Xuan 1992). The precollectivization allocation may have influenced land allocation at the time of decollectivization. There are reports that some households simply went back to farming land they had originally handed over to the cooperative or collective or land they had some historical claim to.[7] While there was no legal commitment to restore the precollectivization land allocation, that was an option for the local authorities.

The 1988 Land Law did not allow voluntary recontracting of land-use rights, although some informal exchanges were no doubt going on. However, it is a reasonable assumption that most parties would then have been aware that the allocation made in 1988 was likely to be "sticky" in the sense of being unresponsive to changing needs. Thus, land may have had to be allocated in anticipation of the various uncertainties facing households in this setting.

Trade-offs clearly loomed large in the allocation of land. There is both a classic efficiency-equity trade-off and a trade-off between average income and the variance of that income, given uninsured risks. One sign that such trade-offs played an important role, at least in the North, is that the administrative allocation left considerable fragmentation of holdings, with many small, dispersed plots per household (see, for example, the discussion in Lam 2001a). The fragmentation arose to ensure that each member of the commune got both good-quality and low-quality land. This diversification helped reduce risk and promote equity. But it came at a cost to aggregate output; since farmers had to spend more time moving between plots, more land was wasted in defining plot boundaries, and using mechanized equipment was harder.

Land allocation was also seen to have a role in social protection, though the 1988 Land Law was rather fuzzy on this role. It entreated the cooperatives to provide appropriate jobs and good arable land to the families of "war heroes and martyrs," to those who significantly contributed to the revolution, to the injured and those who were not able bodied, and to others facing considerable difficulties. However, the 1988 law then diluted this request by adding that the well-being of these groups was really the responsibility of the local Peoples' Committees and that the Ministry of Labor, War Invalids, and Social Affairs and the Ministry of Finance would devise policies of social assistance to them (Vietnam Communist Party 1988).

Creating a Market

Having assigned the collective land to individual households, the government took the next step of introducing a market in land-use rights. In 1993, an important new land law introduced official land titles in the form of land-use certificates (LUCs) and allowed land transactions. Land was still officially the property of the state, but usage rights legally could be transferred and exchanged, leased, mortgaged, and inherited.[8] Intermittent commune reallocations of land to accommodate changes in household size and composition were expressly prohibited.

The central government's explicit aim in introducing this new land law was to promote greater efficiency in production by creating a market in land-use rights (see, for example, de Mauny and Vu 1998).[9] In the words of the Central Committee's Second Plenum of March 1992:

> The transfer, concession, lease, mortgage and inheritance of the land use right must be stipulated in details by law in the hope of encouraging peasants to reassuringly make investments and do their farming, raising the efficiency of land use, creating conditions for the gradual accumulation of land within a rational limit for commodity development in tandem with the expansion, division and distribution of labor and in association with the industrialization process. (quoted in T. Q. Tran 2005: 186)

The expectation was that these legal changes, recognizing private land-use rights and allowing transferability, would foster investment in the land and land reallocation, thus ensuring higher agricultural output. The presumption was that decentralized decision making in the form of a free market in land-use rights would be better able to promote more efficient resource allocation—taking account of such factors as farmers' abilities, supervision costs of hiring labor, and the microgeographic organization of land plots—than was possible through an administrative assignment of land.

Simply legislating a land market does not mean that one will appear. Land markets appear to be surprisingly thin in developing rural economies even when they are (as in most cases) legal. Given how much economic activity in such economies emanates from the land, one would surely expect to see more transactions in land when a market exists. As Bardhan and Udry (1999: 60) put it: "The market *flow* is a trickle compared to the weighty *stock*." Yet it appears that there are many households with rather small holdings that are keen to acquire land, and many farmers with very large holdings, much of which appears to be of relatively low productivity. Why, then, do those with too much land not sell to those with too little?

Two reasons are usually given to explain this feature of developing economies. The first explanation is that large land parcels have a value to their owners beyond their value as a productive asset, and one that exceeds the value to a poor farmer. Large holdings provide good collateral and enhance the power of the owner. The second explanation concerns credit-market failures, such that tenants or small farmers are unable to borrow enough to finance a purchase.[10] These arguments are not fully persuasive in the present setting. The credit-market failure explanation is credible, but the first is less convincing, given that (as chapter 4 shows) the assignment of land at the time of decollectivization was relatively equitable, though still with many inefficiencies that one would want a land market to address.

However, there are other sources of friction in land-market adjustment—frictions that are specific to a transition economy. Despite the center's aim of creating a free market in land-use rights, local authorities in Vietnam retain a degree of power over land. This was facilitated by ambiguities in the new law. While administrative reallocation of land was explicitly prohibited, the land law also states that all households, including those that have lost land through indebtedness, must be given sufficient land for survival (T. M. Ngo 2004). Thus, a degree of local intervention in land allocation, for equity reasons, might well have been seen to be justified under the new law, despite the ban on administrative reassignment. Local cadres also oversee titling, land-use restrictions and planning, and land appropriation for infrastructure projects. Sikor and Truong (2000: 33) describe well how the reforms with respect to land were mediated by village institutions in Son La, a Northern Uplands province:

> Local cadres were located at the intersection of the state and villages. A large majority of them came from local villages and maintained close ties with their kin and fellow villagers. The close ties between local cadres and villagers influenced the activities of the local state. Local cadres attempted to accommodate villagers' interests, sometimes even when they contradicted national policy.

It would be wrong to see the reform as necessarily undermining the power of the local state over land. Indeed, the staff of one nongovernmental organization (NGO) argued that the pro-market reforms enhanced the power of the state (Smith and Binh 1994). Although both the 1988 and the 1993 land laws extended land-use rights for "stable and long-term use," it is widely believed that some local authorities continue to reallocate land periodically by administrative means (particularly in the North), such as in response to demographic changes. Given the ambiguities and even contradictory stipulations of the law with respect to reallocation on the one hand and landless households on the other, differences in local interpretation and implementation are not surprising.

There is other anecdotal evidence that the continuing power of the local state stalled the reforms in some parts of Vietnam. Writing a few years after the 1993 Land Law, Smith (1997) reports that in one northern province (Ha Tinh), the major commercial bank that lent for agricultural purposes had not yet accepted a single LUC as collateral for a loan. The resistance of local officials to have the land sold to an outsider was one of the reasons given by the bank; another was that the bank was unsure it would ever find a buyer for the land should it foreclose on the loan. However, this experience should not be generalized; indeed, the same study reported cases of LUCs being accepted as collateral in another province.

Transaction costs in buying and selling land through formal means remained high in the aftermath of these reforms. Childress (2004) reports that it takes an average of 60 days to transfer a property in Vietnam, which is greater than the other East Asian countries for which an estimate is given.[11] Taxes levied on land transactions appear to be relatively high in Vietnam, compared with those in other countries in the East Asia region (Childress 2004).

However, it also appears that land transactions can sometimes bypass these costs. There have been reports of land transactions without titles (de Mauny and Vu 1998; Kerkvliet 2006; Smith 1997). A quasi-market appears to have also emerged, to avoid the high formal transaction costs. Local cadres would undoubtedly be aware of the trades in land-use rights going on but bypassing the more formal channels. The high transaction costs and constraints on access to credit have probably meant that the rural poor, in particular, rely on more informal means of obtaining access to farmland, including leasing arrangements; we present some survey-based evidence on this issue in chapters 3 and 5.

The fact that land transactions could avoid the formal trappings of titling and fees to some extent does not mean that the reforms were irrelevant. The assignment of land-use rights and the freedom to enter transactions in those rights were clearly crucial. It is one thing for a local cadre to turn a blind eye to certain informal land transactions among local residents, or even to encourage the process, but quite another for cadres and residents to be conspicuously out of step with central policy dictates and the overall thrust of development policy.

These observations suggest that one would be naïve to think that simply legislating the prerequisites for a competitive land market in this setting would make it happen and that it would happen only within the strict confines of the formal legal processes. The reality is more complex and uncertain, including the role of the local state. The legal reforms alone do not, of course, ensure that the subsequent transactions and reallocations of land will make the rural economy any more efficient. Given the pervasive involvement of the local state, and the risks of capture by local elites, the "free market" could yield outcomes that are neither more equitable nor more efficient than the prereform economy. Neither should it be presumed that the local power structures will work against the reform's objectives of promoting a more efficient rural economy. In principle, the continuing power of local cadres could have served either to undermine the expected efficiency gains from the center's reforms (to ensure that other distributional goals were achieved) or to help secure those gains. Indeed, given the historical context outlined, the local state may well have had a crucial role to play in ensuring that the center's legal reforms aiming to create a land market delivered on the efficiency goals.

Debates

At the time of writing, debates continue about both the efficiency and the equity implications of these major institutional reforms, echoing debates going back 50 years between those who favor a family farm model for organizing the rural economy and those who prefer the (pro-Mao) "Chinese model" of collectivized farming. In the former model, production decisions are decentralized, and price incentives play an important role in determining the choices made; in the collectivized-farming model, land is farmed by large brigades and run by cadres that assign the work, monitor progress, and allocate shares of net output to people according to the amount of work done.

There were many advocates of the family farm model in Vietnam at the end of the war with the French, but they lost the debate at that time. The push for collectivization in Vietnam (as in China) was in part a matter of political ideology. Collectivization would (it was argued) put the poorest peasants in charge of production as the final blow (after the redistributive land reform) to the landlord class. It would ensure a classless society. It was also (in part) a practical solution to the problem of ensuring that the center controlled the agricultural surplus needed to finance industrialization; later, the cooperatives came to be seen as a practical solution to the need to feed and support the soldiers and their families during Vietnam's war with the United States.

There were also economic arguments made in favor of collectivization—arguments that mirror the subsequent debates about the pro-market agrarian reforms of the 1980s and 1990s. These arguments concerned both the efficiency and the equity of the rural economy. Proponents argued that collectivized farming would be more efficient because it could exploit economies of scale and reduce coordination problems, such as in developing and maintaining irrigation systems. This does not seem a particularly convincing argument. For most crops (including the main food staple, rice), neither China nor Vietnam was likely to move very quickly toward the type of capital-intensive farming technology for which there are significant economies of scale. Labor was abundant, not scarce. And for millennia, traditional village societies in settled agriculture (such as in most of Vietnam) have been able to deal with coordination problems in supplying local public goods without forming production cooperatives.

The equity argument is less easily dismissed. By this view, the cooperatives were needed to make the equity gains achieved by the revolution permanent. It was claimed that the degree of equity that had been achieved in the family economy through the initial redistributive land reform would eventually vanish, as better-off farmers acquired the land of poor farmers, such as when the latter had a bad crop year.

By the 1980s, however, it seems that few people supported collective farming. As discussed above, the equity case for collectivization was always about equity within communes, while the persistent between-area inequalities were left largely untouched by the collective mode of organizing the rural economy. But the main concern was the evident inefficiency of collective agriculture. In other words, the (within-place) equity gains were no longer considered enough to compensate for the loss of output caused by the poor incentive structure of collective farming. However, while few people appeared to be defending the cooperatives and collectives in the 1980s, there was plenty of room for debate and conflict over the implementation of their dismantling, notably in how the land would be allocated to households (as we have already discussed).

Both at the time and since, the 1993 Land Law was clearly far more contentious than the 1988 Land Law. Kerkvliet and Selden (1998: 51) summarize the debate at the time:

> In Vietnam, the rights and obligations of rural landholders were spelled out in a 1993 land law passed by the national Assembly following extensive public debate. Significantly, not only Party officials but many villagers opposed privatization of land ownership rights. While favoring the long-term distribution of use rights to the fields, many preferred periodic redistribution in order to maintain equity, a pattern with roots in pre-revolution village praxis.

This was essentially a debate between those who favored moving toward a free market in land-use rights—the post-1993 Vietnamese model—and those who favored the Chinese model in which periodic administrative reallocations of land remained the norm.

Supporters of Vietnam's pro-market approach argued that it would increase aggregate output by allowing land to be reallocated toward more efficient farmers. Hayami (1994: 15) saw Vietnam's 1993 Land Law as the key step toward more efficient agriculture, asserting that "it is not necessary to be overly concerned about an inequitable agrarian structure emerging." Ten years later, the Hanoi-based Center for Rural Progress (2005) argued that an active land market in the Mekong Delta contributed to more rapid poverty reduction by allowing more efficient farmers to accumulate more land, fostering diversification and increasing farmers' access to credit.[12]

Our research points to evidence that land allocation has become more efficient since the 1993 Land Law. Chapter 5 shows that since 1993, agricultural land has been reallocated in a way that attenuated the initial inefficiencies in the administrative assignment of land at the time of decollectivization; households that started with an inefficiently low (high) amount of cropland under the administrative assignment tended to increase (decrease) their holdings over time.

The chapter also shows that there was polarization among those who started off with too little land; while most of these households acquired more land, a minority sold or transferred all their farmland, possibly to take up nonfarm activities or to pay off debts. Rising landlessness stemmed in part from inefficiencies in the initial administrative allocation.

Both supporters and critics of land-market reforms have referred to the implications for the pace of urbanization. Supporters argue that the efficiency-promoting role of these reforms would entail an increase in the supply of labor to nonfarm activities, which tend to be concentrated in urban or peri-urban areas, given agglomeration economies in production. Critics have agreed but have argued that higher urbanization is undesirable, because it fosters urban slums and depresses urban wage rates. Chapter 6 examines the implications of rising landlessness for the urbanization process in Vietnam, although we argue that focusing on urbanization per se leaves ambiguous implications for what we really care about, namely, the absolute levels of living of people.

While to some observers a reform that first equalized holdings of such an important asset and then made it a market good is expected to be in the interests of poor people, a number of critics have argued instead that Vietnam's agrarian strategy has exacerbated long-term poverty by promoting rural landlessness. This is a similar argument to that made many decades earlier (in both China and Vietnam) by advocates of collectivization, who believed that the equity in land allocation achieved through the redistributive land reforms undertaken after the socialist revolutions was not sustainable over time. Differences in ability, in household human-capital endowments, and in the incidence of idiosyncratic shocks would entail that some farmers would do better than others and eventually buy up the land of those less successful, thus re-creating the old land-based class structures that the revolution had sought to overturn.

In Vietnam in the 1990s, there were similar concerns about rising landlessness and an emerging rural proletariat, stemming from the agrarian reforms. A former prime minister of Vietnam wrote an influential article as early as 1997, raising his concerns about the problem of rising landlessness in the North's Red River Delta region (Houghton 2000). There have been many anecdotal reports of rising landlessness, notably (but not only) in the South's Mekong Delta region (see, for example, de Mauny and Vu 1998; Lam 2001b). A report by ActionAid staff exemplifies these concerns; while presenting no supportive evidence, the report predicted that the reforms would lead to "a greater concentration of land ownership, a greater disparity in wealth throughout the rural community and a possible increase in the phenomenon of landlessness and full-time agricultural wage labour" (Smith and Binh 1994: 17).

Writing more than 10 years later, Akram-Lodhi (2004, 2005) argues that Vietnam's reforms have not been pro-poor but have created "peasant class differentiation" (2005: 107): "The evidence ... demonstrates the rapid growth of a class of rural landless who are largely separated from the means of production, who survive by intermittently selling their labour, and who are the poorest segment of rural society" (2005: 73). Similarly, Zhou (1998) argues that the privatization of land-use rights in Cambodia, the Lao People's Democratic Republic, and Vietnam has been detrimental by fostering rural landlessness and urban slums. Zhou (1998: 19) sees the rise in rural landlessness in Vietnam as a vindication of the Chinese policy:[13] "The fact that new landlessness has appeared immediately after the land tenure reform in the low wage economy of Cambodia, Laos and Vietnam already shows that this model is inferior to the Chinese." This echoes Dong's (1996: 918) argument (also in defense of China's land policy) that "the distribution of land among peasants must necessarily be equal so as to meet their basic needs in life and to enhance their employability. Otherwise the landless and near-landless will suffer from malnourishment."

Critics of land markets have been concerned that the poorest would be forced into becoming landless and (hence) dependent on wage labor, which (it is believed) makes them worse off. The potentially coercive role of the local state is often pointed to as a reason for why rising landlessness in the wake of these reforms would be poverty increasing. The interaction between land markets and local governance has been a recurrent issue. The expropriation of agricultural land by the local state in the process of land-use conversion has often entailed protests by expropriated farmers who feel that they have not received fair compensation. Critics often claim that the poor incur the largest costs; for example, Yeh and Li (1999) and Guo (2001) argue that poor farmers in China are inadequately compensated for land expropriations. Concerns about these issues have been prominent in high-level policy discussions within China and in the international press (see, for example, *The Economist* 2006 and Yardley 2006). Vietnam's greater reliance on markets for land allocation might be expected to help in setting fair prices. However, the local state in Vietnam continues to play an active role in setting the terms of land-use conversions, and there have also been numerous protests by poor farmers about inadequate compensation and claims of misconduct by local officials in charge of the conversion process (see, for example, V. S. Nguyen 2004). In our own fieldwork in Vietnam, we often heard claims that the provincial government's "guiding prices" used for compensating farmers when their land was expropriated for nonfarm use were well below market prices.

Nevertheless, some of the efforts made by local governments to avoid rising landlessness may well have also had perverse effects. There are reports that in response to central Communist Party concerns about rising landlessness in the late 1990s, some local officials in the Mekong Delta tried to stop poor families from selling their land (de Mauny and Vu 1998). Whether this would be in the interests of such families is a moot point. The consequent devaluation of their main nonlabor asset could make the poor worse off, depending on whether any compensation is provided locally to those prevented from selling their land as a response to some negative shock. It is likely that land transfers still happened despite such policies, though the transactions would become informal and possibly take place on less-favorable terms than for those forced to sell their land more formally because of adverse shocks.

The concerns about land markets have also interacted with concerns about equity between specific social groups, notably ethnic minorities and women. There are more than 50 distinct ethnic groups in Vietnam, and the minorities (non-Kinh) account for 15 percent of the population. They are concentrated in the upland and mountainous areas of the Central and Northern Highlands. Poverty rates tend to be higher among the minorities, in part because of lower land quality and poorer education, although lower returns to these characteristics also play an important role in explaining their lower living standards (van de Walle and Gunewardena 2001).

While land is generally extremely important to their livelihoods, the production and land-use practices of Vietnam's minority groups have tended to be quite different from those of the ethnic majority. The minorities rely much more on shifting cultivation practices and forestry and have relied historically on communal tenure arrangements (whereby community members work together to enforce customary laws). These arrangements do not fit easily in the emerging model of individually assigned rights over specific land parcels. The reforms to land laws did not initially recognize community ownership of land. Since the reforms began, conflicts over land have been common in the upland areas, notably in the Central Highlands, where there has been substantial in-migration of mostly Kinh farm households. Many of the conflicts over land at the time of decollectivization involved minority groups as well, including cases in which they hoped to reclaim land that had been collectivized by Kinh communities (Kerkvliet and Selden 1998). In response to the ethnic conflicts over land, there have been calls for reviving community management of land in those regions as an alternative model to that of individually assigned land-use rights (see, for example, Vuong 2003). Antipoverty policies in Vietnam have emphasized the needs of the minority groups. This has taken various forms, including both direct relief efforts and poor-area programs for developing physical and human infrastructure and social services.[14]

Gender issues have also been a concern. Communism espoused equality for women, although the practice clearly fell well short of that ideal (Wiegersma 1988). The fact that so many men were away fighting in the war during the 1960s and 1970s had given women a higher economic profile, including as cadres and managers of the cooperatives. But in Vietnam, as in many other countries, formal rights over land have tended to be held disproportionately by men. The LUCs introduced by the 1993 Land Law were issued at household level with space for only one name, which was typically the (male) household head. There have been concerns that this practice gave women little or no right over the main productive asset, limiting their access to credit and making them vulnerable to a breakup of the family (T. Q. Tran 2001; T. V. A. Tran 1999). (Divorced women were often left without enforceable land rights.) A government decree in 2001 clarified that the LUC must be in the names of both the husband and the wife, but it remains unclear how well this rule has been implemented. The government department responsible for rural land titling lacked the capacity to implement this decree. A World Bank pilot project demonstrated how LUCs can be reissued in an efficient way to accommodate both names and how cadastral records can be updated (World Bank 2002).

As chapter 4 reveals, female-headed households were disadvantaged in the initial allocation of land at the time of decollectivization. We show that not only was this inequitable but also that it came at a cost to aggregate efficiency.

Another concern about the adverse welfare impacts of the agrarian reforms relates to what can be called the "induced effects" of land markets, in which local institutions play an important role. The commune's control over land came with responsibilities to help with nonland inputs and to provide certain social services, including insurance. With a land market, farmers were increasingly left to their own devices; when their land became marketable, it was felt that farmers could use their land as collateral to obtain credit or sell some or all of it to cope with shocks. The retreat of the local state from its traditional welfare role has been a prominent concern for critics of the land-market reforms (see, for example, the discussions in de Mauny and Vu 1998 and Smith 1997).

It should also be noted that the attribution of poverty to landlessness among critics of the reforms has sometimes been questionable.

Suppose that a household suffers a serious health crisis and has to sell its land. The household becomes both poor *and* landless. This would not have happened if there had been a ban on selling land. But the existence of a land market did not cause the poverty; indeed, the absence of a market could entail even greater poverty, by effectively devaluing the household's main asset.

The criticisms of the reforms also reflect a mistrust of labor markets, although it has rarely been clear that this mistrust has been well founded. For example, in coming to the conclusion summarized above, Dong (1996) alludes to an efficiency-wage argument (citing Dasgupta and Ray 1986 and Moene 1992), whereby workers with too few assets end up unemployed in equilibrium. However, Dong does not establish that the poor would be better off without land markets, or even that the efficiency-wage hypothesis is plausible in the Vietnamese or Chinese context.

Lags and adjustment costs have also prompted concerns about the implications of labor-market outcomes for poor people. Welfare losses can occur with lags in labor-market adjustment and distortions in land markets, particularly in a situation where many people would be unfamiliar with the workings of the market economy. If many people sell their land-use rights when that becomes an option, the increase in labor supply will drive down the wage rate. Suppose that the decision to sell one's land is made *before* the new labor-market equilibrium is revealed—the outcome of which is unanticipated—and that there is a sufficiently large transaction cost to prohibit buying back land; this can arise if the value of the land to the new owner exceeds the prior purchase price, as would be the case when the land purchases allow the consolidation of previously fragmented plots. With a fall in the wage rate attributable to the reform, some farmers who sell their land will eventually find that they are worse off.

Regional Differences

In almost all these respects, there were important regional differences, most notably between the North and the South.[15] High inequality in landholdings and high rates of landlessness had been a long-standing feature of the rural economy in the South prior to reunification in 1975 (at the end of the war with the United States) (Wiegersma 1988). There had been attempts to address land issues in the South prior to 1975. The South's land-reform programs prior to reunification had initially consisted of lease price control and ownership ceilings that were particularly favorable to large landowners. These were followed in 1970 by an ambitious effort at land redistribution and titling under the LTT program (Callison 1983; Pingali and Xuan 1992; Wiegersma 1988). This progressive social program was clearly motivated at least in part by the American belief that the pervasive inequalities in rural areas had fueled much grassroots opposition to the Saigon government and so made the war harder to win. Another factor was the need to ensure a more secure rural tax base. Observations from village studies at the time suggest a rather mixed success, with the LTT program working better in some places than others, depending in large part on the power of local landlords, including their power over the judiciary (Wiegersma 1988: chapter 9). It is also notable that this type of program was essentially designed to help tenant farmers and middle peasants but largely bypassed the landless.

After 1975, farmers in the South's Mekong Delta resisted collectivization, and by the time of the 1988 Land Law, less than 10 percent of the region's farmers had been organized into agricultural cooperatives. In contrast, virtually all of the cropland in the North and in the South's central coastal provinces—where joining the cooperatives was seen as a means of rebuilding after the war—was collectivized by the time of the reform (V. L. Ngo 1993; Pingali and Xuan 1992). Southern Vietnamese farm households that participated in collective agriculture did so for a much shorter period, while many never fully participated, notably in the Mekong Delta.

However, the allocation of land in the South was still administratively determined, and land was periodically reallocated (Pingali and Xuan 1992); the difference with the more collectivized North is that, in the South (especially the Mekong Delta), most farmers continued to farm individually rather than collectively. Resolution 10 allowed farmers in the South to recover land owned prior to 1975, though former "landlords" were explicitly barred from doing so (Pingali and Xuan 1992). There are reports that in the Mekong Delta the implementation of Resolution 10 often entailed restoring the land allocation that prevailed prior to reunification (ANZDEC Limited 2000; Hayami 1994). As previously noted, that allocation was the outcome of a series of prior land reforms.

Historical differences meant that the South—most notably the Mekong Delta and the Southeast (the region around Ho Chi Minh City)—was more open to the idea of a market economy than the North. This was undoubtedly an important factor in the higher rural per capita income growth found in the South, fueled in part by improvements in farmers' terms of trade arising from external trade reforms in the 1990s (Houghton 2000). Benjamin and Brandt (2004) report a 95 percent increase in real income per person in the South over 1993–98, versus 55 percent in the North. Such rapid growth in real incomes may well have dampened the pressure to secure the efficiency gains from land reallocation in the South.

Given this historical difference between the North and the South, heterogeneity in the impacts of reform can be expected. The North's more deeply entrenched traditions of collectivized agriculture and egalitarian norms within villages (predating the introduction of the cooperatives), with their relatively closed village economies, are likely to have created lower initial inequality in some key dimensions than found in the South.[16] The distribution of land was more equitable in the North.[17] The collectivization of agriculture in the North over roughly a generation fostered a more equitable allocation by the time of decollectivization. In the South, the fallback position was the preunification land allocation, and the realized allocation was more unequal than in the North (chapter 4). It is also likely that nonland inputs to farming were more dependent on individual wealth in the South (Akram-Lodhi 2005). Lower inequality in the North may well have made it easier to achieve cooperative outcomes, including more efficient assignments of land-use rights.[18] The pressures toward further land consolidation are likely to be stronger in the South.[19]

Another regional difference that could well have bearing on land allocation can be found in the performance of (formal and informal) institutions that deal with risk. The safety net in rural areas of Vietnam is largely community based; central and provincial programs tend to have very limited coverage (van de Walle 2004). Villages in the North are widely believed to be better organized socially than in the South, so that when a farm household in the North suffers a negative shock (such as crop damage or ill health), it will probably not need to sell land to cope. For example, writing about Son La province, Smith (1997: 11) reports that "there is a tendency for the local authorities to seek to protect households from the dangers of a market in land, despite the provisions of the 1993 Law. This constitutes an attempt to protect poor households who may be tempted to sell their land for short term gain and lose their principal means of subsistence." By contrast, an Oxfam team in the province of Tra Vinh in the Mekong Delta (in which the NGO had been working for many years) reported: "The crucial problem is that there are no safety nets for helping households who encounter temporary crises. . . . It is no surprise that many families resort to transferring or mortgaging their land, discounting the future to cope with the current crisis" (de Mauny and Vu 1998: 23).

This difference between the North and the South is no doubt a legacy of the lower penetration of market institutions in the North during French rule, the longer period of collective organization in the North, and village economies that have been traditionally less open to outsiders (Luong 1992; Wiegersma 1988). However, the more equal land allocation in the North after breaking up the collectives could well have facilitated this difference by making it easier to continue to achieve quasi-cooperative arrangements within communities.[20] Better insurance in the North is likely to have also made it easier for land transactions to be made on efficiency grounds. Land reallocations in the South, by contrast, are likely to have been less flexible, since land would have been more likely to be held as insurance than in the North.

Labor markets also differed. Agricultural wage markets were much more developed in the South for the historical reasons already outlined. Evidence suggests that farmers in the North are likely to have faced more remunerative options for supplying skilled labor than those found in the South. The wage regressions reported for 1998 by Gallup (2004) indicate appreciably higher returns to schooling in the rural North than in the rural South. Indeed, Gallup finds that the wage return to schooling (the coefficient on years of schooling in an ordinary least squares regression for the log wage rate) is not significantly different from zero in the rural South. However, this could reflect sample selection bias, to the extent that better-educated people leave rural areas for skilled work in urban areas.

There is a corresponding schooling gap between the North and the South.[21] We calculate (from the surveys described later) that mean years of schooling in 1993 were 7.3 years for farm households in the North's Red River Delta versus 4.3 years in the South's Mekong Delta.[22] It is also likely that aggregate demand for agricultural labor has been stronger in the South than in the North, given the South's larger farms and higher agricultural growth rate in the 1990s (Benjamin and Brandt 2004).

There is likely to be heterogeneity in impacts within one area at a given time, which can also fuel debate. Consider the different views of Akram-Lodhi (2004, 2005) and the Center for Rural Progress (2005). Both studies draw (in part) on fieldwork in the Mekong Delta, conducted at about the same time, yet they come to very different conclusions, one favoring the view that the postreform rise in landlessness was poverty increasing and the other claiming the opposite. This may partly reflect horizontal inequalities in economic and social change, whereby similar people ex ante fare differently; two researchers can then come back from fieldwork at the same time in the same area with very different stories, depending on whom they talked to. This speaks to the need for representative survey data when attempting to form generalizations.

Later chapters explore what light survey data can cast on these issues. However, the debate will not be resolved by data alone. There are also differences in the value judgments made. Some observers see rising land inequality as a bad thing per se, even if it comes with falling poverty. Here we assume that while inequalities in various dimensions may be instrumentally important to absolute levels of living, the latter are the overriding consideration.

Conclusions

This chapter describes the historical context of the debates over land policy in Vietnam, as well as how deep and intertwined historical and geographic differences have shaped the country's reform process and the responses of local authorities and farm households.

It is clear that the major legal reforms did not appear out of nowhere. In the case of every major land policy intervention in this period, the historical evidence suggests that the reforms legalized practices that already existed informally in some communes, with or without the connivance of local cadres. Land was being sold, rented, mortgaged, and bequeathed in some areas before the 1993 Land Law legalized such market activities. Neither did the reforms create a sudden change in local practices throughout the country. Some communes continued to reallocate land by administrative fiat long after this practice was formally disallowed by the 1993 law.

Nonetheless, the legal formalization through the various decrees and land laws was clearly crucial for scaling up, and it legitimized forces for change that were bubbling up in a geographically piecemeal fashion throughout rural Vietnam. Data on land transactions indicate greater activity in the years after 1993 in all methods of land acquisition legalized by the land law (Brandt 2006: table 12).

After the review of our data in the following chapter, much of the rest of this book aims to assess whether the observed changes in landholdings accorded with the overall efficiency objectives of the land reforms and whether the efficiency gains came at a cost to equity. As we emphasize, many of the same historical and geographic factors underlying the land-reform process also confound any attempt to neatly attribute the subsequent economic changes to the reforms alone. The economic outcomes are best seen as the joint product of the center's legal reforms and the diverse nonmarket forces in the local political economy that in some cases helped spur reform and in others entailed continuing resistance.

Notes

1. The LTT program evolved out of a research study done by the Stanford Research Institute for the U.S. Agency for International Development, which found that 80 percent of the tenants interviewed wanted to own their own land; the study also revealed widespread beliefs that the large landholdings found in the South were socially unjust (Wiegersma 1988: 189–90). The basic design of the LTT program echoed the redistributive land reforms undertaken with U.S. assistance elsewhere in East Asia in the period after World War II.

2. Wiegersma (1988: chapter 7) discusses the strengths and weaknesses of collectivized farming in Vietnam.

3. Wiegersma (1988: 145) argues that the war with the United States had delayed the reforms needed to properly address the problems of collectivized farming in Vietnam.

4. Use rights for cropland were granted for 10 to 15 years; longer periods applied to tree crops. Some flexibility was allowed in that 10 to 15 percent of the cooperative's land could be kept aside for new households and demobilized soldiers and was available for hire by households in the meantime (T. Q. Tran 1997).

5. Although Resolution 10 affirms the right to transfer land use and legate it to one's offspring, such rights were not fully guaranteed legally (Bloch and Oesterberg 1989). The rights to exchange, lease, or mortgage land were extended only in the 1993 Land Law.

6. Article 27 of the 1988 Land Law stipulates that household allocations not exceed 10 percent of the total farmland area of each concerned village. It further decrees regional per capita land ceilings for those contracting land for long-term use from state-operated farms. It has been claimed that ceilings were officially set at 2 hectares in the Red River Delta and 3 hectares in the South (ANZDEC Limited 2000), though there is no mention of this in Resolution 10 or the 1988 Land Law.

7. Smith and Binh (1994) quote a number of Son La households in the North as professing, in 1994, to be farming the same land they had at the time of the departure of the French. Thi Que Tran (1997) claims that land was redistributed according to original household contributions to the cooperatives in some areas.

8. Some restrictions on transactions remain, depending on the category of land. There are ceilings on holdings (although these can be bypassed by paying taxes), land can be leased for no more than three years, and official approval is needed for all transactions (Marsh and MacAulay 2006; T. M. Ngo 2005).

9. This was one element of a set of reforms to increase agricultural output. Other reforms include relaxing trade restrictions, which improved farmers' terms of trade (see Benjamin and Brandt 2004).

10. Good expositions of these and other arguments as to why land markets are thin can be found in Bardhan and Udry (1999: chapter 6) and Binswanger, Deininger, and Feder (1995).

11. The other countries included in the comparisons were Cambodia, Indonesia, the Lao People's Democratic Republic, the Philippines, and Thailand; all take less time than in Vietnam, although the figure given for the Philippines is 14–800 days.

12. Also see Asian Development Bank (2004). These claims are based on largely informal interviews with local authorities and a small number of households; the selection process for the latter appears to have favored places where the land reforms were more successful. See the discussion in section 2.2, especially pages 2–4, of Center for Rural Progress (2005).

13. Zhou (1998) aims to refute Hayami (1994), who argued that introducing a free market in land would promote more efficient agriculture in the transition economies of East Asia (also see Zhou 2001).

14. Vu (2005) provides an overview of these efforts.

15. The differences between (a) the upland areas of the Central Highlands and Northern Uplands and (b) the more lowland regions are also notable, though these differences overlap substantially with the ethnic dimensions of land, which we have already discussed.

16. The egalitarian tradition in northern Vietnam has also been contrasted to China by Van Luong and Unger (1998), who argue that the government of China pursued inequality-increasing development policies that would have been politically infeasible in Vietnam.

17. This difference shows up in the results from the Vietnam Living Standards Survey of 1993 (chapter 3). The coefficient of variation in the log of allocated annual agricultural land was 8.3 percent in the North's Red River Delta, versus 15.3 percent in the South's Mekong Delta. (Among the five regions for which the sample size was deemed adequate, these were the regions with the lowest and highest land inequality, respectively.)

18. For an excellent review of the theoretical arguments as to why high inequality can impede efficiency, see Bardhan, Bowles, and Gintis (2000).

19. This is consistent with the observations made by Taylor (2004), based on fieldwork in the Mekong Delta.

20. On the various ways that inequality can impede cooperation, see Bardhan, Bowles, and Gintis (2000).

21. Across regions of Vietnam, the rate of return to schooling rises with mean schooling (Gallup 2004).

22. This difference persisted; in 2004, the corresponding mean years of schooling were 8.0 in the North's Red River Delta and 4.8 in the South's Mekong Delta.

3

Data and Summary Statistics

This chapter begins with a general discussion of the four key nationally representative household consumption surveys that are used throughout this study. The first section focuses on general characteristics of the surveys and the commonalities across them; this discussion is relevant to all chapters of this book. The following three sections each deal with the details specific to the analysis of a specific stage of the agrarian transition. The second section turns to the data issues concerning our analysis of land allocation at decollectivization in chapter 4, many of which are also relevant to the analysis in chapter 5. The third section focuses on the data in the context of the analysis in chapter 5 of land reallocations following the initial allocation to households. The next five sections discuss the data used in chapters 6 and 7. Trends in poverty and landlessness across the four household surveys are examined in the fourth section. The fifth section discusses a pseudo-panel that we have created to look at changes in landlessness over time (chapter 6). The sixth section examines the detailed land module included in the 2004 household survey, and the seventh section discusses that survey's community and self-assessed welfare measures, both of which we use in chapters 6 and 7. The final section provides some basic information on a complementary data source that we also use in chapters 6 and 7.

The Vietnam Living Standards and Household Living Standards Surveys

The main data sources that we use in this study are the unit-record (household-level) data from four nationally representative surveys by Vietnam's General Statistical Office (GSO) for 1992/93, 1997/98,

2002, and 2004. The Vietnam Living Standards Surveys (VLSSs) of 1992/93 (called herein the 1993 VLSS) and 1997/98 (called herein the 1998 VLSS), with sample sizes of 4,800 and 6,000, respectively, were sponsored by the World Bank under the Living Standards Measurement Study (LSMS).[1] While the larger 2002 and 2004 Vietnam Household Living Standards Surveys (VHLSSs) (with samples of 30,000 and 9,000, respectively) are not LSMS surveys, the GSO made considerable efforts to ensure reasonable comparability with the earlier VLSSs, notably in the consumption modules. They are well-designed surveys by international standards, and they have received considerable technical support from international agencies, including the World Bank and the United Nations Development Programme.

The 1993 sample is self-weighted, while the other surveys used stratified random cluster sampling so that sampling weights need to be applied. Clustering is at commune level, the smallest administrative division. For the most part, we focus on rural areas, for which sample sizes are 3,800, 4,300, 22,600, and 6,900 for 1993, 1998, 2002, and 2004, respectively. All four surveys are representative of urban and rural areas and of the seven regions that Vietnam is commonly divided into—namely, the Northern Uplands, the Red River Delta, the North Central Coast, the South Central Coast, the Central Highlands, the Southeast, and the Mekong Delta. With the exception of the 2002 survey, estimates cannot be considered statistically representative at the province level. Geographic heterogeneity across communes is to be expected, given likely differences in the shadow price of land and differences in production functions (in that a different state of nature is revealed in different locations).

The 1993 VLSS was completed just before the 1993 Land Law. A subsample was reinterviewed in 1998, allowing us to form a household panel dataset, which we exploit in our analysis of the land reallocation process after the 1993 Land Law (chapter 5), as well as to examine the issue of rising landlessness over time (chapter 6). A subsample of those interviewed in 2002 was also resurveyed in 2004. However, there is no such panel link between the 1998 and 2002 surveys.

As in most countries, it is difficult to ensure that all types of households are properly represented in the surveys. In Vietnam, the GSO relies heavily on the list of registered households in the sampled communes when drawing its sample of households. This approach raises a concern about households that are more geographically mobile and that are not yet registered in their new commune of residence. Migration within Vietnam has increased substantially in recent years. Despite this, administrative hurdles to establishing new residency and registration have not eased. Similarly, statistical measures have not been adapted to deal with the changing circumstances. Thus, by all accounts, this group is underrepresented in these surveys (World Bank 2004). Since the rural landless are naturally more mobile, we could well be underestimating the extent of landlessness—and probably more so with more recent surveys.

Throughout this study, we follow past practice in applied development economics in using a comprehensive measure of household real consumption per person as our welfare metric. We can construct a comparable measure of this metric across the four surveys. The consumption aggregate includes the value of consumption from own production, the imputed expenditures on housing, and the depreciated value of consumer durables. It is deflated by a monthly price index to allow for variation in the time of the household interviews and by a spatial price index to take account of regional price variation, and it is expressed in real January 1998 prices (see Glewwe 2003, 2005; World Bank 1995, 2000). Figure 3.1 gives the frequency distribution of log consumption per person for 1993 and 2004; panel a is for rural Vietnam as a whole. (Panel b is for the landless, which we return to.) However, while household consumption is our primary welfare indicator, later in this chapter we provide some results on alternative measures using community-level assessments of individual poverty and self-assessments, both of which are available in the 2004 survey.

The main poverty measure we use is the head-count index—the proportion of the population living in households with consumption per person below the poverty line. However, at times we also use the squared poverty gap index, which penalizes inequality among the poor (Foster, Greer, and Thorbecke 1984). The poverty line is from Glewwe, Gragnolati, and Zaman (2002) and aims to measure the cost of a set of basic food and nonfood consumption needs.

The Initial Land Allocation

In chapter 4, we use the 1993 survey for assessing impacts of privatization of land-use rights over annual agricultural land (or cropland). The subsample is the 2,810 rural farming households in the VLSS for which there are complete data. Some 400 households had to be dropped because of missing data on key variables. There are also 419 households in the survey's rural farming sample without any allocated irrigated or nonirrigated agricultural land identified. Our reading of the literature and casual observations suggest that this is due to genuine measurement error. It is unlikely that there is

Figure 3.1 Frequency Distributions of Consumption, 1993 and 2004

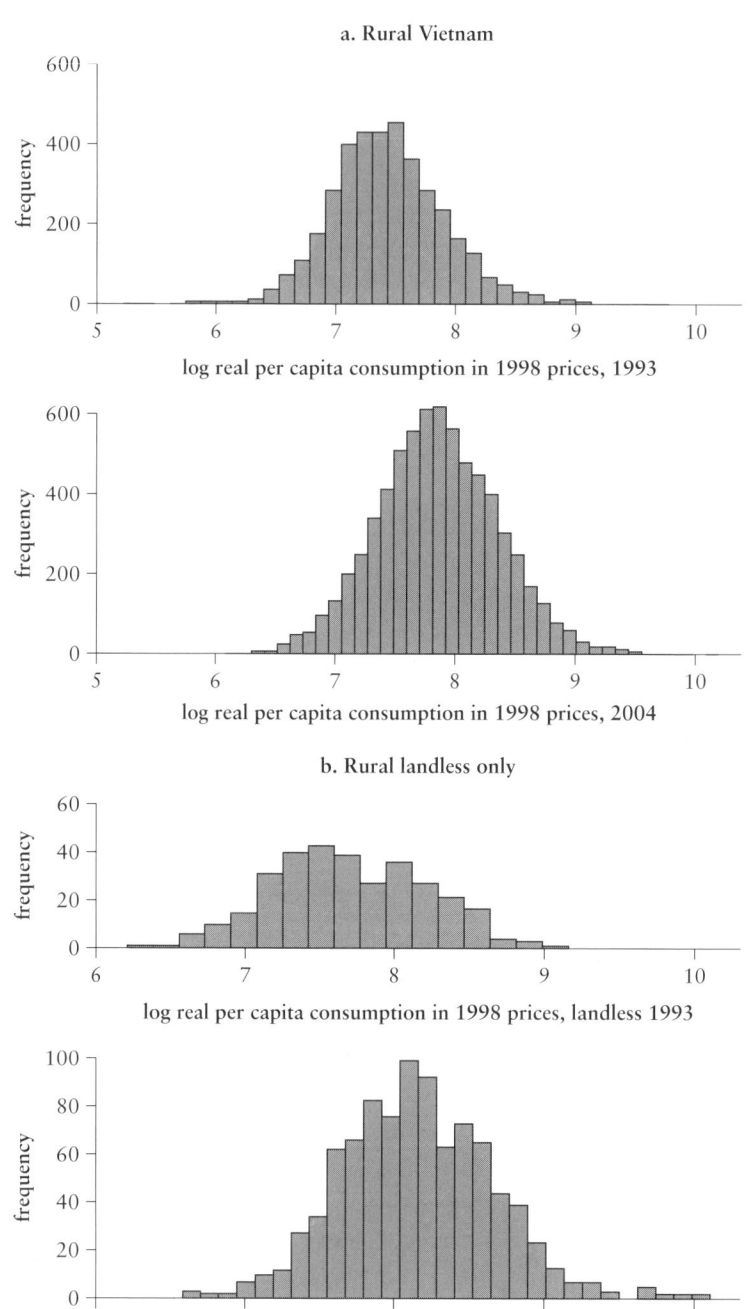

a. Rural Vietnam

log real per capita consumption in 1998 prices, 1993

log real per capita consumption in 1998 prices, 2004

b. Rural landless only

log real per capita consumption in 1998 prices, landless 1993

log real per capita consumption in 1998 prices, landless 2004

Sources: 1993 VLSS and 2004 VHLSS.

actual censoring, such that some farming households were deliberately left out of the land privatization, because doing so would probably have created conspicuous destitution, which would not have been accepted at the time in rural Vietnam. Under that assumption, we focus solely on the sample of farming households with complete data.

While the sample size does not permit estimation of a separate model for each commune, our regressions include a complete set of commune dummy variables so that the regression's intercept is allowed to be different for each commune. We conduct the analysis both nationally and separately for the Northern Uplands, Red River Delta, North Central Coast, South Central Coast, and Mekong Delta regions. We leave out the Central Highlands, where land is mostly perennial, and the Southeast, where there were too few observations in the sample. (After excluding nonfarming households and those with missing data, we are left with a sample of only 99 observations in the Southeast.)

The land situation has evolved during the 1990s—reflecting changing official attitudes toward the market economy and the role of land, as well as consequent policy and legal reforms. This is apparent in the surveys. There were some changes in land categories and definitions between the 1993 and 1998 VLSSs and again between these and the two later surveys. In this and the next two sections, we try to clarify these land concepts and the way we have chosen to define the land variable in the different parts of the research.

All the surveys identify a number of types of land, including annual cropland, perennial land, forestland, water surface land, and "other" land, which includes swidden, bald hill, and newly cleared land.[2] In examining the initial allocation of land to households at decollectivization, we focus on annual cropland.[3] There was also an allocation mechanism for perennial land, forestland, and water surface land. However, since these other land types followed a much slower and haphazard allocation process, we limit our analysis of the allocation of land to households at decollectivization to annual irrigated and nonirrigated cropland.

Within annual cropland, the 1993 survey identifies five land types:

- *Allocated land.* This land is allocated to households by the cooperative or productive group under Resolution 10 (Vietnam Communist Party 1988). Allocated land accounts for the bulk of the North's cropland.
- *Long-term-use land.* Predominant in the South, this land differs from allocated land only in that the farmer owes no contracted output (in addition to obligatory taxes for all allocated land) to the cooperative or productive group that allocated the land.

- *Auctioned land.* This term refers to a part of the cooperative's or commune's land reserved for bidding by households. It has a three- to five-year tenure, depending on the region.
- *Private land.* This land comprises land inherited and used by households as a garden area, as well as an area known as *5 percent land* that was given to households for their private use at the beginning of collectivization and was meant to be equal to 5 percent of the commune's agricultural land. Private land requires no payment.
- *Sharecropped or rented land.* This land is rented from other households under various contracts including sharecropping agreements.

What chapter 4 refers to as "allocated land" is annual cropland, either irrigated or nonirrigated. In the survey, such land is referred to as either "allocated land" or "long-term-use land." It includes all allocated land, whether or not actually cultivated by the household.

We aggregate irrigated and nonirrigated land using region-specific weights to obtain irrigated-land equivalents. To calculate the weights, we estimated region-specific regressions of farm profit on total irrigated and nonirrigated annual cropland, all other land amounts, a wide array of household characteristics, and commune effects. The ratio of the coefficients on nonirrigated land to that on irrigated land was then used as the weight on nonirrigated land to calculate an allocated irrigated-land equivalent for each household. A detailed description of these calculations and of our definition of farm profit is given in annex 3A.

The 1993 survey asked respondents to assign their total annual cropland into the categories "good," "medium," and "poor" quality. Unfortunately, the questionnaire design does not allow us to separately identify quality for allocated land versus other land types. So we cannot use these quality assessments in calculating our measure of allocated irrigated-land equivalents. These quality assessments are problematic from other points of view. The categories are probably quite well defined within communes, but they are unlikely to be comparable between communes. Nor can it be assumed that they would account fully for omitted heterogeneity in land quality in our main results. The exogeneity of these land-quality variables is also questionable. Against these considerations, excluding these variables adds to concerns about omitted heterogeneity in land quality. So, as controls for quality, we include each household's proportions of good irrigated and nonirrigated land in the regressions discussed in chapter 4.[4] We also test robustness to dropping these variables.

In the analyses for both chapters 4 and 5, we treat private land in a special way. A nonnegligible amount of land is classified this way, and it falls under all usages (annual, perennial, and water surface land). Thus, a household's cultivated land can differ from its allocated land. Rural households typically have their own private residential land with a garden area. However, the category of private land is clearly broader than residential land or garden area. Private land has typically been with the household for a long time, and the amounts were clearly known at decollectivization. So it is reasonable to treat private land as exogenous, and we control for it in our analysis. By contrast, we treat all other land, including land obtained through rental arrangements, as endogenous, so that it does not appear in the models.[5]

These data were collected five years after the 1988 Land Law (though prior to the 1993 Land Law). In trying to explain the allocations, we therefore want to use variables that reflect the situation around 1988. We have no explicit information on the methods for allocating land-use rights in the communes. Some observers mention that household size (Hayami 1994; V. L. Ngo 1993) and available labor in the family were factors.[6] Our demographic variables include household size and the dependency ratio. Household size is that reported in the 1993 survey minus all members younger than 6 years of age, and the dependency ratio is one minus the ratio of working-age members (between 20 and 65 years for men and 20 and 60 years for women) to all household members minus those younger than 6 years.

In studying land allocation in chapter 4, we allow for effects of the gender of the head of household; whether that person was born locally; whether he or she reports practicing the Christian or Buddhist religions (as opposed to no religion, animism, or "other"); and whether he or she belongs to an ethnic group other than the majority Kinh or the relatively well-off Chinese. We also allow for whether the household reports cultivating swidden land. This aims to capture an ethnocultural particularity of those farmers who practice shifting cultivation. Since at least the 1960s, the government has pursued policies to sedentarize such groups by apportioning land to them (Bloch and Oesterberg 1989). Resolution 10 also states that practical measures should be adopted to promote permanent agriculture and settlement. One might therefore expect these households to get more allocated land as a result.

We also control for whether a household contains a handicapped adult of working age.[7] Such an individual could influence the land allocation decision negatively, through effects on productivity. Against that, the Vietnamese government has had a number of policies bestowing preferential treatment to the disabled and to those individuals and their families who suffered in the wars. A handicapped adult might thus be favored. However, this variable will not fully capture the possibility that soldiers and their families were treated differently from others, as decreed by Resolution 10 (Vietnam Communist Party 1988) and alleged by Vinh Long Ngo (1993). We test for this possibility by adding a dummy variable for whether the household or one of its members receives social subsidy transfers from the government. Receipt of this transfer—targeted to the disabled, wounded veterans, and families of war heroes—appears to be the best way to identify such households in our data. There are, however, possible concerns about the endogeneity of this variable (notably if people who are not poor select out of the program). So we do our analysis both with and without it.

In common with the other surveys, the 1993 survey does not identify members of the Communist Party. However, we do know if a household member worked for the cooperative or collective, a social organization, a state-owned enterprise, or the government for five years or more, either in a primary or secondary job. On a priori grounds, it is unclear how these variables would influence land allocation. Other sources of employment may entail a substitution effect, with the commune allocating less land to such households. Conversely, these variables may well come with a power effect, whereby households with such employment have more power over local decisions.

The cooperatives and collectives had owned the farm capital stock (tools, machinery, draft animals) that also had to be allocated among farm households. It is sometimes claimed that this process more easily allowed local officials to favor themselves, their families, and their friends than the more visible land allocation process. It is possible that the most egregious abuse and corruption occurred in the distribution of collectively owned farming implements and draft animals rather than that of land. If so, we would expect to find positive impacts on consumption through the returns to land for favored households. We test this by including in the consumption equation an interaction effect between land and whether a household member worked for a cooperative or collective at or prior to decollectivization. This test is imperfect because it allows only for favoritism through household member ties, but it is the best we can do with the data.

Table 3.1 gives summary statistics on the variables that we use from the 1993 dataset, by region. The Mekong Delta had both the highest mean consumption and the highest land per person (reflecting its lower population density). The Mekong Delta also had the lowest mean schooling (as discussed in chapter 2). The North Central Coast is the region with lowest mean consumption in our baseline. Most other variables are similar between regions.

Table 3.1 Variable Definitions and Descriptive Statistics, 1993

Variable definition	Northern Uplands		Red River Delta		North Central Coast		South Central Coast		Mekong Delta		Full sample	
	Mean	SD	Mean	SD	Mean	SD	Mean	SD	Mean	SD	Mean	SD
Log household real consumption expenditure	15.24	0.52	15.21	0.54	15.11	0.53	15.39	0.62	15.67	0.53	15.31	0.58
Real consumption expenditure per capita (thousand D)	947.67	474.91	1,114.44	506.65	899.98	391.30	1,146.17	556.84	1,422.44	847.95	1,117.79	628.68
Religion: 1 if household head is Buddhist or Christian (0 if other, animist, or none)	0.33	0.47	0.26	0.44	0.18	0.38	0.12	0.32	0.56	0.50	0.31	0.46
Ethnic: 1 if household head is of ethnicity other than majority Kinh or Chinese	0.35	0.48	0.08	0.26	0.03	0.18	0.08	0.28	0.08	0.27	0.12	0.32
Local born: 1 if household head is born locally	0.80	0.40	0.95	0.22	0.89	0.31	0.85	0.36	0.83	0.38	0.86	0.35
Age of household head	40.38	13.59	43.51	14.53	45.44	15.31	47.90	15.26	46.65	14.26	44.46	14.75
Gender of household head: 1 if male	0.81	0.39	0.76	0.43	0.80	0.40	0.76	0.43	0.79	0.41	0.78	0.41
Log household size, excluding those < 6 years old	1.35	0.48	1.17	0.49	1.27	0.50	1.38	0.47	1.47	0.48	1.30	0.50
Dependency ratio: 1 − ratio of working-age members to all members > 6 years old	0.46	0.25	0.42	0.28	0.45	0.28	0.47	0.25	0.49	0.24	0.45	0.26

(Continued on the following page)

Table 3.1 (Continued)

Variable definition	Northern Uplands		Red River Delta		North Central Coast		South Central Coast		Mekong Delta		Full sample	
	Mean	SD	Mean	SD	Mean	SD	Mean	SD	Mean	SD	Mean	SD
Working-age adult member who is handicapped	0.01	0.09	0.01	0.09	0.01	0.08	0.02	0.13	0.00	0.00	0.01	0.08
State-owned enterprise: household member has primary or secondary occupation in a state-owned enterprise and had it 5 years ago	0.01	0.08	0.03	0.19	0.01	0.11	0.01	0.08	0.01	0.11	0.02	0.14
Government job: household member has worked for the government in a primary or secondary occupation for 5+ years or did so 5 years ago or retired from the government[a]	0.07	0.25	0.04	0.21	0.07	0.28	0.05	0.23	0.08	0.30	0.06	0.25
Social subsidy: dummy for receipt of government transfers to war heroes, martyrs, and disabled	0.10	0.30	0.12	0.32	0.13	0.34	0.09	0.29	0.05	0.22	0.10	0.30
Household head's years of education	6.25	3.71	7.23	3.70	7.05	3.80	4.56	3.79	4.31	3.13	6.16	3.83

	Mean	SD	Mean	SD	Mean	SD	Mean	SD	Mean	SD	Mean	SD
Other household adults' years of education	9.81	9.25	10.68	8.56	11.17	9.54	10.20	9.93	9.77	9.55	10.44	9.24
Log allocated irrigated land equivalent (m^2)	7.20	0.73	7.45	0.62	7.40	0.79	7.60	0.73	8.42	1.29	7.59	0.93
Allocated irrigated land equivalent (m^2)	1,679.57	1,117.37	2,007.70	997.03	2,084.14	1,312.36	2,621.58	2,403.59	7,296.94	6,514.12	3,003.26	3,646.40
Household's private irrigated land (m^2)	159.62	238.56	157.05	167.05	86.21	157.35	136.42	545.33	279.17	1,505.35	155.89	648.13
Household's private nonirrigated land (m^2)	242.92	401.20	113.38	521.38	250.95	389.62	310.03	598.75	209.02	1,561.83	218.54	921.38
Household's private perennial land (m^2)	278.72	507.38	120.70	353.67	90.71	204.60	188.53	463.52	903.74	1,672.80	343.75	1,453.46
Household's private water surface land (m^2)	58.32	163.23	60.73	176.88	30.01	116.36	0.00	0.00	116.26	1,102.29	55.74	459.87
Household cultivates swidden land = 1	0.29	0.45	0.04	0.19	0.04	0.20	0.23	0.42	0.02	0.14	0.10	0.31
Share of good irrigated land	0.18	0.34	0.51	0.39	0.31	0.35	0.24	0.38	0.11	0.30	0.31	0.39
Share of good nonirrigated land	0.28	0.40	0.18	0.37	0.68	0.43	0.24	0.38	0.59	0.49	0.37	0.46
Number of observations	484		956		506		276		443		2,810	

Source: 1993 VLSS.

Note: SD = standard deviation; D = dong; m^2 = square meters.

a. Government work is identified through professional codes 20 and 21.

The 1993–98 Household Panel: Land Reallocations

In studying the land reallocation process in the wake of introducing land markets in chapter 5, we use the household panel data from the 1993 and 1998 VLSSs. The surveys contain a balanced panel of 4,308 households. We limit our sample to the 2,559 rural farming households in the panel that had allocated annual agricultural land in 1993.

An issue of potential concern in using panel data is attrition of households across the two surveys. Some of the households interviewed in the first survey may not have been available for interview in the second, follow-up, survey. For example, they may have moved during the intervening period or no longer be willing to participate in the survey. In the case of the 1993–98 VLSS panel, attrition was low: 9 percent of the households covered in the first survey were not in the second. If such attrition is random, then it is of no concern for our analysis. However, nonrandom attrition could bias our results. Tests for attrition bias rely on one's having the baseline characteristics of both those who stayed in the panel and those who left. Hence, one can estimate the probability of attrition at the household level as a function of those characteristics; under the null hypothesis that attrition is random, the baseline characteristics will have no explanatory power. If there are signs of systematic factors influencing attrition, then one can use the same regressions for the probability of attrition to correct for the bias in the regressions of interest estimated on the panel dataset; for example, one can use the estimated probabilities of attrition conditional on baseline characteristics to reweight the data. In the context of the VLSS panel for 1993–98, Falaris (2003) has studied attrition but does not find that it is a serious concern for regressions for schooling, labor-force participation, self-employment, wages, and fertility. Similarly, van de Walle and Cratty (2004) and De Brauw and Harigaya (2007) test for selective attrition in a model of consumption estimated on the VLSS panel for 1993–98 and find that correcting for attrition makes very little difference to their results. When we analyze land reallocations, we test for bias in that context.

Table 3.2 provides summary statistics from the panel for 1993–98. Notice that there was a net increase in total allocated land for the panel sample, reflecting new land brought under cultivation.

As in chapter 4, here we focus on allocated *annual* agricultural land because of its importance in production and total area, and because its allocation began earlier and has progressed more rapidly than for other land types. Here our aim is to study changes in the

Table 3.2 Variable Definitions and Summary Statistics, 1993–98

Variable definition	Full sample Mean	Full sample SD	Kept allocated annual land in 1998 Mean	Kept allocated annual land in 1998 SD	No allocated annual land in 1998 Mean	No allocated annual land in 1998 SD	Mekong Delta Mean	Mekong Delta SD	Full sample minus Mekong Delta Mean	Full sample minus Mekong Delta SD
Log change in allocated irrigated-land equivalent (m²)	0.142 (n = 2,361)	0.66	0.142	0.66	0	0	0.002 (n = 308)	0.75	0.163 (n = 2,053)	0.64
Change in allocated irrigated-land equivalent (m²)	206.708	3,527.38	494.22	3,203.79	−3,221.619	5,078.94	−521.438	6,891.17	337.633	2,459.15
Log real per capita 1993 consumption expenditure (thousand 1993 D)	13.801	0.46	13.789	0.44	13.952	0.59	14.053	0.48	13.756	0.436
Real per capita 1993 consumption expenditure (thousand 1993 D)	1,100.111	604.98	1,076.842	548.77	1,377.579	1,030.01	1,432.131	824.85	1,040.412	535.13
Change in real per capita consumption 1993–98 (thousand 1998 D)	813.883	408.29	809.698	403.83	863.765	456.25	1,009.039	653.47	778.777	334.60
Proportional efficiency loss (log efficient allocation minus log actual in 1993)	−0.016	0.78	−0.072	0.72	0.651	1.17	0.038	0.94	−0.085	0.74
Religion: 1 if household head is Buddhist or Christian (0 if other, animist, or none)	0.307	0.46	0.305	0.46	0.338	0.47	0.572	0.50	0.260	0.44
Ethnic: 1 if household head is of ethnicity other than majority Kinh or Chinese	0.121	0.33	0.116	0.32	0.177	0.38	0.087	0.28	0.127	0.33
Local born: 1 if household head is born locally	0.861	0.35	0.867	0.34	0.783	0.413	0.844	0.364	0.864	0.34
Age of household head	44.758	14.69	44.496	14.54	47.874	16.09	47.385	14.18	44.285	14.73
Gender of household head: 1 if male	0.791	0.41	0.792	0.41	0.778	0.42	0.787	0.41	0.791	0.41

(Continued on the following page)

Table 3.2 (Continued)

Variable definition	Full sample		Kept allocated annual land in 1998		No allocated annual land in 1998		Mekong Delta		Full sample minus Mekong Delta	
	Mean	SD	Mean	SD	Mean	SD	Mean	SD	Mean	SD
Log household size in 1993	1.516	0.44	1.520	0.44	1.468	0.49	1.652	0.45	1.492	0.44
Dependency ratio: 1 − ratio of working-age members to all members in 1993	0.564	0.19	0.563	0.19	0.576	0.21	0.573	0.19	0.562	0.19
Working-age adult member is handicapped	0.007	0.09	0.008	0.09	0	0	0	0	0.009	0.09
State-owned enterprise: household member has primary or secondary occupation in a state-owned enterprise and had it 5 years ago	0.018	0.14	0.017	0.14	0.035	0.21	0.013	0.11	0.019	0.15
Government job: household member has worked for the government in a primary or secondary occupation for 5+ years or did so 5 years ago or retired from the government[a]	0.059	0.25	0.056	0.25	0.096	0.30	0.085	0.31	0.055	0.24
Social subsidy: dummy for receipt of government transfers to war heroes, martyrs, and disabled	0.103	0.30	0.095	0.29	0.197	0.40	0.044	0.20	0.114	0.32
Household head's years of education	6.107	3.83	6.197	3.81	5.035	3.98	4.213	3.09	6.448	3.858
Other household adults' years of education	10.648	9.22	10.76	9.22	9.343	9.16	10.197	9.70	10.729	9.13

Variable										
Household's private irrigated land (m²)	158.853	658.68	169.018	680.34	37.641	269.42	300.949	1,579.04	133.303	245.43
Household's private nonirrigated land (m²)	228.824	955.31	224.399	951.56	281.581	999.96	215.256	1,638.92	231.263	771.23
Household's private perennial land (m²)	349.057	1,492.13	312.983	1,436.01	779.207	2,001.22	935.467	1,656.14	243.616	1,435.91
Household's private water surface land (m²)	55.913	478.74	52.806	442.33	92.965	794.15	121.842	1,169.92	44.059	154.66
Household cultivates swidden land = 1	0.108	0.31	0.107	0.31	0.126	0.33	0.021	0.142	0.124	0.33
Share of good irrigated land	0.304	0.39	0.318	0.39	0.131	0.32	0.109	0.30	0.339	0.39
Share of good nonirrigated land	0.374	0.46	0.362	0.46	0.520	0.49	0.587	0.49	0.335	0.44
Number of household members ≥ 16 years in 1993 who died by 1998	0.109	0.33	0.104	0.33	0.162	0.40	0.131	0.35	0.105	0.33
Number of household members ≥ 50 years in 1993 who died by 1998	0.089	0.30	0.085	0.30	0.146	0.37	0.113	0.33	0.085	0.30
Change in number of disabled adults 1993–98	−0.004	0.15	−0.005	0.15	0	0.10	−0.005	0.12	−0.004	0.15
Change in number of able-bodied working-age household members 1993–98	−0.138	1.19	−0.141	1.20	−0.106	1.13	−0.172	1.45	−0.132	1.14
Household has new individual age 8–99 in 1998	0.216	0.60	0.213	0.60	0.247	0.59	0.321	0.78	0.197	0.56
Number of observations	2,559		2,361		198		390		2,169	

Sources: 1993 and 1998 VLSSs.

Note: SD = standard deviation; D = dong; m² = square meters.

a. Government work is identified through professional codes 20 and 21.

allocated annual land amounts following the 1993 Land Law. Nonirrigated-land amounts are converted into irrigated-land equivalents as described in the previous section and annex 3A, using the same weights calculated from the 1993 VLSS data. As also described in the previous section, our allocated land variable in 1993 comprises the questionnaire categories "allocated" and "long-term-use" annual land. By 1998, this distinction was no longer enforced. The 1998 VLSS refers to allocated land as either long-term-use or "contract" land. The latter is also allocated to households for long-term and stable use, but its land-use title is held by a state-managed farm or enterprise rather than the household. This category of land was subsumed in either allocated or long-term-use land in the 1993 survey. We consider it to be part of the allocated land category in 1998. Also in contrast to the 1993 VLSS, where allocated annual land amounts include any area that was rented out, such rented land is recorded separately in 1998 and so must be added to determine the amount of the household's total allocated annual land.

In modeling land reallocation, we control for exogenous household-level variables that describe the household's initial 1993 situation in terms of assets, connections, and possible discriminating variables. These household-level variables include the years of education of the head of household and of other adults; dummy variables for the head of household's religion (1 if Christian or Buddhist, 0 otherwise), ethnicity (1 if the head of household belongs to an ethnic group other than the majority Kinh or relatively wealthy Chinese minority), and place of birth (1 if born locally); and dummies for whether the household contains one or more handicapped adult members, whether the household contains members who work for the government or for a state-owned enterprise, and whether the household receives social insurance fund transfers. Again, we run the model with and without the dummy variable for receipt of social fund transfers, given the possible endogeneity concerns. We also control for the household's private land (as discussed in the previous section), whether or not it cultivates swidden land, and the share of its irrigated and nonirrigated land that is considered to be of good quality by the respondent.

In addition, we include variables that capture changes in the household's characteristics that are exogenous to land allocation—namely, the change in the number of disabled adult members, the change in the number of able-bodied working-age members, the number of new members between 8 and 99 years of age in 1998, and whether an adult or elderly member died between the two surveys.

Overall Comparisons of Poverty and Landlessness, 1993–2004

In measuring landlessness for the analyses in chapters 6 and 7, we use as the land concept the amount of "cultivated land" in the annual, perennial, water surface, and forest categories, which allows us to define *landlessness* similarly across the four surveys. We define a household as landless if it has no land other than land it rents in or residential or swidden land.[8] We make a distinction between "landless" and "noncultivating" households; the latter include those who rent out all of their land.[9] The 2004 survey has the advantage that it included a special module on land (see the section titled "Lessons from the 2004 Land Module"), which we take advantage of in chapters 6 and 7.

As already noted, we do not have panel data spanning the years 1993–2004. Thus, we cannot measure welfare changes over time for those who were farmers in 1993 but landless in 2004. Nor can we trace farmers who became landless and moved to urban areas (which is also impossible with most panels). Observed changes over time will reflect (in part) the changing internal composition of given socioeconomic groups. For example, if relatively worse-off farmers sell their land, this will put upward pressure on the poverty rate among the landless. Comparing a poverty measure for the landless over time, we cannot say how much is caused by changing living conditions among the initially landless compared with low living standards among those who become landless.

Table 3.3 provides summary statistics on poverty and landlessness across the four household surveys. For rural Vietnam, the landlessness rate increased by two-thirds over the period, to slightly more than 12 percent in 2004. (These are population weighted; the proportion of households that were landless rose from 8.4 percent to 13.6 percent.) In all years, the poverty rate is higher for those with land than for the landless. Similarly, mean consumption is higher for the landless. There was a sharp contraction in the incidence of poverty, which occurred at roughly the same rate for those with land as for those without land. From 1993 to 2004, the proportionate gain in consumption was higher for those with land; the ratio of the mean consumption for the landless relative to those with land fell between 1993 and 2004 from 1.33 to 1.24, though within the period it fell (to 1.21 in 1998) and then rose (back to 1.33 in 2002).

Table 3.3 also gives an inequality measure, the *mean log deviation* (MLD), defined as the log of mean consumption minus the

Table 3.3 Poverty, Inequality, and Landholding Status in Rural Vietnam

Population/ survey year	Population with land				Landless population			
	Percentage	Mean consumption	Consumption inequality (MLD)	Poverty rate (%)	Percentage	Mean consumption	Consumption inequality (MLD)	Poverty rate (%)
Rural Vietnam								
1993	92.2	1,626.9	0.114	70.04	7.8	2,163.2	0.174	50.87
1998	93.1	2,135.0	0.124	45.90	6.9	2,588.3	0.199	40.51
2002	86.1	2,338.9	0.133	38.60	13.9	3,116.5	0.162	25.11
2004	87.7	2,823.9	0.148	25.99	12.3	3,514.4	0.162	18.14
Majority ethnic groups								
1993	91.4	1,708.5	0.108	66.20	8.6	2,248.3	0.165	47.38
1998	92.7	2,274.0	0.114	39.13	7.3	2,784.7	0.155	34.66
2002	84.4	2,499.8	0.117	31.44	15.6	3,168.2	0.160	23.40
2004	86.1	3,046.2	0.125	18.06	13.9	3,582.3	0.159	16.60
Minority ethnic groups								
1993	96.6	1,215.4	0.103	89.39	3.4	1,038.0	0.090	97.12
1998	95.0	1,516.5	0.097	76.04	5.0	1,259.1	0.216	80.14
2002	96.0	1,544.2	0.113	73.96	4.0	1,995.0	0.144	62.16
2004	96.0	1,775.6	0.132	63.36	4.0	2,270.0	0.146	46.41

Sources: 1993 and 1998 VLSSs and 2002 and 2004 VHLSSs.
Note: Mean consumption per capita is in thousands of real 1998 dongs. Inequality is measured by the mean log deviation (MLD); poverty is given by the head-count index based on a constant real poverty line.

DATA AND SUMMARY STATISTICS   55

mean of log consumption.[10] We find that inequality is higher among the landless than among those with land but that there is a sign of convergence, with increasing inequality among those with land and decreasing inequality among the landless.

Panel b of figure 3.1 shows how the distribution of consumption changed for the landless between 1993 and 2004. The rise in the mean and the fall in poverty are evident, but there is no sign of marked polarization among the landless. Two clear subgroups are not emerging among the landless—one poor and one not.

The patterns for rural Vietnam also hold for the majority ethnic group in all four years (table 3.3).[11] For the minority groups—who are appreciably poorer on average and less likely to be landless—the poverty rate was higher for landless households in the 1990s, but this switched in 2002 and 2004 to the same pattern found for the majority. The (absolute and proportionate) rate of decline in poverty is greater among the landless minorities than for those with land.

Table 3.4 gives a regional breakdown. The landlessness rate is higher in the South, notably in the Southeast and the Mekong Delta. In a number of respects, the Mekong Delta stands apart from Vietnam's other regions. The landless tend to be less poor in all regions except the Mekong Delta. There was a decline in poverty incidence among the landless in all regions, though the rate of poverty reduction for the Mekong Delta's landless is lower than for those with land. In 1993, the landless in the Mekong Delta were about 20 percent more likely to be poor than those with land; by 2004, the landless were twice as likely to be poor. There is little sign of polarization in the consumption distribution among the Mekong Delta landless; similarly to figure 3.1, panel b, the frequency distribution of consumption in the Mekong Delta was no more bimodal in 2004 than in 1993. We do not find any sign that other regions are following in the footsteps of the Mekong Delta; elsewhere, the rate of poverty reduction among the landless has kept pace (or even exceeded) that for the landed.

The rise in landlessness naturally has put upward pressure on the inequality of landholdings. Figure 3.2 gives the Lorenz curves for annual cropland (panel a) and perennial cropland (panel b). We find that the 2004 Lorenz curve was nowhere above that for 1993 for either annual or perennial cropland, implying an unambiguous increase in the inequality of landholding for any standard inequality measure (satisfying the transfer axiom; see Atkinson 1970).

Did unemployment rise with the increase in landlessness? The open unemployment rate is known to be low in Vietnam and to have fallen in the postreform period; Houghton (2000) estimates an overall unemployment rate from the 1998 VLSS of 1.6 percent, less

Table 3.4 Poverty, Inequality, and Landholding Status, by Region

Region/survey year	Population with land				Landless population			
	Percentage	Mean consumption	MLD	Poverty (%)	Percentage[a]	Mean consumption	MLD	Poverty (%)
Northern Uplands								
1993	97.8	1,342.1	0.081	85.41	2.2 (13)	1,816.6	0.238	62.86
1998	98.0	1,701.8	0.099	66.30	2.0 (18)	3,619.3	0.132	10.61
2002	96.6	2,019.4	0.125	50.58	3.4	3,639.7	0.110	7.89
2004	97.2	2,457.7	0.150	37.40	2.8	4,365.6	0.128	5.43
Red River Delta								
1993	98.0	1,557.4	0.080	73.74	2.0	2,584.9	0.087	21.59
1998	99.6	2,291.1	0.089	36.10	0.4 (10)	2,106.0	0.029	40.85
2002	92.6	2,449.9	0.104	30.59	7.4	4,668.8	0.159	3.90
2004	94.3	2,996.8	0.106	16.29	5.7	4,467.3	0.105	3.27
North Central Coast								
1993	96.5	1,428.9	0.080	79.43	3.5	1,680.3	0.094	58.16
1998	98.3	2,018.6	0.114	50.95	1.7 (18)	1,719.8	0.029	71.09
2002	91.3	2,005.4	0.108	51.35	8.7	2,596.7	0.159	37.27
2004	93.2	2,369.7	0.123	37.49	6.8	3,070.3	0.129	21.67
South Central Coast								
1993	90.2	1,642.4	0.136	65.80	9.8	2,582.7	0.174	35.75
1998	98.3	2,109.0	0.133	43.56	1.7 (13)	3,052.2	0.235	44.05
2002	83.6	2,292.4	0.118	34.50	16.4	2,927.5	0.150	20.40
2004	86.7	2,764.8	0.154	26.13	13.3	3,020.2	0.093	16.33

Central Highlands							
1993	92.8	1,506.6	0.161	72.87	7.2 (12)	1,921.7	0.086	72.73
1998	90.9	2,033.4	0.146	49.38	9.1	1,021.7	0.274	82.68
2002	96.8	1,753.8	0.155	62.17	3.2	2,092.4	0.123	55.81
2004	97.0	2,322.5	0.171	42.43	3.0 (17)	2,879.8	0.099	5.38
Southeast							
1993	78.3	2,067.2	0.147	50.84	21.7	2,534.7	0.196	36.26
1998	74.3	3,397.0	0.131	12.47	25.7	3,732.7	0.159	14.51
2002	62.0	3,218.7	0.126	15.85	38.0	3,624.6	0.154	14.05
2004	62.7	4,043.1	0.138	8.35	37.3	4,511.5	0.194	7.04
Mekong Delta							
1993	86.0	1,943.5	0.131	54.63	14.0	1,888.0	0.165	64.05
1998	84.1	2,189.9	0.086	40.27	15.9	2,085.4	0.130	50.81
2002	75.1	2,790.1	0.130	25.02	24.9	2,603.1	0.153	35.75
2004	77.1	3,232.0	0.129	14.83	22.9	2,883.4	0.152	29.26

Sources: 1993 and 1998 VLSSs and 2002 and 2004 VHLSSs.

Note: Mean consumption per capita is in thousands of real 1998 dongs. Inequality is measured by the mean log deviation (MLD); poverty is given by the head-count index based on a constant real poverty line.

a. Numbers of respondents for small samples (under 20) are given in parentheses.

Figure 3.2 Lorenz Curves for Annual and Perennial Cropland in Rural Vietnam, 1993 and 2004

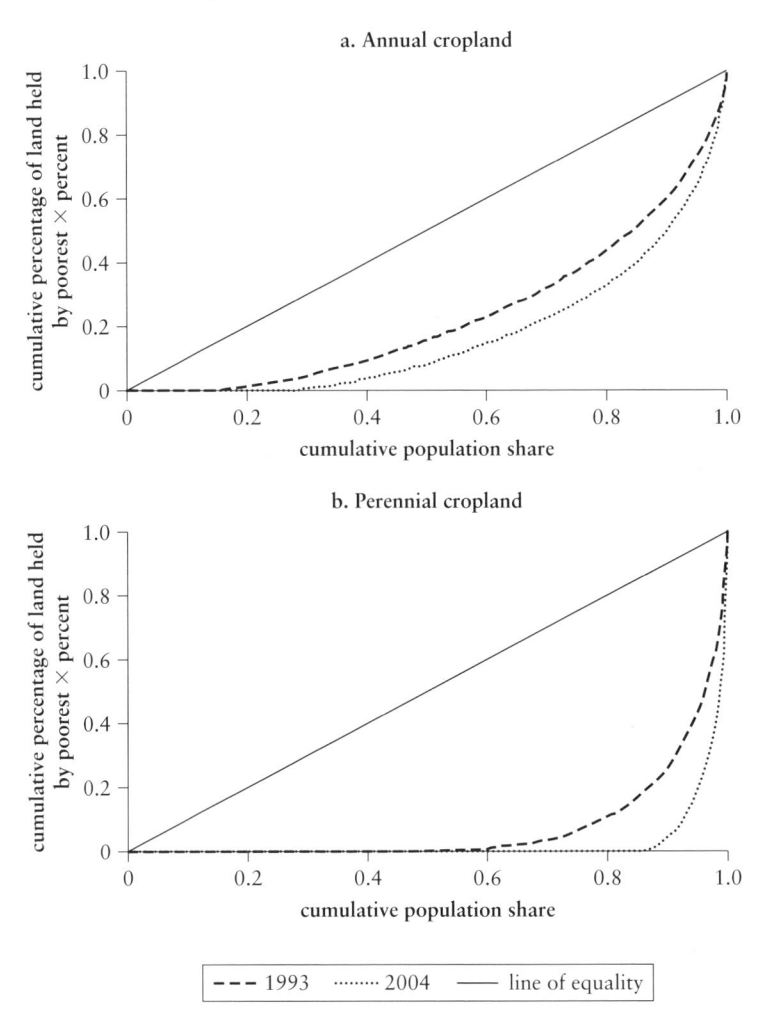

a. Annual cropland

b. Perennial cropland

--- 1993   2004   —— line of equality

Sources: 1993 VLSS and 2004 VHLSS.

than half of the rate in 1993. Using adults who report that they did not work because they could not find work in the past 12 months, we find that only 2.6 percent of landless rural households in 2004 had an unemployed adult, and this figure was almost identical in 1993 (2.5 percent).[12] The rate was lower in the Mekong Delta (2.1 percent in 2004; 1.6 percent in 1993). However, time-use data might well reveal higher rates on underemployment, depending on the season.

Did those who became landless start to rent in land? From the 1993 VLSS, we calculate that 8.9 percent of rural households rented in land; this figure rose to 10.7 percent in the 2004 VHLSS. Among the landless, as we have defined them, the proportion of households that rented in land actually fell over time, though the change was small, from 7.7 percent in 1993 to 6.5 percent in 2004. Those who became landless do not appear to have turned to land rental.

A Pseudo-Panel Based on Age Cohorts for 1993–2004

As we have noted, we do not have a household-level panel dataset spanning the entire period of interest; the 1993 sample was reinterviewed in 1998 but not in 2002 or 2004. This is a limitation; for example, we cannot track those who became landless to see what happens to their standard of living. But that would also be difficult with a household panel such as that for 1993–98. Such datasets typically do not trace rural residents who move to urban areas.

There is another way of studying the process of rising landlessness, which has not been used in any previous research on this topic to our knowledge. We can construct a "pseudo-panel" from the repeated cross-sectional surveys by calculating the means of all relevant variables by age cohorts. By using the national (urban plus rural) sample, we can ensure valid inferences from such a pseudo-panel, in that each cross-section gives a sample that is representative of the same population subgroup at each of the two dates. By contrast, if we did the analysis for only the rural sample, then a bias would arise from selective migration to urban areas. Notice that in using pseudo-panel data in this way, we are not only making up for the lack of a true panel spanning the period, but also addressing a data inadequacy of most such "true panels," given that movers are rarely traced after they move.

We can also use pseudo-panel data to study the incidence of urbanization. As chapter 2 noted, the implications for the pace of urbanization of reforms that encourage some farmers to leave their land have never been far from the concerns raised by both sides of the debates on Vietnam's agrarian transition.

We use the 1993 and 2004 surveys for this purpose. We form means of all relevant variables based on the age of the household head in 1993 and similarly for the corresponding groups in 2004 (age in 1993 plus 11 years). We were able to construct 34 age cohorts with minimum sample sizes of 100 (about half the cohorts had sample sizes over 150).[13] Annex 3B gives the means by age cohorts of the main variables we use here.

We return to use this pseudo-panel dataset for deeper analysis in chapter 6. However, a couple of descriptive points should be noted now. First, since this dataset pertains to Vietnam as a whole, the landlessness rate is for both urban and rural areas. Naturally, then, the landlessness rate is strongly correlated with the urbanization rate, given that most urban residents do not have agricultural land, although the correlation has become weaker over time, reflecting the greater diversification of the rural economy. The correlation coefficients between the landlessness rate and the urban population share are 0.85 and 0.51 for 1993 and 2004, respectively; the correlation between the changes in landlessness and the changes in urbanization is 0.56.

Second, there is also a strong negative correlation between the landlessness rate and the head-count index of poverty. This correlation has also become weaker over time. The correlation coefficients between the landlessness and poverty rates are −0.68 and −0.36 for 1993 and 2004, respectively; the changes in landlessness and the changes in the poverty rate have a correlation of −0.27. As one would expect, similarly high correlations are found between the urban population share and poverty (both in levels and in changes over time). And mean consumption is highly correlated with both the landlessness rate and the urban population share.

Lessons from the 2004 Land Module

The 2004 VHLSS contains a detailed land module, which we make extended use of in chapter 6. It collects plot-specific information on the usual details concerning the type and quality of the land, water access, users of the land, and ways it is used. It is the first of Vietnam's nationally representative household surveys to ask about land-use certificates (LUCs)—whether the plot has an LUC, when it was received, and whose name is on the title registration (with room for two names). In using the 2004 land data, we aggregate plot-specific responses, weighted by plot sizes.

In addition, the module contains a number of interesting sections with retrospective data based on recall, which can be used to better understand the history of household landholdings and provides a view of the development of land markets in recent years. One section questions households on when they started using the plots of land to which they currently have land-use rights and how they initially acquired their use rights—whether through commune allocation, inheritance, auction, purchase, reclamation, or other means. Another section focuses on plot-specific land-use conversions and investments over the past 10 years. Yet another asks about the land transactions carried out over the past 10 years, including whether and how plots were newly acquired (including through allocation from the commune, inheritance, auction, purchase, reclamation, or exchange) or disposed of (including through bequest, sale, exchange, government expropriation, or lease expiration). Chapter 6 makes extensive use of these data.

One of the interesting questions asked in the land module is when households started *using* the plots of land to which they currently have land-use rights. As already noted, the same section also asks how use rights to the plots were acquired. The revealed range of dates of first use is surprising and appears to raise doubts about what role the land reforms played (particularly in the South) if one assumes that acquiring use rights and first using the land necessarily coincided in time. For example, assuming contemporaneity, Brandt (2006) presents a table of the share of total annual land acquired by year and method of acquisition. As noted by Brandt, the table suggests that communes have played a negligible role in land allocation in the South and that most of the land farmed by households in the Mekong Delta was inherited or purchased, much of it prior to 1988.

For a number of reasons, we believe that this interpretation is questionable. For one, it is clear that households were often farming some plots of land for many years before they acquired use rights to those same plots. In much of the country, Contract 100 assigned land management with annual production contracts to households in 1981. That allocation presumably took many of the same factors into account that the communes would consider when allocating land at decollectivization seven years later. Hence, it is likely that in many cases farmers would have been farming at least some of the same land prior to 1988 without having acquired stable land-use rights as these came to be defined by the 1988 Land Law. Similarly, while not succeeding in its push to form fully fledged cooperatives or even collectives in much of the South, the communist government nevertheless took over land property rights and reallocated land across households there. This region had been a war zone with widespread population displacement and National Liberation Front domination in many parts. Although eventually households may have been allocated land they had previously farmed and initially brought to the collectives, this would by no means have been an expectation on the part of many farm households after a long period of upheaval and uncertainty about land-use rights and the future of agricultural policy.

The interpretation of the data on the time of first use and on the ways that land was acquired is complex in another respect. In a number of circumstances, it is unclear how households would interpret and answer the question of how land-use rights were acquired. If at decollectivization in 1988 a Mekong Delta household was allocated the land subsequent to the 1988 Land Law that its family had purchased and farmed prior to 1975, would the household say that it acquired the land through the commune, through purchase, or through inheritance? As Brandt (2006: 31) notes:

> In using these data to provide an indication of trends in land market activity, there is an obvious caveat: the further back we go the more likely we underestimate the extent of land market activity. Land that households purchased in the early 1980s, for example, may be subsequently resold or given to children in the form of bequests, in which case it would not be included in land obtained from the market.

Clearly, the same point applies to allocation of land by communes. So we take care in our interpretation of these data and their implications for the effects of the land reforms on market-based activity. What is striking about these data is what they reveal about the degree to which market and state processes are intertwined in Vietnam's land outcomes during this entire period.

Community-Assessed and Self-Assessed Welfare

There are two alternative measures of household welfare available from the 2004 survey. The first is a community-based assessment of poverty status. Respondents were asked whether they were classified as poor by the commune authorities in 1999, in 2003, or at both times. Members of the commune's People's Committee make this list, with verification at public village meetings. In practice, village leaders and the mass organizations appear to play a major role in determining who is on the list. This can also change for reasons that have little to do with real changes in poverty. For example, we have heard anecdotal reports from staff members of nongovernmental organizations working in the field that local officials sometimes trim lists of the poor to ensure that they meet predetermined poverty reduction targets. Being classified as poor by the local authorities is one factor determining eligibility for the antipoverty programs, namely, the Hunger Elimination and Poverty Reduction Program and Program 135 (which we study further in chapter 7).

The second welfare measure is the household's own perspective on how its living standards have altered since 1999, with options of answering "very much improved," "improved," "no change," and "worsened." The survey did not, however, include any measure of

DATA AND SUMMARY STATISTICS   63

the level of (as opposed to change in) subjective welfare (such as the "economic welfare question" studied by Ravallion and Lokshin 2002).

Figure 3.3 shows the relationship between the share of households classified as poor by the commune in both years and consumption for the landless and landed separately. These are nonparametric regressions, using the method for locally smoothed scatter plots

Figure 3.3 Households Classified as Poor by the Commune, 1999 and 2003

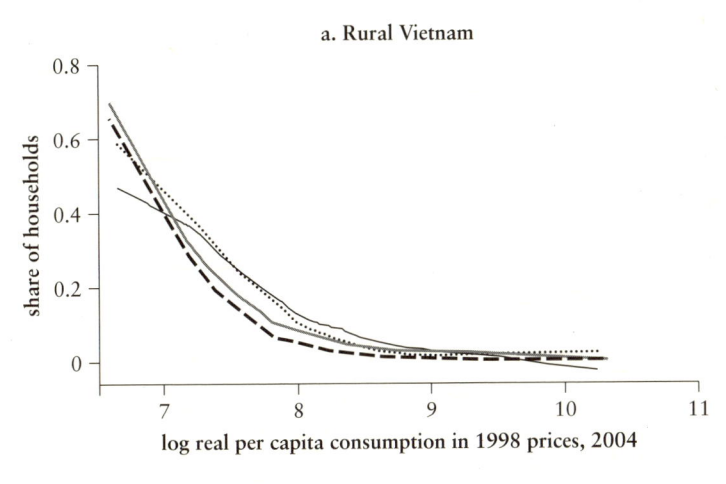

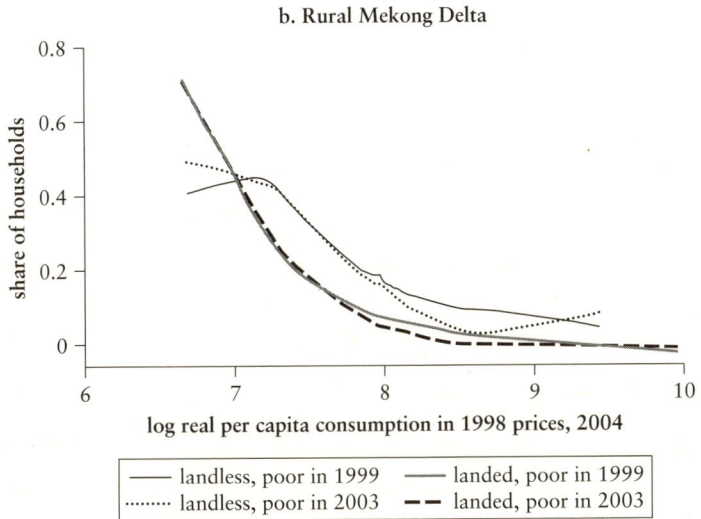

a. Rural Vietnam

b. Rural Mekong Delta

——— landless, poor in 1999   ——— landed, poor in 1999
········ landless, poor in 2003   — — landed, poor in 2003

Source: 2004 VHLSS.

proposed by Cleveland (1979), as programmed in STATA software. There is a stable decreasing and convex relationship between whether one is on this list and consumption per person. (The fact that it is so stable over time is reassuring.) Nationally, and for both dates, we find that equally poor rural landless households were less likely to be identified as poor than households with land, though the disparity had lessened by 2003. The same can also be seen for the Mekong Delta (panel b of figure 3.3).

Turning to the households' self-assessments of welfare change in figure 3.4, we see that once again, conditioning on consumption, the landless poor have a much less favorable view of how they have fared since 1999 than the landed poor. This is true for the entire rural sample as well as for the landless in the Mekong Delta. Thus, at equal levels of consumption, poor landless households feel worse about their living conditions. This could reflect pessimistic long-term expectations about the future and their expected trajectory, or it could indicate a sense of greater vulnerability than is felt by landed households.

Data from the Survey of Impacts of Rural Roads in Vietnam

We also make use of a panel dataset collected for analyzing the impact on living standards of a rural roads project: the Survey of Impacts of Rural Roads in Vietnam (SIRRV). The SIRRV is useful for our purposes because it follows the same households from 1997 to 2003, a period through which the other surveys do not. The SIRRV asked a number of questions that allow us to track changes in land markets over time, complementing the information available in the VLSS and VHLSS. This panel covers close to 3,000 households living in 200 communes located in six provinces: Lao Cai and Thai Nguyen in the north, Nghe An and Binh Thuan in the center, and Kon Tum and Tra Vinh in the south of the country.

A household questionnaire was administered to 15 households in each sampled commune. To ensure samples representative of different socioeconomic groups, the SIRRV used a system of stratified sampling whereby five households were randomly selected from each of three lists, containing the poorest, middle, and richest thirds of each commune's households. These household classifications were based on a welfare ranking periodically done by the commune authorities. They are undoubtedly somewhat subjective, but stratified sampling on this basis should ensure a sample that is reasonably representative of each commune's socioeconomic groups.

Figure 3.4 Self-Assessed Increases in Living Standards, 1999–2004

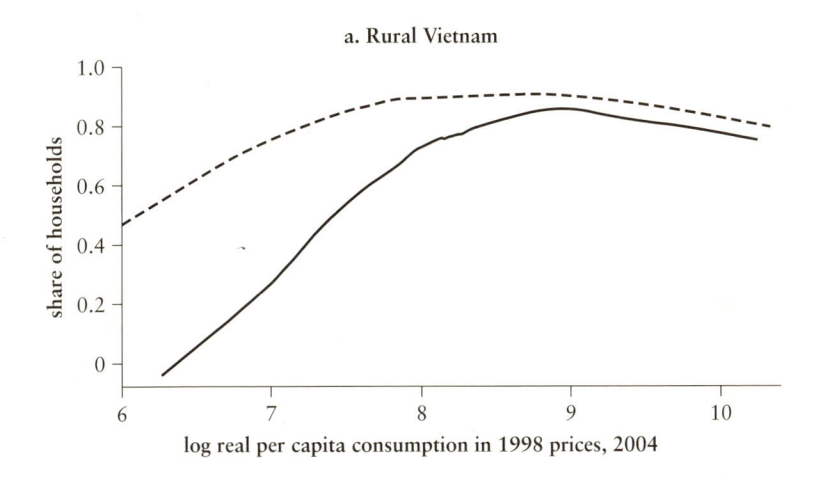

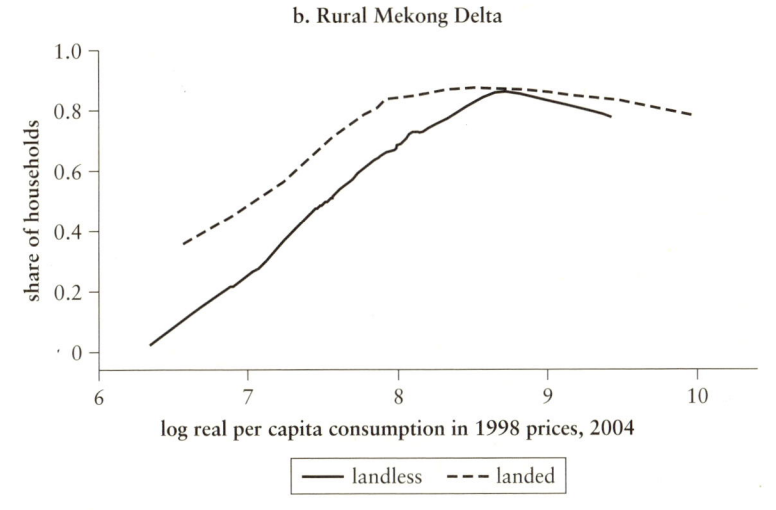

a. Rural Vietnam

b. Rural Mekong Delta

——— landless --- landed

Source: 2004 VHLSS.
Note: The vertical axis is the proportion of households saying that their standard of living had increased since 1999.

Unfortunately, the data do not include a household-level indicator of welfare such as consumption expenditures. However, drawing on extensive information on household characteristics common to the SIRRV and to the 1998 VLSS and 2004 VHLSS, we use regression techniques to predict consumption expenditures for SIRRV households.

Using the rural samples from the VLSSs, we regressed the log of real per capita expenditures on a large set of household characteristics that can be expected to be highly correlated with household consumption and that also exist, similarly defined, in the SIRRV household data.[14] The regression coefficients are then used to predict real 1998 and 2004 log per capita consumption expenditures for the 1997 and 2003 SIRRV households using the corresponding variables in the SIRRV.[15]

Actual mean per capita consumption for the 1998 VLSS rural sample is 2,515.605 (with a standard deviation of 1,467.065), while predicted mean consumption for the SIRRV sample in 1997 is 2,332.896 (with a standard deviation of 1,110.707). For 2004, actual mean per capita consumption in the rural sample is 3,367.183 (with a standard deviation of 2,147.307), and the calculated mean of consumption for SIRRV 2003 is 3,418.321 (with a standard deviation of 1,819.55). The results from this procedure allow us to draw implications for household welfare and rank the SIRRV households into welfare groups.

Annex 3A: Irrigated-Land Equivalents

Annual agricultural land can be either irrigated or nonirrigated. To facilitate our analysis of land allocation and reallocation (chapters 4 and 5), we convert all allocated annual agricultural land into an equivalent amount of allocated irrigated land for each household. In calculating irrigated-land equivalents, we start with a measure of farm profits—farm crop income net of variable costs—calculated from the 1993 VLSS as follows. First, we compute total revenue from agricultural production. This includes crops evaluated at harvest prices (missing values are replaced by average community prices), the value of crop by-products consumed or sold, and incomes from leasing out land and farm production equipment. From this total revenue, we subtract total production costs. These include the costs of hired labor, seeds and young plants, fertilizer, manure, insecticide, animal rental, transport, packaging and storage, equipment rental, repair and maintenance fees, fuel oil and electricity, an accounting depreciation charge for owned farming equipment (5 percent), land and other taxes, and fees to the cooperative or the government. Transformation of homegrown crops or livestock income is not included. The costs of household labor inputs on the family farm are also omitted (van de Walle 2003).

Next, we estimate region-specific regressions of farm profit on total irrigated and nonirrigated annual cropland, perennial land, forestland, and other land amounts (including swidden, bald hill, and newly cleared land), and commune effects.[16] Controls were also included for household characteristics (the head's religion, ethnicity, age and age squared, and whether born locally; household size and size squared; the share of male adults in the household; and the years of primary schooling of the head of household and of other adults). Table 3A.1 gives the regressions for farm profits by region.

We then take the ratio of the coefficients on nonirrigated to the coefficients on irrigated land for each region as the weight on nonirrigated land and calculate an allocated irrigated-land equivalent amount for each household in a specific region. Our estimated weights for nonirrigated land are 0.241 for the Northern Uplands, 0.407 for the Red River Delta, 0.495 for the North Coast, 0.838 for the Central Coast, and 0.906 for the Mekong Delta. These weights seem plausible on the basis of our knowledge of the regions.

Thus, irrigated and nonirrigated land amounts are aggregated into square meters of irrigated-land equivalents using region-specific weights. The same weights, estimated using the 1993 VLSS, are used to create the allocated irrigated-land equivalents in both 1993 and 1998.

(*Chapter continues on the following page.*)

Table 3A.1 Determinants of Farm Profits

Variable definition	Northern Uplands	Red River Delta	North Central Coast	South Central Coast	Mekong Delta	Full sample
Religion	−235,405.6	−198,855.7	−214,888.5	−157,535.6	35,471.5	−46,667.1
	(−1.12)	(−2.04)	(−2.58)	(−1.37)	(0.14)	(−0.46)
Ethnicity	−427,411.3	−373,835.5	−44,234.1	−198,095.3	303,292.3	169,283.2
	(−2.20)	(−2.65)	(−0.17)	(−0.51)	(1.16)	(1.09)
Born locally	−122,289.7	1,033.5	230,786.8	−107,960.5	579,389.3	18,258.1
	(−0.98)	(0.01)	(0.95)	(−0.90)	(1.27)	(0.14)
Age of head of household	24,355.9	29,321.6	−12,267.5	−24,907.4	−10,448.4	8,797.8
	(1.32)	(1.92)	(−0.96)	(−1.06)	(−0.15)	(0.67)
Age^2 of head of household	−218.7	−236.2	184.0	308.045	138.8	−42.9
	(−1.00)	(−1.52)	(1.48)	(1.20)	(0.24)	(−0.34)
Household size	222,636.9	63,895.3	−9,125.0	69,883.3	189,781.8	168,622.6
	(1.35)	(0.96)	(−0.09)	(1.43)	(0.61)	(2.85)
Household size^2	3,903.7	2,030.02	1,750.5	964.6	−4,118.0	−1,829.3
	(0.36)	(0.33)	(0.24)	(0.65)	(−0.19)	(−0.55)
Share of male adults	411,804.5	−130,818.7	−243,968.4	−401,261.6	423,927.7	−21,108.2
	(0.94)	(−0.50)	(−1.13)	(−1.17)	(0.38)	(−0.08)
Education of head of household	10,885.5	30,195.9	30,897.6	9,956.3	112,153.8	34,967.1
	(0.43)	(3.39)	(2.80)	(0.78)	(1.77)	(2.83)
Education of other adults	−4,643.3	4,844.7	6,284.7	15,550.5	56,444.8	23,026.6
	(−0.43)	(0.76)	(0.76)	(2.40)	(2.58)	(3.61)

Allocated irrigated annual land	330.8	610.3	535.1	138.4	217.4	236.4
	(3.54)	(9.15)	(13.19)	(3.27)	(7.18)	(10.72)
Allocated nonirrigated annual land	79.8	248.2	264.7	116.0	197.0	174.7
	(4.39)	(2.80)	(3.87)	(1.86)	(3.73)	(4.76)
Perennial land	321.1	429.7	−90.7	137.8	97.7	208.1
	(1.94)	(7.37)	(−0.58)	(0.62)	(0.92)	(2.52)
Forestland	55.4	65.3	5.5	100.6	n.a.	40.7
	(1.40)	(2.64)	(0.17)	(1.43)		(1.63)
Other land	20.1	65.5	123.5	27.3	n.a.	−21.3
	(1.56)	(4.49)	(3.45)	(0.32)		(−0.48)
Constant	−105,171.9	−1,901,731.0	490,262.2	1,387,672.0	−240,235.7	793,103.9
	(−0.14)	(−4.22)	(1.00)	(2.05)	(−0.09)	(1.63)
R^2	0.512	0.632	0.660	0.358	0.420	0.499
Root mean square error	1.2e+06	8.5e+05	6.8e+05	9.0e+05	3.0e+06	1.6e+06
F statistic	$F(15,18)=473.65$	$F(14,31)=728.43$	$F(14,17)=1{,}060.05$	$F(10,11)=103.90$	$F(13,24)=102.42$	$F(14,119)=251.08$
$P > F$	0.0000	0.0000	0.0000	0.0000	0.0000	0.0000
Number of observations	591	989	543	333	586	3,406

Source: 1993 VLSS.

Note: n.a. = not applicable. The dependent variable is farm profit. Commune fixed effects are included. *T*-ratios in parentheses are based on standard errors corrected for heteroskedasticity and clustering. The full sample regression also includes observations for the Central Highlands and the Southeast regions. Observations in the region-specific regressions differ from those for regressions in chapter 4 because the latter dropped observations when there were missing data on variables not included in these regressions.

Annex 3B

Table 3B.1 Means of Key Variables by Age Cohort, 1993 and 2004

Age	Mean consumption, 1993 (thousand 1998 D)	Mean consumption, 2004 (thousand 1998 D)	Head-count index, 1993 (%)	Head-count index, 2004 (%)	Landlessness rate, 1993 (urban + rural) (%)	Landlessness rate, 2004 (urban + rural) (%)	Urban population share, 1993 (%)	Urban population share, 2004 (%)
24	1,660.76	3,122.29	72.94	24.95	11.42	24.54	10.61	20.93
26	1,559.84	3,208.93	79.25	26.34	14.77	26.90	8.45	20.57
27	1,645.62	3,124.34	72.89	25.41	14.58	21.20	12.37	18.55
28	1,526.01	3,213.13	79.56	22.94	16.67	24.03	10.83	20.89
29	1,627.92	3,411.78	75.49	21.83	11.90	23.89	13.64	23.28
30	1,745.37	3,741.99	66.51	19.87	18.45	28.00	14.58	24.84
31	1,867.74	3,930.26	65.97	20.33	20.60	26.94	17.70	23.02
32	1,696.48	3,760.51	72.16	18.05	17.10	27.36	16.07	31.60
33	2,034.88	3,951.11	62.97	17.86	23.74	29.06	26.71	26.82
34	1,922.32	4,227.60	67.54	15.83	21.20	28.35	20.71	30.29
35	1,843.58	4,133.01	63.76	14.45	23.41	29.88	23.03	28.86
36	1,588.87	3,983.21	72.77	16.99	15.18	28.26	12.00	26.57
37	2,107.92	4,375.80	59.45	14.61	25.89	28.09	26.57	29.71
38	1,765.47	4,557.24	64.65	12.61	21.46	30.27	20.86	27.84

39	1,785.88	4,168.01	68.51	19.65	23.80	27.78	19.51	27.67
40	1,844.77	4,138.81	63.48	12.16	19.12	30.93	17.36	32.06
41	1,990.11	3,985.05	63.52	10.12	27.22	27.17	21.28	25.00
42	2,034.02	4,891.23	55.44	11.87	20.75	30.01	22.86	30.54
43	2,039.75	3,827.96	59.52	16.45	18.19	24.77	21.60	27.04
44	1,880.66	4,403.69	64.09	18.48	28.52	37.67	23.53	33.72
46	2,062.90	4,567.73	51.68	11.40	24.11	34.85	26.83	26.79
48	1,986.65	4,099.51	58.86	13.17	24.73	29.54	21.71	27.94
50	1,956.69	4,604.77	50.15	13.21	22.01	32.93	22.98	28.10
52	2,064.32	4,309.53	57.90	12.89	20.32	32.19	22.84	24.49
54	2,196.85	4,113.25	56.47	17.48	21.44	29.25	21.39	29.39
56	1,925.95	3,899.12	57.42	21.90	19.14	27.99	17.83	21.39
58	1,984.31	4,024.38	54.66	16.27	25.23	32.74	24.11	23.65
60	2,135.30	4,055.45	51.76	22.38	28.24	25.00	23.75	24.34
62	2,063.67	3,770.46	45.82	25.45	26.24	28.53	24.20	27.54
64	2,123.13	3,866.77	48.24	20.75	27.12	26.14	23.49	22.02
66	2,354.14	4,042.38	44.20	18.30	25.66	30.55	25.44	20.00
68	2,067.54	3,616.98	56.64	17.91	23.45	37.68	23.08	25.00
71	2,146.48	3,622.32	45.56	9.82	20.91	33.28	17.50	28.72
74	1,866.34	3,465.05	64.11	32.22	16.60	34.18	16.07	30.43

Sources: 1993 VLSS and 2004 VHLSS.
Note: D = dong. Age cohorts are missing when there were insufficient observations.

Notes

1. These surveys are publicly accessible, subject to standard conditions. For further information on the LSMS, see http://www.worldbank.org/lsms/.

2. *Swidden* is hilly or mountainous land that is cleared through burning, farmed for a few years, and then abandoned or, more commonly today, left fallow for a few years. This form of cultivation is practiced primarily by ethnic minorities.

3. Annual cropland is used for annual crops such as rice or groundnuts. We hereafter refer to allocated annual agricultural or cropland simply as *allocated land*.

4. Very few households reported having "poor-quality" irrigated or "good-quality" nonirrigated land. So we aggregated the categories into two; by "good-quality nonirrigated land," we mean good or medium quality.

5. Throughout the analysis all land amounts are expressed in square meters.

6. For example, Thi Que Tran (1997) describes one local allocation rule as giving a full share to members of working age (defined as 16 to 60 years for men and 16 to 55 years for women), one-half share to those older than working age and to those 13 to 15 years old, and one-third share to the youngest. See also Hayami (1994).

7. We create this variable for men age 21 to 65 and women age 21 to 60 who did not work during the past 12 months or look for work in the past seven days and give being handicapped as the main reason.

8. We tested an alternative definition that excludes auction land and land contracted from state farms. This definition gives a slightly higher landlessness rate (14.5 percent of households) in 2004, but because it can be calculated only for 1998 and 2004, we stick with the first definition.

9. A limitation of the 2002 survey is that it asks only about the amount of land that is cultivated by households, whether they have long-term-use rights to the land, or whether they are renting it in. While we know if the household rents out land, we cannot identify how much and, hence, the total amount over which the household has use rights.

10. This is the E(0) measure in the generalized entropy class and is also Theil's L measure. It ranges from zero for perfect equality to infinity for the case of complete inequality where one person has everything. The measure has a number of desirable properties, including exact additive decomposability by subgroups, which we exploit later.

11. Although the Chinese represent a tiny minority, they tend to be well off and more similar to the Kinh majority than to other minority groups. For this reason, we include them with the majority group.

12. For 1993, one can also calculate an unemployment rate for whether work was wanted but could not be found in the past seven days; this gives an even lower rate for rural areas of 0.5 percent (Gallup 2004).

DATA AND SUMMARY STATISTICS 73

13. These sample sizes appear to be adequate for us not to be too worried about attenuation biases in pseudo-panel data (see Verbeek and Nijman 1992).

14. The explanatory variables (80 for 1998 and 84 for 2004, not including the province dummies) include household durables and farm equipment, area of different types of landholdings, housing characteristics, household demographics, occupation and employment status, and province dummies.

15. Corrections are made for heteroskedasticity and clustering using the STATA robust and cluster commands. For the 1998 consumption model: the adjusted R^2 is 0.687, with $n = 4,225$. For 2004, the adjusted R^2 is 0.654, and $n = 6,633$.

16. We exclude water surface land from the farm profits regressions because we are unable to adequately calculate net profits for it. The questionnaire does not allow a separation of expenses incurred in raising water products from that of raising livestock, and assumptions must also be made about consumption from the household's production.

4

Welfare Impacts of Privatizing Land-Use Rights

This chapter assesses the impacts on household living standards of the first stage of Vietnam's agrarian reforms, namely, the privatization of land-use rights undertaken at the time of breaking up the collectives and cooperatives. Following common practice, one can define the *impact* of a policy reform or economic change as the difference between the observed, postintervention value of the relevant outcome indicator—such as mean consumption or a poverty measure—and its value under an explicit counterfactual, such as the absence of the intervention or some alternative policy or event. In assessing the impacts of a program, one compares the "treated" group with an observationally similar comparison group that did not receive the "treatment."[1] This is appropriate for "assigned programs," meaning that some units get the program and some do not, though even then one often has to worry about spillover effects, whereby the costs and benefits of the intervention spill over to the comparison group.

However, here there is an important difference. Decollectivization was a national policy, so we cannot observe a comparison group of nonparticipants. That is, of course, quite common for many policies that affect household welfare; many of the things we would like to evaluate are not assigned programs. To infer impacts without a comparison group, we need to make assumptions about how the economy works under the counterfactual. In other words, we need an economic model.

We begin by outlining the model we use to infer the welfare impacts of decollectivization, and then we present our estimates and empirical results using the 1993 Vietnam Living Standards Survey (VLSS) discussed in chapter 3. For data and variable-specific issues concerning this chapter's analysis, we refer readers to chapter 3, notably "The Initial Land Allocation."

Models of the Actual and Counterfactual Land Allocations

Motivated by the observations in chapter 2, we test whether the local implementation of decollectivization served distributional goals—possibly reflecting capture by local elites—at some loss to aggregate consumption. We construct a model that allows us to estimate that loss and to compare the observed allocation of annual agricultural land against explicit counterfactuals. This section describes the model; a more formal treatment can be found in annex 4A.

As a starting point for our analysis, it should be noted that the allocation of annual cropland at decollectivization had to be determined in advance of the realization of the uncertainties facing households in this setting, such as future health shocks, agro-climatic conditions affecting farm yields, or policy changes. Furthermore, given uncertainty over whether the allocation could be renegotiated once the state of nature was revealed, commune authorities were likely to proceed as though it could not be. We assume that there is a fixed and known ex ante probability distribution across the possible states of nature, meaning that widespread agreement exists on the likelihood of any specific state of nature—such as high output prices or crop failure—occurring, and a unique probability can be attached to each possible event.

Motivated by our observations in chapter 2, we allow a potentially wide range of possible decision-making processes at the local level. The actual process might be anything from administrative decree (according to the cadre's personal preferences) to a complex bargaining game. We assume only that the outcome (however it is reached) can be represented by the maximum of a nonnegatively weighted sum of welfare levels across all farm households. The weight attached to the expected utility of a household depends on a vector of exogenous household characteristics. Naturally, different weighting functions imply different distributions of land and utility. If the weights tend to be negatively (positively) correlated with household welfare, then one can say that the outcome will tend to be "pro-poor" ("pro-rich").

The utility of each farm household in a given state of nature is assumed to depend solely on its consumption. The household receives an exogenously fixed amount of land under the administrative allocation, which yields a known farm output in each state of nature. (For now we treat land as homogeneous; in the empirical work, we allow for observable heterogeneity, and we consider the consequences of latent heterogeneity later in this chapter.) The household also has (positive or negative) nonfarm income that depends on household characteristics. At the time of the reform, agricultural labor markets were thin and virtually nonexistent in the north of Vietnam, so to simplify the exposition, we close off this market in our model (though we note the possible implications of relaxing this assumption). We also ignore saving and dissaving, as well as borrowing and lending; incorporating these features would complicate the model in unimportant ways for our purposes. The household's consumption is then equal to its income. We make the standard assumption that the production functions are increasing and strictly concave in the amount of land allocated to each household for all states of nature: that is, the marginal product of land in a given state of nature is positive, and it declines as the amount of land increases. Utility is, in turn, an increasing concave function of consumption (that is, a strictly positive marginal utility of consumption that falls as consumption increases).

The commune selects an allocation of the total available annual cropland across all the households living in that commune, and it does this before the state of nature is revealed. The realized land allocation maximizes the weighted sum of expected utilities (see annex 4A). The allocation to a given household equates the household-specific weighted expected marginal utility of land (marginal utility of consumption times the marginal product of land) with the shadow price of land in the commune.

We do not attach any normative significance to the allocations generated by maximizing the weighted sum of expected utilities; our use of a positively weighted sum of utilities as an objective function is motivated only by the desire to have a reasonably flexible representation of the potentially diverse objectives of local cadres and others involved in the actual allocation process.

But how might we assess the actual allocations? There are potentially many counterfactual allocations of interest, depending on the weight one attaches to equity versus efficiency. We focus here on just two counterfactuals. One of these will be an equal allocation of each commune's land per capita. This is a natural equity benchmark, though it is not the only possible one. For example, other possibilities might include equalizing expected consumption or expected utility. The other counterfactual we use is the allocation that maximizes the commune's aggregate current (state-specific) consumption (see annex 4A for details). We call this the *consumption-efficient allocation*. This allocation equates the marginal products of land across all households in a given commune. We can then derive the consumption loss from the actual allocation, as measured relative to this counterfactual.

Both the equal land and the consumption-efficient allocations are natural benchmarks for assessing the actual land allocation. The consumption-efficient allocation is also of special interest since it coincides with the competitive-market solution, allowing costless recontracting in each state of nature. This is because the land allocation across households that maximizes consumption equates the marginal product of land across all households; otherwise, aggregate output, and hence consumption, could rise by a small reallocation of land. However, that is exactly what a competitive market does, since everyone faces the same land price (controlling for quality) and so will choose an amount of land that equates its marginal product with that price, so as to maximize own utility. (See annex 4A for a proof of this claim.)

The assumption that utility depends solely on consumption is crucial to this competitive-market interpretation of the consumption-efficient allocation. If holding land gives utility independently of consumption, then the market allocation of land will differ from the consumption-maximizing one. For example, if land provides insurance against risk, it will have value independent of current consumption. Then our interpretation of the consumption-maximizing allocation as the market solution also requires that risk markets worked perfectly. Since we have no basis for assigning a value to land independently of the current consumption it generates, we cannot calculate a "conditional-market" solution (conditional on other market failures).

Nonetheless, the consumption-maximizing allocation remains a natural benchmark even without accepting the conditions required for interpreting it as the market solution. By comparing the actual allocation with that benchmark, we are able to quantify the equity-efficiency trade-off facing the administrative land allocation carried out at decollectivization.

Empirical Implementation

There was no nationally representative household survey prior to decollectivization; when the communes controlled all production, household surveys made little sense for most purposes. Furthermore, even if there had been a survey prior to the reform, there was no household-level assignment of land-use rights under collectivized farming. So a conventional preintervention baseline is impossible in this setting.

The 1993 VLSS provides us with survey data on a random sample of farm households collected some three years after the decollectivization was completed. These data are taken to reveal household circumstances in one state of nature. We then assess this observed land allocation against the consumption-efficient allocation for that state of nature, as well as against the equal land per capita allocation.

We make the following assumptions on functional forms:

Assumption 4.1. Utility is given by log consumption

(4.1) $$U(C_{ij}) = \ln C_j(L_i, X_i),$$

where C_{ij} is the consumption of household i in the jth state of nature when allocated L_i of land and having characteristics X_i.

Assumption 4.2. Log consumption is given by

(4.2) $$\ln C_{ij} = a_j + b_j \ln L_i + X_i c_j + \varepsilon_{ij},$$

where $0 < b_j < 1$ and ε_{ij} is a zero-mean i.i.d. (independent and identically distributed) error term uncorrelated with L_i and X_i.

Assumption 4.3. The welfare weights attached to the expected utilities by the commune authorities take the form

(4.3) $$\ln w_i = X_i d + v_i,$$

where v_i is a zero-mean error term uncorrelated with X_i.

Assumptions 4.1–4.3 imply that the administrative land allocation can be written in explicit form as the regression model

(4.4) $$\ln L_i = \ln\left(\sum_{j=1}^{m} p_j b_j / \mu\right) + X_i d + v_i,$$

where p_j is the probability of state $j = 1, m$. Equation (4.4) identifies directly the parameters of the implicit welfare weights of the local land allocation authority. Substituting equation (4.4) into equation (4.2) generates the reduced-form equation for consumption:

(4.5) $$\ln C_{ij} = a_j + b_j \ln\left(\sum_{j=1}^{m} p_j b_j / \mu\right) + X_i(b_j d + c_j) + \varepsilon_{ij} + b_j v_i.$$

The consumption-efficient allocation maximizes aggregate consumption, given the available land. Annex 4A outlines the formal analysis of this optimization problem. Given equation (4.2), the required allocation of land solves $\ln L_{ij}^* = \ln(b_j/\lambda_j) + \ln C_{ij}^*$, which can be written as:

(4.6) $$\ln L_{ij}^* = \frac{a_j + \ln(b_j/\lambda_j)}{1 - b_j} + \frac{X_i c_j}{1 - b_j} + \frac{\varepsilon_{ij}}{1 - b_j}.$$

Comparing equations (4.4) and (4.6), one can see that if $c_j/(1 - b_j) = d$, then the actual allocation responds to changes in X the same way as the consumption-efficient allocation in state j. So if the two allocations are essentially the same, then we should be able to accept the restriction that $d = b_j d + c_j$ when imposed on the reduced-form equations, (4.4) and (4.5). If we cannot accept this restriction, then it is of interest to calculate the consumption-efficient land allocation, $(L_{1j}^*, L_{2j}^*, \ldots, L_{nj}^*)$, from which we can then measure the distribution of consumption losses implied by the actual allocation, using the fact that the proportionate consumption loss for household i is $(L_{ij}^*/L_i)^{b_j} - 1$.[2]

One possible concern about this empirical model is that we identify effects of land allocation only on current consumption. We do not look at impacts on farm output per se. Consumption is clearly the more appropriate welfare indicator for our purposes. Current income is likely to be far more heavily influenced by transient factors that would not presumably have much impact on the local allocation of longer-term land-use rights. However, by the same token, one would probably prefer to measure consumption over a longer period than is possible with a single survey round. Given the data limitation, we must assume instead that current consumption reveals longer-term consumption up to some random error term.

Another possible concern is that while allocated land is endogenous in this model, it is taken to be exogenous to household consumption ($\text{Cov}(v, \varepsilon) = 0$). This is a standard assumption in past empirical work for Vietnam and in other settings in which land allocation is done administratively rather than through markets (see, for example, van de Walle 1998; Wiens 1998). The assumption can also be defended on the grounds that the end of the land allocation preceded the survey-based consumption measure by about three years.

However, the assumption that the land allocation is exogenous to consumption can still be questioned. Our estimates of the parameters of equation (4.2) will be biased if omitted variables jointly influence the welfare weights and consumption levels. The most serious concern in this respect is heterogeneity in land quality. Higher land quality will probably result in higher consumption at given land quantity. Assuming that the quality differences are public knowledge within the commune, the administrative land allocation will take them into account, with more land being used to compensate for lower quality. We include available controls for differences in the average quality of landholdings, though latent heterogeneity will still create a negative correlation between the error terms in the estimated consumption equation and the land allocation equation ($\text{Cov}(v, \varepsilon) < 0$).

Notice, however, that our test for systematic differences between the efficient and actual land allocations is robust to heterogeneity in land quality. Our test is based on the reduced-form coefficients in equations (4.4) and (4.6); it does not require the (potentially biased) parameters of equation (4.2). In contrast, our estimates of the parameters of the implicit equation for the efficient allocation in equation (4.6) *do* require the parameters of the structural model in equation (4.2). So bias caused by latent heterogeneity in land quality will contaminate our estimates of the efficient allocation.

In principle, this problem could be dealt with by introducing an instrumental variable that influences land allocation but not consumption conditional on land; that is, at least one element of the parameter vector d in equation (4.3) would have to be set to zero, while leaving the corresponding element of c unrestricted. However, there is no theoretical basis for such an exclusion restriction; anything that can be included from our dataset could presumably have been observed or anticipated by the local authorities.

It should also be noted that while there is likely to be heterogeneity in land quality across plots within communes, it was common to combine land from different plots when forming a package for each household mean (Lam 2001a). Hence, the variance across households in the average quality of their allocations can be considerably less than the underlying interplot variance. For example, Tanaka (2001) finds that such plot fragmentation in North Vietnamese villages was used to produce land parcels of relatively even quality. Then heterogeneity in land quality would not be a problem for our analysis.

Regressions for Consumption and Allocated Land

For the sample as a whole and each region, we can convincingly reject the null hypothesis (with probability less than 0.00005) that the observed land allocation responded the same way to household characteristics as the consumption-efficient allocation that one would have expected from a competitive-market-based privatization, under our assumptions. The reduced-form regressions for consumption and test statistics for the hypothesis that the two allocations are the same can be found in table 4.1. So we proceeded to estimate the efficient allocation.

The structural model of consumption (equation 4.2) is given in table 4.2. The results are generally unsurprising. Household consumption is a rising function of household size, with an elasticity less than unity. In most regions, consumption is higher for households

Table 4.1 Reduced-Form Regressions for Consumption

Variable	Northern Uplands	Red River Delta	North Central Coast	South Central Coast	Mekong Delta	Full sample
Religion	−0.10	−0.003	−0.03	0.13	−0.02	−0.01
	(−1.96)	(−0.06)	(−0.56)	(1.60)	(−0.62)	(−0.25)
Ethnicity	−0.06	−0.17	−0.09	−0.67	0.21	−0.09
	(−1.14)	(−1.84)	(−0.71)	(−2.40)	(2.15)	(−2.39)
Born locally	−0.07	0.03	0.10	−0.13	−0.04	−0.02
	(−1.55)	(0.49)	(1.47)	(−1.64)	(−0.62)	(−1.02)
Age of head of household	−0.001	0.02	−0.003	0.01	0.01	0.01
	(−0.11)	(2.56)	(−0.40)	(1.03)	(1.02)	(2.15)
Age^2 of head of household $\times 10^3$	0.05	−0.16	0.03	−0.09	−0.09	−0.07
	(0.45)	(−2.46)	(0.34)	(−0.82)	(−0.88)	(−1.77)
Log household size	0.52	0.53	0.57	0.67	0.50	0.57
	(8.58)	(12.56)	(10.92)	(7.93)	(8.02)	(23.64)
Dependency ratio	−0.11	−0.07	−0.14	−0.25	−0.09	−0.13
	(−1.31)	(−1.22)	(−1.94)	(−1.89)	(−0.91)	(−3.61)
Gender of head of household	0.08	0.04	0.02	0.05	−0.05	0.02
	(1.86)	(1.19)	(0.54)	(0.67)	(−0.90)	(0.94)
Disabled adult in household	−0.36	−0.01	−0.44	−0.04	n.a.	−0.17
	(−2.20)	(−0.04)	(−2.43)	(−0.22)		(−2.08)
Government job	0.08	0.14	0.09	0.29	0.20	0.12
	(1.34)	(2.66)	(1.83)	(2.58)	(3.03)	(4.25)
State-owned enterprise job	0.47	0.09	−0.04	0.49	0.11	0.11
	(2.43)	(1.60)	(−0.28)	(1.66)	(0.61)	(2.23)
Education of head of household	0.02	0.03	0.02	0.03	0.01	0.03
	(3.77)	(6.50)	(5.04)	(3.28)	(1.69)	(10.25)
Education of other adults	0.01	0.01	0.01	0.01	0.01	0.01
	(4.32)	(6.35)	(6.21)	(1.64)	(4.16)	(10.87)

	(1)	(2)	(3)	(4)
Social subsidy recipient	0.01	0.04	0.04	0.02
	(0.15)	(0.98)	(0.90)	(0.71)
Private irrigated land $\times 10^3$	0.18	0.27	0.24	0.07
	(2.46)	(3.00)	(2.22)	(5.83)
Private nonirrigated land $\times 10^3$	0.01	−0.004	0.10	0.01
	(0.27)	(−0.13)	(2.02)	(1.25)
Private perennial land $\times 10^3$	0.07	0.11	0.04	0.02
	(1.75)	(2.59)	(0.53)	(3.66)
Private water surface land $\times 10^3$	0.19	0.18	0.33	0.05
	(2.01)	(2.79)	(2.54)	(3.26)
Cultivates swidden land	0.08	−0.06	−0.09	−0.01
	(1.77)	(−0.88)	(−0.83)	(−0.31)
Share of good irrigated land	0.03	0.02	0.08	0.05
	(0.38)	(0.32)	(1.47)	(2.02)
Share of good nonirrigated land	−0.03	0.001	−0.01	0.02
	(−0.47)	(0.04)	(−0.17)	(0.78)
Constant	13.87	n.a.	n.a.	13.88
	(71.90)			(137.88)
R^2	0.670	0.668	0.700	0.657
Root mean square error	0.309	0.320	0.301	0.349
F statistic	25.220	40,785.07	32,665.58	39.568
$Prob > F$	0.0000	0.0000	0.0000	0.0000
Number of observations	484	956	506	2810
Test of $\gamma/(1-\beta) = b$	$F(36, 894) =$	$F(53, 1{,}804) =$	$F(39, 932) =$	$F(129, 5{,}340) =$
	8.68	179.15	151.65	28.37
$Prob > F$	0.0000	0.0000	0.0000	0.0000

(Additional columns appear between (2) and (4):)

	(2a)	(3a)
Social subsidy recipient	−0.08	−0.10
	(−0.84)	(−1.00)
Private irrigated land $\times 10^3$	0.08	0.02
	(1.48)	(1.33)
Private nonirrigated land $\times 10^3$	0.03	0.02
	(0.56)	(1.32)
Private perennial land $\times 10^3$	0.02	0.05
	(0.24)	(3.77)
Private water surface land $\times 10^3$	n.a.	0.03
		(1.53)
Cultivates swidden land	−0.01	0.20
	(−0.09)	(1.23)
Share of good irrigated land	−0.04	0.12
	(−0.59)	(1.38)
Share of good nonirrigated land	0.01	0.01
	(0.14)	(0.20)
Constant	14.13	14.62
	(46.60)	(47.99)
R^2	0.641	0.522
Root mean square error	0.397	0.387
F statistic	14.003	10.360
$Prob > F$	0.0000	0.0000
Number of observations	276	443
Test of $\gamma/(1-\beta) = b$	$F(31, 486) =$	$F(42, 796) =$
	6.66	31.45
$Prob > F$	0.0000	0.0000

Source: 1993 VLSS.

Note: n.a. = not applicable. The dependent variable is log household consumption expenditure. Commune fixed effects were also included. *T*-ratios in parentheses are based on standard errors corrected for heteroskedasticity and clustering.

Table 4.2 Determinants of Consumption

Variable	Northern Uplands	Red River Delta	North Central Coast	South Central Coast	Mekong Delta	Full sample
Religion	−0.09	−0.01	−0.04	0.12	−0.06	−0.02
	(−2.07)	(−0.14)	(−0.54)	(1.18)	(−1.00)	(0.82)
Ethnicity	−0.06	−0.19	−0.12	−0.65	0.14	−0.07
	(−0.86)	(−2.34)	(−1.23)	(−2.90)	(1.90)	(−1.65)
Born locally	−0.08	0.03	0.10	−0.14	−0.06	−0.04
	(−1.57)	(0.78)	(1.53)	(−3.65)	(−0.86)	(−1.29)
Age of head of household	−0.0002	0.02	−0.003	0.002	0.01	0.01
	(−0.02)	(2.32)	(−0.32)	(0.21)	(0.47)	(1.83)
Age^2 of head of household × 10^3	0.04	−0.16	0.03	0.01	−0.05	−0.06
	(0.42)	(−2.19)	(0.33)	(0.15)	(−0.45)	(−1.46)
Log household size	0.45	0.46	0.53	0.53	0.45	0.48
	(6.90)	(7.62)	(10.24)	(6.24)	(6.92)	(15.73)
Dependency ratio	−0.07	−0.03	−0.12	−0.19	−0.11	−0.07
	(−0.65)	(−0.41)	(−1.71)	(−1.73)	(−1.19)	(−2.00)
Gender of head of household	0.07	0.03	0.01	0.03	−0.08	0.01
	(1.65)	(0.75)	(0.37)	(0.61)	(−1.34)	(0.34)
Disabled adult in household	−0.35	0.003	−0.43	−0.07	n.a.	−0.16
	(−3.81)	(0.01)	(−1.37)	(−0.61)		(−1.68)
Government job	0.10	0.15	0.10	0.30	0.18	0.14
	(2.13)	(3.10)	(1.70)	(4.15)	(3.72)	(4.83)
State-owned enterprise job	0.54	0.11	−0.04	0.50	0.05	0.13
	(4.16)	(2.26)	(−0.58)	(1.45)	(0.40)	(2.74)
Education of head of household	0.02	0.03	0.02	0.03	0.01	0.03
	(3.87)	(5.45)	(4.48)	(4.93)	(1.46)	(9.48)
Education of other adults	0.01	0.01	0.01	0.01	0.01	0.01
	(4.72)	(7.74)	(4.89)	(1.89)	(4.21)	(11.32)

Social subsidy recipient	0.01	0.04	0.04	−0.03	0.03
	(0.17)	(1.10)	(0.56)	(−0.52)	(1.15)
Log allocated irrigated-land equivalent	0.10	0.08	0.05	0.21	0.13
	(2.82)	(2.30)	(2.39)	(3.81)	(7.45)
Private irrigated land $\times 10^3$	0.14	0.24	0.24	0.05	0.03
	(3.34)	(2.32)	(3.01)	(1.04)	(2.54)
Private nonirrigated land $\times 10^3$	0.02	−0.002	0.09	0.05	0.01
	(0.31)	(−0.05)	(2.50)	(0.77)	(0.98)
Private perennial land $\times 10^3$	0.06	0.11	0.04	0.03	0.02
	(3.47)	(1.73)	(0.40)	(0.51)	(1.76)
Private water surface land $\times 10^3$	0.19	0.18	0.31	n.a.	0.04
	(2.15)	(3.40)	(4.16)		(1.50)
Cultivates swidden land	0.07	−0.08	−0.09	−0.02	−0.01
	(1.15)	(−0.86)	(−0.70)	(−0.26)	(−0.24)
Share of good irrigated land	−0.004	0.03	0.08	−0.06	0.04
	(−0.06)	(0.57)	(1.21)	(−0.63)	(1.47)
Share of good nonirrigated land	0.02	0.004	−0.01	−0.04	0.02
	(0.25)	(0.10)	(−0.27)	(−0.54)	(0.81)
Constant	13.32	13.42	13.38	12.71	13.47
	(41.53)	(49.55)	(50.75)	(28.17)	(68.80)
R^2	0.679	0.671	0.703	0.666	0.673
Root mean square error	0.305	0.318	0.300	0.383	0.340
F statistic	53.10	971.45	456.46	71.89	92.43
$Prob > F$	0.0000	0.0000	0.0000	0.0000	0.0000
Number of observations	484	956	506	276	2,810

Source: 1993 VLSS.

Note: n.a. = not applicable. The dependent variable is log household consumption expenditures. Commune fixed effects were also included. *T*-ratios in parentheses are based on standard errors corrected for heteroskedasticity and clustering.

with a member who holds a job in the government or a state-owned enterprise (SOE). It is increased by higher household education. Consumption rises with the amount of allocated annual land in all regions. Recall that our theoretical model requires that the elasticity of consumption to allocated land (the coefficient on the log of allocated land) must be between zero and unity. We find that the estimated elasticity is significantly positive and significantly less than unity in all regions and nationally. Possibly more surprising is that, quantitatively, the elasticity is much closer to zero than to unity. Clearly, the lower this elasticity, the less responsive the consumption-efficient land allocation will be to differences in household characteristics and the less consumption will respond to differences in land allocation. So our first empirical finding suggests that land allocation may well be less important to living standards in this setting than one might have imagined.

Table 4.3 gives the regressions for the actual land allocation (equation 4.4) and the estimated parameters of the implied equation for the consumption-efficient allocation (equation 4.6). Note that the latter equation does not require a separate regression, but rather its parameters are retrieved using the parameters of the regression for log consumption (equation 4.5). There is diversity between regions in how much the two allocations differ, notably between the North (the Northern Uplands, Red River Delta, and North Central Coast) and the South (the South Central Coast and Mekong Delta). For example, in the North, the actual allocation is more responsive to household size than the efficient allocation would have been. This reverses in the South. The dependency ratio significantly and negatively affects the actual allocations in the North but not in the South. The negative coefficient on the dependency ratio indicates that the administrative allocation in the North put higher weight on household members who were of prime working age than the consumption-efficient allocation would have required.

In the North (except for the Northern Uplands), being in a minority group significantly increases the administrative allocation but decreases the efficient allocation (though only significantly so in the Red River Delta). In the other two regions, there is less difference in how ethnicity affected the two allocations. The positive and significant effect of being a minority household in the northern regions probably captures the fact that the minorities were given more land as a result of having contributed more to the collectives originally, as allowed by Resolution 10.

Having a household member with a government job or a job in an SOE tended to reduce the administrative allocation, though the effect is generally not significant. But these characteristics would have

Table 4.3 Actual Land Allocations Compared to Consumption-Efficient Allocations

Variable	Northern Uplands		Red River Delta		North Central Coast		South Central Coast		Mekong Delta		Full sample	
	Actual	Efficient	Actual	Efficient	Actual	Efficient	Actual	Efficient	Actual	Efficient	Actual	Efficient
Religion	−0.12	−0.10	0.05	−0.01	0.13	−0.04	0.04	0.16	0.16	−0.07	0.08	−0.03
	(−1.48)	(−2.03)	(0.66)	(−0.14)	(0.93)	(−0.54)	(0.47)	(1.16)	(1.86)	(−1.00)	(1.24)	(−0.81)
Ethnicity	0.02	−0.07	0.31	−0.21	0.46	−0.12	−0.12	−0.83	0.36	0.17	0.01	−0.08
	(0.39)	(−0.85)	(2.56)	(−2.29)	(2.78)	(−1.22)	(−0.47)	(−2.73)	(1.51)	(1.91)	(0.11)	(−1.65)
Born locally	0.03	−0.09	−0.03	0.03	−0.09	0.11	0.02	−0.18	0.15	−0.08	0.05	−0.04
	(0.72)	(−1.59)	(−0.54)	(0.78)	(−0.51)	(1.51)	(0.38)	(−3.69)	(1.73)	(−0.87)	(1.07)	(−1.29)
Age of head of household	−0.01	−0.0002	−0.0003	0.02	−0.01	−0.003	0.05	0.002	0.03	0.01	0.003	0.01
	(−0.49)	(−0.00)	(−0.81)	(2.29)	(−0.88)	(−0.32)	(2.23)	(0.22)	(1.75)	(0.47)	(−0.46)	(1.82)
Age² of head of household × 10³	0.08	0.04	−0.07	−0.17	0.04	0.03	−0.49	0.02	−0.21	−0.06	−0.06	−0.07
	(0.44)	(0.42)	(−0.81)	(−2.17)	(0.27)	(0.33)	(−2.32)	(0.14)	(−1.39)	(−0.45)	(−0.75)	(−1.45)
Log household size	0.72	0.50	0.79	0.50	0.70	0.56	0.66	0.68	0.24	0.56	0.70	0.56
	(6.63)	(8.01)	(14.38)	(9.41)	(5.18)	(10.79)	(4.39)	(7.50)	(2.21)	(8.08)	(11.93)	(18.70)
Dependency ratio	−0.50	−0.07	−0.48	−0.03	−0.39	−0.13	−0.29	−0.24	0.09	−0.14	−0.42	−0.08
	(−2.59)	(−0.66)	(−6.91)	(−0.41)	(−2.52)	(−1.71)	(−1.34)	(−1.68)	(0.50)	(−1.21)	(−6.07)	(−2.02)
Gender of head of household	0.07	0.08	0.07	0.03	0.15	0.02	0.10	0.03	0.16	−0.10	0.09	0.01
	(0.77)	(1.69)	(1.90)	(0.75)	(2.43)	(0.37)	(1.19)	(1.68)	(1.21)	(−1.34)	(2.82)	(0.35)
Disabled adult in household	−0.13	−0.39	−0.09	0.003	−0.09	−0.46	0.12	−0.09	n.a.	n.a.	−0.05	−0.19
	(−1.19)	(−3.81)	(−0.70)	(0.00)	(−0.45)	(−1.36)	(0.57)	(−0.61)			(−0.64)	(−1.68)
Government job	−0.22	0.11	−0.12	0.16	−0.20	0.11	−0.05	0.38	0.10	0.22	−0.16	0.16
	(−1.28)	(2.17)	(−1.90)	(2.93)	(−1.63)	(1.71)	(−0.29)	(3.48)	(0.92)	(3.74)	(−2.75)	(4.77)
SOE job	−0.77	0.60	−0.23	0.12	0.13	−0.05	−0.05	0.63	0.34	0.06	−0.17	0.15
	(−2.26)	(3.90)	(−4.09)	(2.22)	(0.43)	(−0.57)	(−0.13)	(1.35)	(0.88)	(0.40)	(−2.32)	(2.69)
Education of head of household	−0.01	0.02	−0.01	0.03	−0.01	0.03	−0.02	0.04	0.02	0.01	−0.001	0.03
	(−1.06)	(3.81)	(−1.10)	(5.26)	(−1.10)	(4.38)	(−2.53)	(4.35)	(1.46)	(1.45)	(−0.30)	(9.12)
Education of other adults	−0.01	0.01	0.002	0.01	0.01	0.01	0.004	0.01	0.01	0.01	0.003	0.01
	(−1.31)	(4.81)	(0.74)	(6.95)	(0.86)	(5.04)	(0.84)	(1.87)	(1.45)	(4.09)	(1.29)	(11.04)
Social subsidy recipient	0.01	0.01	−0.08	0.05	0.04	0.04	−0.19	−0.04	−0.37	−0.03	−0.09	0.04
	(0.07)	(0.17)	(−1.61)	(1.09)	(0.37)	(0.57)	(−1.58)	(−0.52)	(−3.50)	(−0.30)	(−2.26)	(1.15)

(Continued on the following page)

Table 4.3 (Continued)

Variable	Northern Uplands Actual	Northern Uplands Efficient	Red River Delta Actual	Red River Delta Efficient	North Central Coast Actual	North Central Coast Efficient	South Central Coast Actual	South Central Coast Efficient	Mekong Delta Actual	Mekong Delta Efficient	Full sample Actual	Full sample Efficient
Private irrigated land $\times 10^3$	0.47 (2.79)	0.15 (3.41)	0.40 (3.28)	0.26 (2.28)	0.08 (0.71)	0.25 (2.95)	0.14 (5.79)	0.06 (1.07)	0.03 (2.05)	0.02 (1.55)	0.15 (3.14)	0.03 (2.54)
Private nonirrigated land $\times 10^3$	−0.03 (−0.66)	0.02 (0.30)	−0.01 (−0.21)	−0.003 (0.00)	0.17 (1.62)	0.09 (2.49)	−0.09 (−1.85)	0.06 (0.78)	−0.004 (−0.16)	0.03 (1.24)	−0.01 (−0.69)	0.01 (0.97)
Private perennial land $\times 10^3$	0.02 (0.27)	0.07 (3.59)	0.03 (0.62)	0.12 (1.68)	0.05 (0.38)	0.04 (0.40)	−0.08 (−2.32)	0.04 (0.50)	0.02 (0.62)	0.05 (3.63)	0.01 (0.57)	0.02 (1.76)
Private water surface land $\times 10^3$	−0.02 (−0.11)	0.21 (2.17)	0.04 (0.77)	0.19 (3.51)	0.35 (2.62)	0.33 (4.42)	n.a.	n.a.	0.06 (6.50)	0.02 (0.71)	0.06 (5.00)	0.05 (1.50)
Cultivates swidden land	0.12 (1.10)	0.08 (1.26)	0.23 (2.32)	−0.09 (−0.87)	0.05 (0.40)	−0.10 (−0.69)	0.05 (0.40)	−0.02 (−0.26)	0.47 (7.90)	0.14 (4.08)	0.08 (0.93)	−0.01 (−0.24)
Share of good irrigated land	0.30 (1.20)	−0.01 (−0.00)	−0.03 (−0.74)	0.04 (0.57)	−0.10 (−0.78)	0.09 (1.20)	0.05 (0.52)	−0.07 (−0.62)	0.05 (0.48)	0.14 (1.57)	0.01 (0.18)	0.05 (1.48)
Share of good nonirrigated land	−0.43 (−2.89)	0.02 (0.24)	−0.20 (−3.46)	0.004 (0.10)	0.03 (0.44)	−0.01 (−0.26)	0.22 (3.30)	−0.05 (−0.53)	−0.02 (−0.38)	0.02 (0.04)	−0.04 (−0.89)	0.02 (0.81)
Constant	5.73 (18.39)	n.a.	6.88 (38.40)	n.a.	4.78 (12.97)	n.a.	6.61 (15.73)	n.a.	7.00 (17.44)	n.a.	5.88 (13.74)	n.a.
R^2	0.543		0.630		0.627		0.610		0.771		0.675	
Root mean square error	0.512		0.389		0.503		0.482		0.648		0.545	
F statistic	(14, 15) = 135.92		(20, 31) = 2,020.27		(16, 17) = 2,120,200.0		(10, 11) = 230.57		(18, 22) = 1,066.59		(21, 109) = 874.10	
Prob > F	0.0000		0.0000		.000		0.0000		0.0000		0.0000	
Number of observations	484	484	956	956	506	506	276	276	443	443	2,810	2,810

Source: 1993 VLSS.

Note: n.a. = not applicable. The dependent variable for "actual" is the log of the allocated irrigated-land equivalent held by each household. Commune fixed effects were also included. T-ratios in parentheses are based on standard errors corrected for heteroskedasticity and clustering. The coefficients under "efficient" are derived from the first-order conditions for maximizing aggregate consumption based on the regressions in table 4.2.

resulted in a higher efficient allocation—suggestive of greater access to credit or productive inputs by these households. Again, there are some regional differences in these effects. For example, there is no significant effect of a job in an SOE on the efficient allocation in the South; the significant national effect stems from the Northern Uplands and Red River Delta.

Administrative allocations responded positively to male household headship, and much more so than the efficient allocation. This finding offers support for the claim of Scott (1999) that female-headed households are generally not treated equally in local administrative allocation decisions. Generally, education of the household head had no significant effect on the actual allocation (the sole exception is in the South Central Coast, where higher education reduced the allocation). The education of others in the household was also insignificant in the actual allocation. However, the consumption-maximizing allocation would have favored households with higher education, presumably reflecting complementarities between education and land productivity. The Mekong Delta is the one exception.

Receipt of a social subsidy reduced the actual land allocation nationally, though at the regional level this effect was confined solely to the Mekong Delta. This finding provides some support for the claims that war veterans and their families were unequally treated in the land allocation process in the South. In contrast, we found this variable to be insignificant in the consumption equation for all regions (suggesting that the social transfer compensated fully for the income loss attributable to war disability). The efficient allocation would have ignored whether the household received social subsidies. All other results were robust to including this variable.

The practice of cultivating swidden land increased the administrative allocation in the Red River Delta and the Mekong Delta, but not elsewhere. The positive effect in those regions can be interpreted as a policy effort to discourage this form of land usage (on the assumption that lack of access to regular annual cropland encouraged swidden farming). The efficient allocation in the Mekong Delta would also have given weight to this characteristic, but considerably less so than the actual allocation.

As discussed in chapter 3, while we do not know from our data how farm capital was allocated, we can test for an interaction effect between allocated irrigated-land equivalents and a dummy for whether a household member worked for a cooperative. On doing so, we found no sign of any effect on consumption in the national or individual regional samples. However, in testing an interaction with private land amounts, we find a significant positive effect of water surface land on consumption in the national sample and in the Red River Delta and Northern Uplands. There was also a significant negative interaction effect with private perennial land in the North Central Coast and a significant negative interaction effect with nonirrigated private land in the South Central Coast, though at the same time there was a positive interaction with private irrigated land in that region. On balance, our results suggest that having a job in a cooperative provided no advantage in deriving benefits from a given land allocation, though there are signs of limited impact on the productivity of other land types (notably water surface land in some regions).

In the aggregate sample, the proportion of good-quality land (whether irrigated or not) had no significant effect on either the actual or efficient allocation. This finding holds in all regions except the Northern Uplands and Red River Delta, where there is an indication that households with higher-quality nonirrigated land tended to get lower total land allocations. Other coefficients in both equations were little affected by dropping these land-quality variables (given possible endogeneity concerns).

Welfare Comparisons

The first section of table 4.4 gives various summary statistics on welfare outcomes for the actual allocation, namely, mean consumption and measures of inequality and poverty. (The inequality and poverty measures are described in chapter 3.) The second section in table 4.4 gives results for the simulated consumption-efficient allocation at the survey date, for which we give mean consumption and inequality. The third section is for an equal allocation, in which the irrigated-land equivalent is equalized on a per capita basis across all households within the commune.

Recall that the socialist mode of agricultural production had been in place for a shorter time in the South and that the Mekong Delta, in particular, had been far less collectivized than the North and the South Central Coast (though still subject to other controls under socialist agriculture).[3] So the land allocation in the South at the time of decollectivization was undoubtedly more influenced by the precommunist allocation, as determined by historical land rights and prior land reforms (chapter 2). Thus, it is notable that, relative to the consumption-efficient allocation, we find that the actual allocation in the South entailed a greater loss of aggregate consumption, with just over a 5 percent consumption loss in the Mekong Delta and just under in the South Central Coast (table 4.4). One possible explanation is that the historical (preunification) land allocation

Table 4.4 Mean Consumption, Inequality, and Poverty under Alternative Land Allocations

Indicator	Northern Uplands	Red River Delta	North Central Coast	South Central Coast	Mekong Delta	Full sample
Actual allocation						
Mean consumption (thousand D) per household	4,725.08	4,594.56	4,183.38	5,725.08	7,300.91	5,258.28
Inequality in per capita expenditures	0.10	0.09	0.08	0.12	0.13	0.12
Head-count index of poverty (%)	81.32	67.52	85.14	61.98	49.92	68.46
Squared poverty gap index (×100)	13.01	7.39	13.46	9.72	5.64	9.27
Consumption-efficient counterfactual						
Maximum consumption (thousand D) per household	4,821.80	4,656.41	4,227.62	6,000.31	7,688.66	5,448.44
Percentage loss (1 − actual/efficient)	2.01	1.33	1.05	4.59	5.04	3.49
Inequality of consumption under the efficient land allocation	0.12	0.10	0.09	0.19	0.18	0.15
Head-count index of poverty under the efficient land allocation (%)	78.39	66.69	83.96	59.66	50.53	66.33
Squared poverty gap index under the efficient land allocation (×100)	13.56	8.08	13.71	11.98	6.72	10.33
Equal land counterfactual						
Mean consumption (thousand D) at equal land per household	4,773.22	4,620.38	4,205.75	5,829.24	7,546.89	5,345.51
Percentage loss	1.01	0.56	0.53	1.79	3.26	1.63
Inequality of consumption at equal land allocation	0.10	0.09	0.08	0.12	0.12	0.12
Head-count index of poverty at equal land allocation (%)	79.62	66.99	84.65	61.13	46.44	66.51
Squared poverty gap index at equal land allocation (×100)	12.70	7.41	13.33	9.17	4.55	8.93

Source: 1993 VLSS.
Note: D = dong. Inequality is given by the difference between log mean consumption per capita and the mean of log consumption per capita.

had become less efficient over time (given restrictions on land markets under communism) but was nonetheless the more natural fallback position in both the Mekong Delta and the South Central Coast. Ironically, then, it can be argued that because socialist agriculture had been more short-lived in the South, the region could not achieve the potential efficiency gains available to the North from land reallocation under decollectivization. The history of Vietnam meant that the North of the country was in a somewhat better position to achieve a relatively efficient land allocation.

Both the efficient and the equal land allocations would have resulted in a lower poverty rate than the actual allocation, though the differences are small (two percentage points overall). This is somewhat deceptive since the poverty line turns out to be close to the intersection of the cumulative distribution functions. However, the poverty lines used here are higher (in real terms) than those used in Vietnam at the time of the 1988 allocations (Dollar and Glewwe 1998). So it can be argued that poverty incidence would have been higher under the efficient allocation when assessed by the local standards of poverty at the time.

These observations are reinforced by figure 4.1, which plots percentage losses from the actual allocation (relative to the consumption-maximizing allocation) against actual consumption and a nonparametric regression function. It can be seen that the losses from the actual allocation tend to rise with consumption, both nationally and within each region. Nationally, mean consumption gains are about 15 percent for the poorest, with losses of about 20 percent for the richest (comparing end points on the regression function in panel a of figure 4.1). The mean proportionate gains are roughly linear in log consumption. The point where the mean gain is zero is fairly close to the poverty line (indicated by the vertical line). The gains to the poorest are also reflected in the squared poverty gap measures in table 4.4, which are higher for the consumption-efficient allocation.

It is evident from figure 4.1 that there are large interregional differences in the conditional variance of the losses. The relationship between welfare losses and consumption levels is less precise (though still positive) for the Mekong Delta and the South Central Coast, where there are clearly other factors at play in determining the incidence of the losses relative to the consumption-efficient allocation. Again, historical (preunification) allocations are likely to have had greater influence in these southern regions.

An equal allocation of land (in terms of its irrigated equivalent) across all households would have achieved a close approximation to the levels of mean consumption and inequality observed in the data.

WELFARE IMPACTS OF PRIVATIZING LAND-USE RIGHTS

Figure 4.1 Distribution of Consumption Losses Relative to the Efficient Allocation

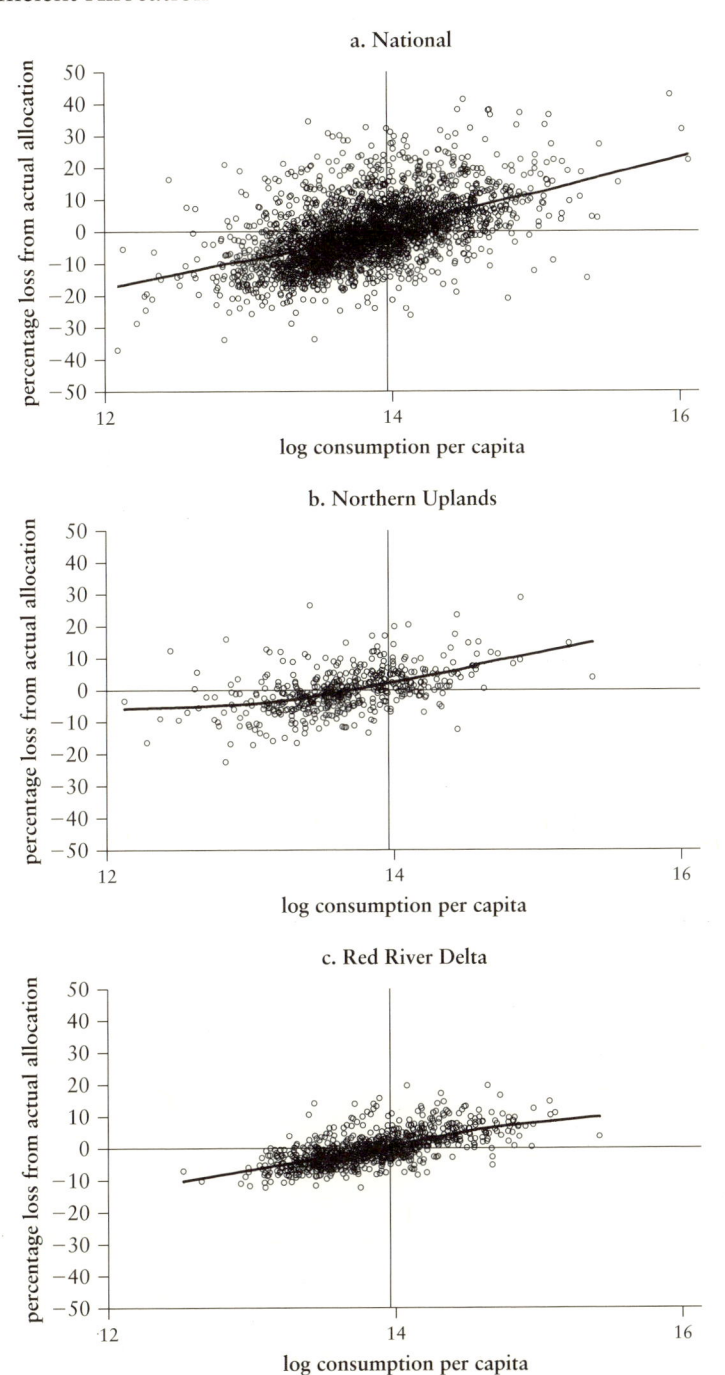

a. National

b. Northern Uplands

c. Red River Delta

(*Continued on the following page*)

Figure 4.1 (Continued)

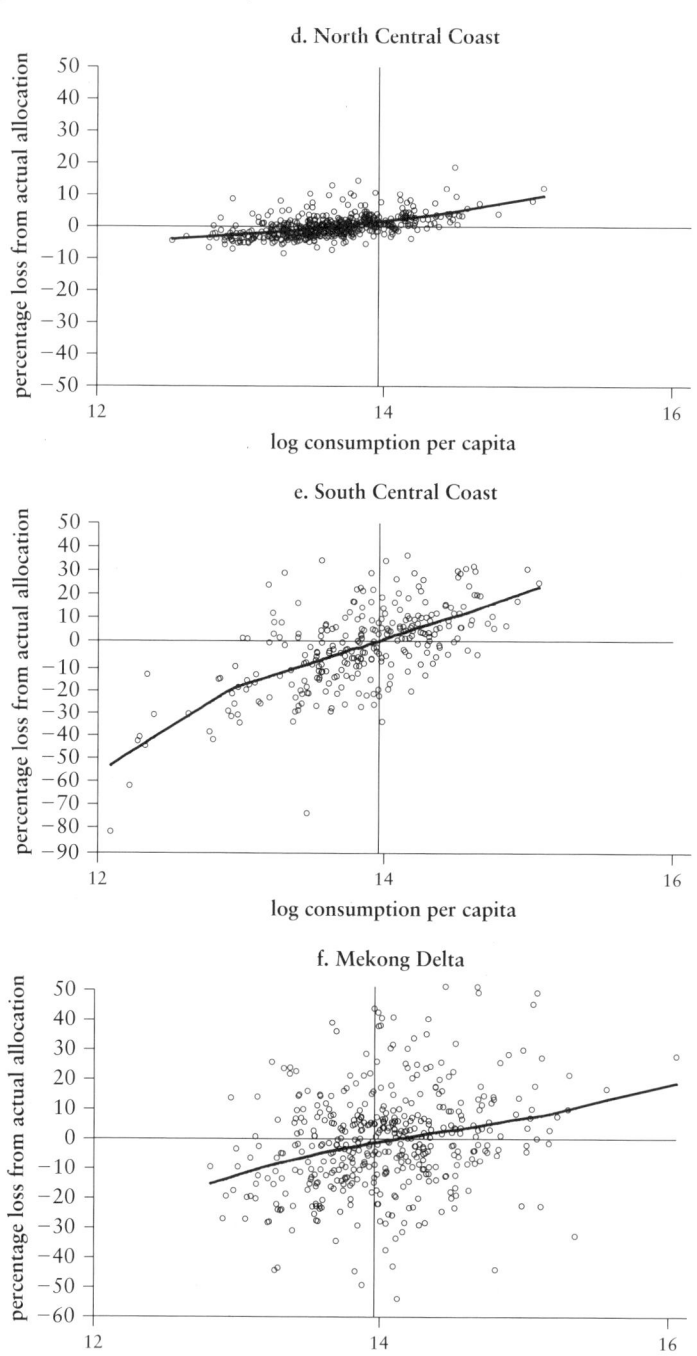

d. North Central Coast

e. South Central Coast

f. Mekong Delta

Source: 1993 VLSS.

There were, of course, deviations from equal land allocation in practice, but the overall outcomes for the distribution of consumption were similar. However, under the equal land allocation, the poorest are generally better off relative to the actual allocations, as evidenced by lower squared poverty gap indices. It is notable again that the region where the equal allocation differed most from the actual is the Mekong Delta, followed by the South Central Coast.

It might be conjectured that the market-based allocation would have achieved substantially higher average consumption if only land could have been redistributed between communes. To address this question, we repeat in table 4.5 the simulations reported in table 4.4, except that we ignore commune boundaries when making the calculations. Thus, the calculation entails maximizing aggregate consumption over the entire region, subject only to the aggregate amount of (irrigation-equivalent) land in the region. In practice, this would, of course, require moving households between communes, which was rare in Vietnam. However, this simulation gives an idea of how much immobility constrains the problem.

Maximum attainable consumption would, of course, have been higher by allowing households to move between communes, so that only aggregate land endowments at the regional level mattered. The difference is not large, however (comparing tables 4.4 and 4.5). The actual allocation within communes, without redistribution between them, entailed losses in mean consumption of between 1 and 5 percent as compared with 1 to 13 percent for a consumption-maximizing land allocation with redistribution allowed. Impacts on poverty are similar. The head-count index of poverty is lower everywhere, whereas compared with the actual allocation, the very poorest households would have a worsening under the efficient allocation with mobility across communes. When we compare the outcomes under the actual allocation with those resulting from the equalization of land at the regional level, we find the losses in consumption to be slightly lower—ranging from 1 percent to 10 percent. This scenario shows the largest impact on poverty. Both the rate and the severity of poverty would be lower under a regionwide equal land allocation relative to the actual land allocation.

Again, the Mekong Delta stands out as having high unrealized consumption gains from land reallocation. If mobility were possible within the region, the actual land allocation would entail a 9 percent loss of aggregate consumption relative to the consumption-maximizing allocation and 8 percent relative to an equal allocation; in both cases this is about twice the overall mean consumption loss (table 4.5). Lack of mobility under communism appears to have come at an unusually large cost in the Mekong Delta. This finding

Table 4.5 Mean Consumption, Inequality, and Poverty with Mobility between Communes

Indicator	Northern Uplands	Red River Delta	North Central Coast	South Central Coast	Mekong Delta	Full sample
Consumption-efficient counterfactual						
Maximum consumption (thousand D) per household	4,836.77	4,674.56	4,245.88	6,111.00	8,386.24	5,580.24
Percentage loss	2.31	1.71	1.47	6.32	12.94	5.77
Inequality under efficient allocation	0.12	0.10	0.09	0.19	0.22	0.15
Head-count index of poverty under efficient allocation (%)	78.20	66.42	82.90	59.17	49.56	64.56
Squared poverty gap index under efficient allocation ($\times 100$)	13.27	8.03	13.61	11.55	6.53	9.46
Equal land counterfactual						
Mean consumption (thousand D) at equal land per household	4,792.57	4,639.76	4,226.55	5,938.66	8,105.72	5,488.36
Percentage loss	1.41	0.97	1.02	3.60	9.93	4.19
Inequality at equal land	0.10	0.09	0.08	0.12	0.15	0.11
Head-count index of poverty at equal land allocation (%)	79.19	67.11	83.76	60.29	46.80	65.00
Squared poverty gap index at equal land allocation ($\times 100$)	12.42	7.35	13.22	8.72	4.28	8.08

Source: 1993 VLSS.

Note: D = dong. Inequality is given by the difference between log mean consumption per capita and the mean of log consumption per capita.

is consistent with our casual observations that household plot sizes vary greatly within the region.

Conclusions

Returning to the debates summarized in chapter 2, we find it hard to reconcile the results of this chapter with the picture that many commentators have painted of an inegalitarian land allocation captured by relatively well-off local cadres. Although there were clearly geographic heterogeneity and "hot spots" as discussed in chapter 2, overall this decentralized reform resulted in a more equitable outcome than one would have expected from a consumption-efficient allocation, as would have been achieved by competitive markets. It seems that an effort was made to protect the poorest and reduce overall inequality at the expense of aggregate consumption. Clearly, both equity and efficiency were valued positively.

In the concluding chapter of this book, we consider why the historical record of seemingly widespread abuse in the land-privatization process appears to have been so wrong. Next, we turn to the second key stage of the agrarian reform process to see whether the achievements of this first stage were undermined once the legal trappings of a land market were introduced.

Annex: Theoretical Model

This annex outlines in more formal terms our theoretical model of the actual and counterfactual allocations of land. We make three key assumptions, as follows:

Assumption 4A.1. There is a fixed and known ex ante probability distribution $p = (p_1, \ldots, p_m)$ for the m possible states of nature, where p_j denotes the probability of state j occurring.

Assumption 4A.2. The outcome of the actual decision-making process can be represented by the maximum of a nonnegatively weighted sum of welfare levels across all farm households. The weight attached to the expected utility of household i is $w_i = w(X_i)$, where X is a vector of exogenous household characteristics.

Assumption 4A.3. The utility of the ith farm household in state j is assumed to depend solely on its consumption of a composite commodity, which depends, in turn, on both own-farm output and nonfarm income.

The household receives L_i of land under the administrative allocation, which yields an output of $F_j(L_i, X_i)$ (net of the cost of nonland, nonlabor inputs) in state $j(=1, \ldots, m)$. The household also has (positive or negative) nonfarm income, $Y_j(X_i)$.[4] At the time of the reform (and since), agricultural labor markets were thin and virtually nonexistent in the northern regions of Vietnam, so to simplify the exposition we close off this market in our model. Consumption is then equal to income:

(4A.1) $\quad C_{ij} = C_j(L_i, X_i) = F_j(L_i, X_i) + Y_j(X_i).$

We assume that the functions $F_j (j = 1, \ldots, m)$ are increasing and strictly concave in L_i for all states of nature; that is, the marginal product of land in state j is $F_{jL}(L_i, X_i) > 0$ and $F_{jLL}(L_i, X_i) < 0$, where the subscripts for L denote partial derivatives (so $F_{jLL} = \partial^2 F_j/\partial L_i^2$). Utility is, in turn, an increasing concave function of consumption, $U_{ij} = U(C_{ij})$, $\partial U/\partial C_{ij} > 0$, $\partial^2 U/\partial C_{ij}^2 < 0$.

The commune selects an allocation of the total available land $n\bar{L}$ across n households, with mean $\bar{L}$. The realized land allocation $(L_1, \ldots, L_n)$ maximizes

(4A.2.1) $\quad \sum_{i=1}^{n} w(X_i) \sum_{j=1}^{m} p_j U[F_j(L_i, X_i) + Y_j(X_i)],$

subject to

(4A.2.2) $\quad \sum_{i=1}^{n} L_i = n\bar{L}.$

The first-order conditions for a solution require that $(L_1, \ldots, L_n)$ satisfies

(4A.3) $\quad w(X_i) \sum_{j=1}^{m} p_j [U'(C_{ij}) F_{jL}(L_i, X_i)] = \mu \quad (i = 1, \ldots, n),$

where μ is the shadow price of land in the commune (the Lagrange multiplier on the aggregate land constraint in equation 4A.2.2).

The efficiency counterfactual is the allocation that maximizes the commune's aggregate current (state-specific) consumption; we can write this as

(4A.4) $\quad (L_{1j}^*, \ldots, L_{nj}^*) = \arg \max \left[\sum_{i=1}^{n} C_j(L_i, X_i) \middle| \sum_{i=1}^{n} L_i = n\bar{L} \right].$

We call this the "consumption-efficient allocation." From the first-order conditions for an optimum, we can see that this equates $F_{jL}(L_i^*, X_i)$ with the multiplier λ_j on aggregate land in equation (4A.4); we write this as

(4A.5) $\quad L_{ij}^* = L_j(X_i, \lambda_j) \quad (i = 1, \ldots, n).$

Mean consumption in state j is then

$$(4A.6) \qquad \overline{C}_j^* = \sum_{i=1}^{n} C_j(L_{ij}^*, X_i)/n.$$

The consumption loss from the actual allocation is then $\overline{C}_j^* - \overline{C}_j$, where $\overline{C}_j$ is the actual mean.

To see why the consumption-efficient allocation coincides with the competitive-market solution allowing costless recontracting in each state of nature, note that in such an allocation, each household's consumption will be $F_j(L_{ij}, X_i) + Y_j(X_i) - \lambda_j L_i$, where λ_j is the market price of land in state j. Demands then equate $F_{jL}(L_{ij}, X_i) = \lambda_j$ over all i, which is exactly the same allocation that maximizes aggregate consumption. Naturally, the market solution will also vary with the joint distribution of the X's as well as with the realized state of nature.

Notes

1. In an experimental evaluation, the assignment is random, while in a nonexperimental evaluation there is purposive placement, entailing a "selection bias" that one must address in the evaluation method. There is a large literature on the methods that can be used to address this problem; for an overview and references, see Ravallion (2008).

2. The simplest procedure to verify this result is to use the constraint on aggregate land availability to solve for the term $[a_j + \ln(b_j/\lambda_j)]/(1 - b_j)$ in equation (4.6).

3. However, the South Central Coast was probably a somewhat special case, given that it had been a war zone, and so collectivization was more easily adopted (V. L. Ngo 1993; Pingali and Xuan 1992).

4. To the extent that some nonfarm income may depend on landholding, one can reinterpret $Y(X)$ as that component of income that is not affected by landholding.

5

Land Reallocation after the Introduction of a Land Market

The second stage of the agrarian reform was to introduce a market in the land-use rights that had been privatized at the time of decollectivization. There are a number of ways that a rural economy might respond to inefficiencies in an initial administrative allocation of land. One way is through a quasi-market process in which individuals take up the new opportunities allowed by the 1993 Land Law. As previously discussed, many households had already engaged in various types of land transactions prior to the 1993 law. Nevertheless, the new law assuredly provided and strengthened the legal and institutional basis for land transactions. It introduced a formal title system, bolstered tenure security, and officially encouraged participation in land transactions. The law served to reaffirm expectations that the market-based land reforms would not be reversed. Those with too much land could now legally rent or sell it to those with too little.

Did land start changing hands in the wake of these reforms? In principle, this could happen through either rental or purchase-sale transactions. A more active rental market had emerged by 1998, though it has since declined (Brandt 2006). The Vietnam Living Standards Surveys (VLSSs) and Vietnam Household Living Standards Surveys (VHLSSs) reveal that 8.3 percent of rural households rented in annual cropland in 1993, 12.4 percent did so in 1998, and 8.6 percent did so in 2004. The rented-in land amounts follow a downward trend as a percentage of total annual land: from 9.8 percent in 1993 to 5.1 percent and 5.5 percent in 1998 and 2004, respectively. Rental of other land types was no higher on average, representing 3.6 percent of the total agricultural land in 2004 (Brandt 2006).

Adjustment through land rental was not, however, encouraged. It should be noted that a number of restrictions remained on land rentals

101

after 1993, including a three-year limit and administratively determined prices (Marsh and MacAulay 2006).[1] Rentals tend often to be temporary arrangements, such as when a family worker is sick or temporarily absent. Indeed, the 2004 VHLSS shows that nationally a vast majority of land rentals are to immediate family (30 percent), other relatives (22 percent), or friends and neighbors (34 percent), leaving only 14 percent going to "others" (Brandt 2006). Interestingly, Brandt also finds that the proportion of these transactions for which there is payment increased from around 25 percent in 1993 to over 80 percent in 2004. This could well be a result of the 1993 Land Law. Auction land—that is, land that effectively is rented from the commune—accounted for 2.1 percent of all cultivated land in 1993 and 2.2 percent in 1998.

But a number of options instead of rental were now legal. The 1998 VLSS indicates that 27 percent of the households in the 1993–98 panel received use rights to new land plots through purchase, exchange, inheritance, or allocation during the previous five years, resulting in a mean change of 1,492 square meters over all panel households. Moreover, 13 percent sold, exchanged, or returned land during the same period (405 square meters per household, on average). Unfortunately, the data do not identify to what extent changes in landholdings between the surveys occurred through market versus administrative reallocations. Nor did the 1998 survey ask whether the household held a land-use certificate (LUC). Scattered anecdotal evidence suggests that some commune authorities continued to control land reallocations, particularly in the North. Drawing again on the 2004 VHLSS, one sees reallocations by communes between 1993 and 1998, though less so after 1998, in all regions of the North (although not in the South). Such administrative reallocations were disallowed under the 1993 Land Law, which aimed to establish free exchange in land-use rights while protecting stable, long-term use and promoting incentives to invest in the land. Administrative reassignments appear to have continued in some communes, side by side with market-based transactions.

In principle, the allocation of two other factors of production could also respond to these agrarian reforms—namely, capital and labor. If a farm household had too much land, then it might invest (to add more capital) or hire labor (or engage in labor exchanges or possibly add family members). The latter option was probably more important in the South (notably in the Mekong Delta), where the greater inequality of landholdings (even before the reform) meant a more active labor market. (Naturally, when land is very unequally distributed, there will tend to be more farmers with too little land for their consumption needs, who then supply labor to farmers with too much land for their needs; if everyone has the same amount of land, the agricultural labor market will tend to be very thin or nonexistent.)

A strand of the literature has thrown some light on investment responses to land-market inefficiencies, although the focus has been more on responses to land titling. In this strand of the literature, the emphasis has been on the scope for land titling to enhance efficiency by promoting greater investment in land, given that its use right was more secure.[2] Research on this issue for Vietnam has suggested that greater security of landholdings, through the issuance of LUCs, did rather little to promote greater investment and, hence, higher productivity of land in Vietnam (Do and Iyer 2007). Identifying the impact of LUCs on farm productivity is difficult, however, given that obtaining an LUC is a choice made by farmers and so is endogenous to other choices affecting productivity.[3] Data permitting, one might instead treat obtaining an LUC as a response to inefficiencies in land allocation or in access to capital; however, as already noted, the 1998 VLSS did not ask about LUCs.[4]

Furthermore, the importance of having a formal title will undoubtedly depend on the context. In a rural setting in which traditions of cooperation mean use rights are well defined and widely respected, an LUC is presumably irrelevant and possibly undesirable, given transaction costs (as discussed in chapter 2). The fact that some villagers felt less of a need to obtain LUCs does not mean that the efficiency gains from privatizing land-use rights and freeing up land markets were any less important.

In this chapter, we aim to see how the allocation of land across farmers responded to this second stage of Vietnam's land reforms. We use the 1993–98 panel discussed in the section "The 1993–98 Household Panel: Land Reallocations" of chapter 3. The main hypothesis to be tested is that land reallocation (by whatever means) during Vietnam's agrarian transition helped offset prior inefficiencies in the administrative allocation. To test this hypothesis, we need to explicitly characterize the extent of inefficiency in the initial allocation. Then we will see how subsequent reallocations of land responded to the measured inefficiencies.

Gainers and Losers from the Initial Administrative Allocation

Following the model of chapter 4, we assume that holding L_i of land allows household $i = 1, \ldots, n$ to consume $C(L_i, X_i)$, where X_i is a vector of exogenous household characteristics and the function C

is assumed to be strictly concave in L. Our efficiency counterfactual is the allocation for a given commune that maximizes the commune's aggregate current consumption (see annex 4A for details). A necessary condition for an efficient allocation is that the marginal consumption gains from extra land, $C_L(L_i^*, X_i)$, are equated with the shadow price of land, λ. The solutions can be written as

(5.1) $\qquad L_i^* = L(X_i, \lambda) \quad (i = 1, \ldots, n).$

We call this the *consumption-efficient allocation*. As discussed in chapter 4, this is also the competitive equilibrium, assuming that utility depends solely on consumption and on allowing costless recontraction in each state of nature. Under the market allocation, demands for land will also equate $C_L(L_i, X_i)$ over all i at the (common) market price of land, λ.

In our empirical implementation, we continue to assume that the consumption function, $C(L_i, X_i)$, takes the form

(5.2) $\qquad \ln C_i = a + b \ln L_i + X_i c + \varepsilon_i,$

where a, b, and c are parameters and ε_i is a white noise error process. Given data on X and estimates of the parameters and error term, we can then calculate the consumption efficient allocation to each household. For $0 < b < 1$, the solution is

(5.3) $\qquad L_i^* = \exp[(\ln(b/\lambda) + X_i c + \varepsilon_i)/(1 - b)].$

The main parameters of interest in this equation are identified from the parameters of equation (5.2). Note that the regression specification in equation (5.2) implies that any element of X that increases (decreases) consumption must also increase (decrease) the efficient allocation of land. This property can be relaxed by adding interaction effects between $\ln L$ and X to equation (5.2). (Recall that chapter 4 reported tests for such interaction effects but found no sign of their presence.)

A special case of the above formulation is obtained when intertemporal behavior is closed off, such that consumption is simply the current period's income, comprising farm output and nonfarm income. In principle, one could base our empirical model on this special case and model farm output instead of consumption (assuming that only farm output depends on land allocation, though this assumption could be relaxed easily). This might seem a natural model, given that we are studying a largely agrarian economy. However, we prefer the more general formulation in which consumption is the key dependent variable for the empirical analysis. In addition to the fact that this allows for intertemporal behavior, consumption is almost certainly measured better than incomes in this setting.

The administrative allocation at decollectivization gives L_i^A of land to household i. The administrative allocation need not be efficient in the sense of maximizing aggregate consumption. We postulate a measure of the land deficit of the administrative allocation relative to the efficient solution defined above of the general form $\tau_i = \tau(L_i^*, L_i^A)$, where the function τ is strictly increasing in L_i^* and strictly decreasing in L_i^A. Naturally, we want the function τ to have the property that $\tau(L, L) = 0$. We ensure this by adopting the following functional form:

$$(5.4) \qquad \tau(L_i^*, L_i^A) = \phi(L_i^*) - \phi(L_i^A).$$

Here ϕ is some strictly increasing function. Thus, it will be the case that τ will be positive (negative) according to whether L_i^* is above (below) L_i^A.

We can embrace a reasonably wide range of possible empirical measures of the land deficit by restricting attention to the class of parametric functions $\phi(L) = (L^\eta - 1)/\eta$, where $\eta \in [0,1]$. The two extreme cases are (a) *proportionate differences*, in which $\eta = 0$, implying that $\tau_i = \ln(L_i^*/L_i^A)$ (noting that $\lim_{\eta \to 0}(L^\eta - 1)/\eta = \ln L$); and (b) *absolute differences*: ($\eta = 1$), whereby $\tau_i = L_i^* - L_i^A$.

Modeling the Postreform Land Reallocation

We observe only a single time interval in the process of land reallocation after legalizing market transactions, and we should not, of course, assume that the process has reached its long-run solution by the end of the period of observation. However, we do assume that the dynamic process will eventually converge to a unique long-run equilibrium that depends on the competitive-market allocation of land to that household, but which can also be influenced by the household's power in local decision making about the allocation of use rights. That power could be exercised through the market or through local-level political processes.

The new allocation observed at a date after the reform is $(L_1^R, L_2^R, \ldots, L_n^R)$. Let $\rho_i = \rho(L_i^R, L_i^A)$ denote a measure of the extent of land reallocation. (We do not assume that $\Sigma L_i^R - L_i^A = 0$. Thus, land "reallocation" can come with higher total acreage.) We clearly want $\rho(L_i^R, L_i^A)$ to be strictly increasing in L_i^R and decreasing in L_i^A with $\rho(L, L) = 0$. We also want to ensure that if $\rho(L_i^R, L_i^A) = \tau(L_i^*, L_i^A)$, then $L_i^R = L_i^*$; that is, if the land gain through reallocation to household i exactly matches the initial efficiency loss, then the household must have reached the market solution. These conditions require that ρ and τ have the same functional form—that is, $\rho_i = \phi(L_i^R) - \phi(L_i^A)$.

To see how land allocation responded to initial inefficiencies in the administrative assignment, we begin by studying the nonparametric regression of ρ on τ:

(5.5) $$\rho(L_i^R, L_i^A) = f[\tau(L_i^*, L_i^A)] + \nu_i,$$

where $f(\tau_i) \equiv E[\rho_i|\tau_i]$, which is the mean (mathematical expectation) of ρ when that mean is formed over the distribution of the random error term ν. In the special case with $f(0) = 0$ and $f'(\tau_i) = 1$ for all τ, there are no systematic nonmarket constraints on land reallocation, so $E\phi(L_i^R) = \phi(L_i^*)$. Adjustment to the market solution is then complete up to the value of a random error term within the period of observation. More generally, one can allow $0 \leq f'(\tau_i) \leq 1$, in which case we have a nonlinear partial adjustment model by which landholdings adjust to any discrepancies between the administrative allocation and the market solution, but in which the process need not be complete in the period of observation. With repeated observations, L_i^* will eventually be reached; this adjustment holds whatever the initial start value (in this case, the administrative allocation at decollectivization). The slope, $f'(\tau_i)$, is the "partial adjustment coefficient" for household i, giving the speed at which initial inefficiencies are eliminated.

The partial adjustment model described here can be questioned from a number of perspectives. One concern is the possibility of measurement error in estimates of the efficient allocation and in the data for the initial land allocation. Classical measurement error in L_i^A or L_i^* will bias the ordinary least squares (OLS) estimate of the linear partial adjustment coefficient. The direction of bias is ambiguous when the measurement error is in L_i^A; the usual attenuation bias will be at least partly offset by the fact that the measurement error also appears positively in the dependent variable.[5] The initial land allocation is likely to have been well known at the farm household and commune level, in part because it was officially and publicly allocated, but also because taxes are land based. So we do not expect sizable bias attributable to measurement error in L_i^A. Measurement error in L_i^* is a different matter; this will impart a downward bias to the partial adjustment coefficient. Since L_i^* is a constructed variable (rather than data), there is no instrumental variables estimator for dealing with this bias. All we can do is test whether land reallocation responds to our measure of initial inefficiency.

A second concern relates to our assumption that initial land allocation does not influence land reallocation independently of the gains and losses from the initial administrative allocation. We refer to this assumption as *homogeneity*.[6] Imposing homogeneity when it does not hold will bias upward (downward) the OLS partial adjustment coefficient if there is convergence (divergence) at a given land deficit relative to the efficient allocation. By adding L_i^A as an additional regressor, we can test homogeneity. Again, any measurement error in L_i^A may induce some bias, which will tend toward showing convergence.

A third concern is that the efficient allocation of land may have changed over time. For example, demographic shocks will no doubt shift the consumption-efficient allocation. This can be thought of as measurement error in our estimate of the loss from the administrative allocation. We address this issue by adding controls for observed changes in household characteristics that are likely to influence the efficient allocation. Latent measurement error will leave some bias.

A final concern is that the local political economy may influence land reallocation, as discussed in chapter 2. To deal with this concern, we can postulate instead a solution, L_i^{R*}, such that the higher $\tau(L_i^{R*}, L_i^*)$ the higher the weight given household i in local decision making about land. This allows some households to acquire more land in the long run than implied by the efficient solution. Thus, $\tau(L_i^{R*}, L_i^*)$ can be thought of as a measure of the household's (competitive or noncompetitive) power over land allocation. We assume that L_i^{R*} depends on assets (education and other types of land), connections (such as having a government job and being a long-standing resident), and possible discriminating variables (such as gender and ethnicity of head of household). We then augment the partial adjustment model for these household characteristics. Notice that the initial administrative allocation may itself be one such factor; if a higher initial administrative allocation gives one the power to acquire more land, then we will see signs in the data of a divergent (nonstationary) process.

Combining these considerations, we also estimate a parametric model:

(5.6) $\quad \rho(L_i^R, L_i^A) = \alpha + \beta\tau(L_i^*, L_i^A) + \gamma \ln L_i^A + \pi Z_i + \nu_i.$

Here Z_i denotes a vector of controls for other (competitive or noncompetitive) factors influencing $\tau(L_i^{R*}, L_i^*)$. The long-run solution to equation (5.6) is obtained by setting $L^R = L^A = L_i^{R*}$ and solving for

(5.7) $\quad L_i^{R*} = \phi^{-1}\left[\phi(L_i^*) + \frac{\alpha}{\beta} + \frac{\gamma}{\beta}\ln L_i^A + \frac{\pi}{\beta}Z_i + \frac{\nu_i}{\beta}\right].$

We also allow the partial regression coefficient of $\rho(L_i^R, L_i^A)$ on $\tau(L_i^*, L_i^A)$ to vary between households according to their characteristics, by augmenting equation (5.6) with appropriate interaction terms between $\tau(L_i^*, L_i^A)$ and Z_i.

This expanded partial adjustment model will not be able to cleanly separate "competitive" from "noncompetitive" forces on land allocation. A nonzero element of the parameter vector π could reflect that characteristic's influence over how the competitive-market allocation has changed over time, or it could reflect its bearing on the ability of a household to distort the market in the household's favor, by exercising (competitive or noncompetitive) power. In this setting, it is hard to imagine any household characteristic that could be unambiguously interpreted as one rather than the other. For example, finding a significant effect of gender or ethnicity is suggestive of a noncompetitive force at work, but we cannot know with certainty in which market it operates; possibly the discrimination is in access to credit rather than to land.

Nonetheless, we will be able to see whether the controls reinforce or offset the adjustment process. We will say that the controls are "cooperant" ("noncooperant") with competitive market forces arising from inefficiencies in the initial administrative allocation if the unconditional adjustment coefficient (setting $\gamma = \pi = 0$) is found to be biased upward (downward) when the controls are added.

Note that there are limits to how many control variables we can add to the partial adjustment model. We cannot include all the postulated determinants of initial consumption as well as initial land allocation since doing so would create a singularity (given that the log efficiency loss is linear in log initial land and X). We must thus impose exclusion restrictions. We follow common practice in panel data econometrics in relying on lagged values to help in identification. In our augmented model based on equation (5.6), the excluded variables from the model for initial consumption are the lagged values (lagged five years prior to 1993) for the demographics (notably household size and the dependency ratio) and the presence of a disabled adult in 1993. While these variables influence consumption, they are assumed to be irrelevant to the post-1993 land reallocation conditional on the initial efficiency loss, initial landholding, and other control variables.

Results

Recall that in measuring land reallocation and the initial land deficit, we assume that $\phi(L) = (L^\eta - 1)/\eta$, where $\eta \in [0, 1]$. To choose a value of η, we regressed $\rho(L_i^R, L_i^A)$ on $\tau(L_i^*, L_i^A)$ across the entire dataset for alternative values of η at 0.1 interval over the [0,1] interval. The best fit (measured by the t-ratio on the partial adjustment coefficient) was obtained at $\eta = 0$, which gave a partial adjustment coefficient for proportionate differences of 0.33 with a t-ratio of 9.8.[7] The coefficient for absolute differences ($\eta = 1$) was 0.17, and

LAND REALLOCATION   *109*

Figure 5.1 Proportionate Land Reallocations from 1993 to 1998 against the Proportionate Land Deficit (Efficient Minus Actual) in 1993

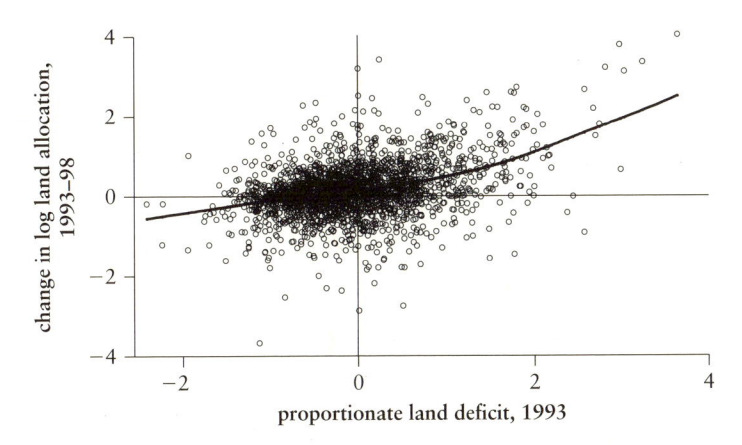

[Scatter plot: x-axis "proportionate land deficit, 1993" ranging from -2 to 4; y-axis "change in log land allocation, 1993–98" ranging from -4 to 4.]

Sources: 1993 and 1998 VLSSs.

between the two, the *t*-ratio declined monotonically. So we chose the proportionate (log difference) specification in all further work. However, this specification has the drawback that we lose some observations with zero land allocation in 1998 (since we cannot take the log of zero); this applies to less than 8 percent of the sample.[8] Later in this chapter, we study this subsample with zero allocated land in the 1998 survey more closely and test for sample selection bias. For the present discussion, we confine attention to the proportionate case.

For the national sample, figure 5.1 plots the proportionate changes (log differences) in land allocation ($\ln(L_i^R/L_i^A)$) between 1993 and 1998 against our measure of the initial land deficit relative to the efficient allocation ($\ln(L_i^*/L_i^A)$). The empirical relationship suggests a tendency for land reallocation to respond positively to the initial inefficiency in the administrative allocation. As already noted, the linear regression coefficient is 0.33, indicating that one-third of the initial disparity between the administrative allocation and the market allocation was eliminated over this five-year period. Figure 5.1 also gives the nonparametric regression function, using Cleveland's (1979) local regression method. The slope is positive but less than unity throughout, though it is clear that $f(0) \neq 0$, reflecting an overall expansion in allocated annual land area over this period.

This relationship between annual land reallocation and the extent of the initial inefficiency is found at different levels of initial welfare. Figure 5.2 gives the plots corresponding to figure 5.1 by quintile of

Figure 5.2 Proportionate Land Reallocations from 1993 to 1998 Relative to the 1993 Efficiency Loss, Stratified by Quintile of 1993 Household Consumption per Person

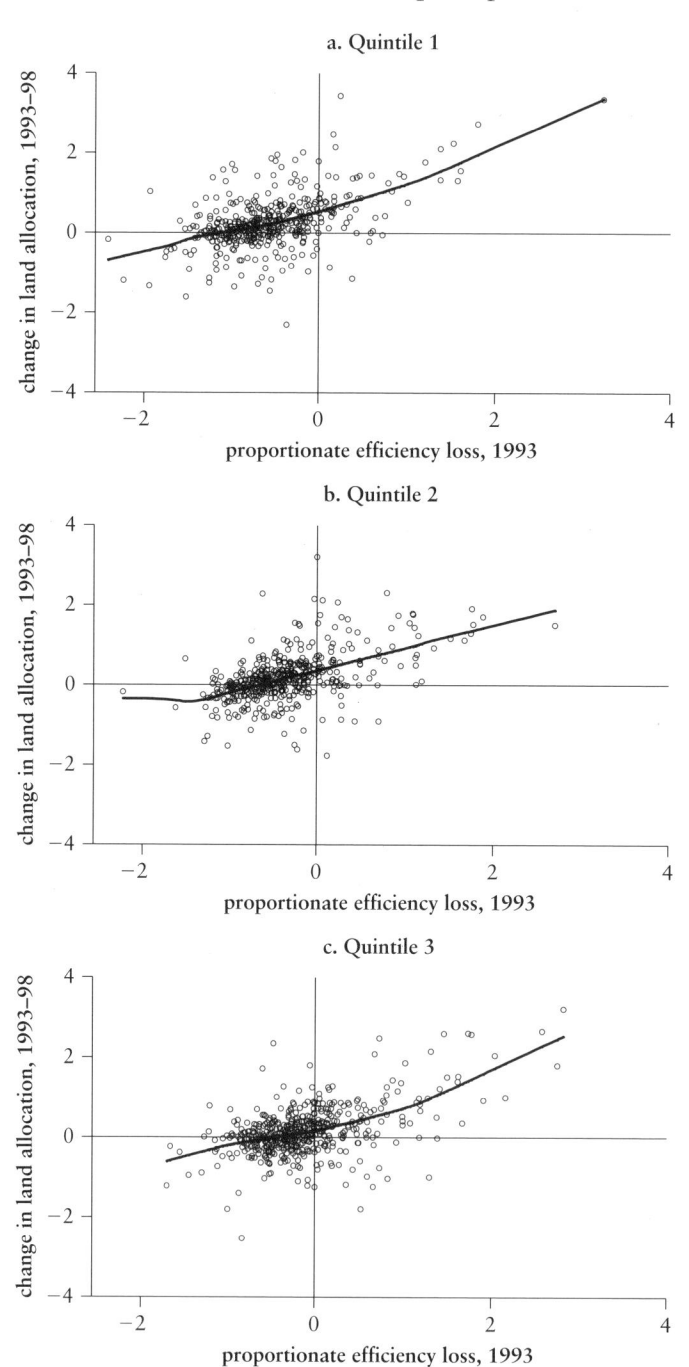

a. Quintile 1

b. Quintile 2

c. Quintile 3

LAND REALLOCATION

Figure 5.2 (Continued)

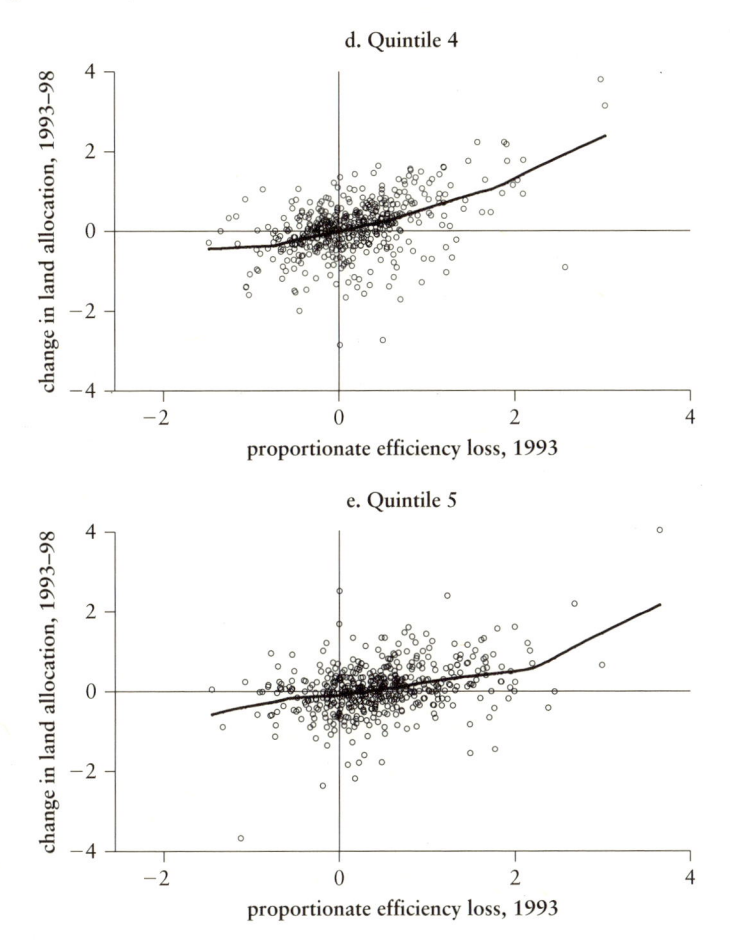

d. Quintile 4

e. Quintile 5

Sources: 1993 and 1998 VLSSs.

consumption in 1993, ranked by consumption per person. Table 5.1 gives the corresponding conditional means. The tendency to adjust over time toward the efficient allocation is evident for all quintiles of initial consumption. We also see a marked tendency in table 5.1 for the gains in allocated annual landholding to fall as consumption rises. This effect appears to be somewhat stronger among those who lost most from the initial administrative allocation, relative to the efficient solution. In other words, the gradient in land increments between those who gained from the efficient allocation and those who lost appears to be steeper for the poor.

Figure 5.1 is suggestive of near-linear partial adjustment toward the market allocation, though still leaving two-thirds of the initial

Table 5.1 Proportionate Gain in Allocated Annual Agricultural Land, 1993–98

Quintiles of households ranked by estimates of loss $(L_i^* - L_i^A)$ from administrative allocation of land 1992/93	Quintiles of households ranked by consumption per person in 1993				
	1 (poorest 20%)	2	3	4	5 (richest 20%)
1 (gained relative to the efficient allocation)	−0.147 (0.527) [147]	−0.190 (0.365) [123]	−0.229 (0.528) [82]	−0.339 (0.596) [56]	−0.152 (0.708) [47]
2	0.249 (0.448) [131]	0.109 (0.511) [157]	−0.028 (0.360) [145]	−0.217 (0.514) [71]	−0.315 (0.657) [19]
3	0.520 (0.685) [110]	0.344 (0.543) [122]	0.208 (0.542) [137]	0.001 (0.584) [111]	−0.043 (0.602) [65]
4	0.960 (0.817) [34]	0.734 (0.841) [46]	0.426 (0.629) [94]	0.280 (0.708) [148]	0.069 (0.542) [154]
5 (lost relative to the efficient allocation)	0.717 (0.624) [10]	0.667 (0.677) [17]	0.771 (1.010) [35]	0.390 (0.838) [93]	0.173 (0.696) [207]
Mean by consumption quintile	0.250 (0.671) [432]	0.174 (0.607) [465]	0.148 (0.632) [493]	0.091 (0.716) [479]	0.062 (0.649) [492]

Sources: 1993 and 1998 VLSSs.
Note: Standard deviation in parentheses; number of sampled households in brackets.

mean proportionate land deficit after five years. We next study the effect of adding controls to the simple partial adjustment model.

On adding $\ln L_i^A$ to the regression of $\ln(L_i^R/L_i^A)$ on $\ln(L_i^*/L_i^A)$, we could reject the null hypothesis implied by homogeneity. The regression coefficient on $\ln L_i^A$ was −0.287 (*t*-ratio of −8.05), while the partial adjustment coefficient fell to 0.217 (7.09). Recall that measurement error in $\ln L_i^*$ will impart a downward bias to our estimate of this coefficient.

Table 5.2 gives the estimated partial adjustment coefficients when various controls are added step by step (cumulatively). We give national results and a breakdown by region. We focus first on the national results. Consistent with figure 5.1, all of our tests indicate a highly significant positive coefficient on the initial efficiency loss, implying that the land reallocation process was in the direction of a more efficient allocation. However, as can be seen from table 5.2, the partial adjustment coefficient falls to less than half the value implied by figure 5.1 when all controls are added. This is the combined effect of relaxing homogeneity and adding the controls, including commune fixed effects. Of all these changes, relaxing homogeneity and adding commune effects do most of the work; with just these two changes, the partial adjustment coefficient falls to 0.155 (*t* = 5.18),

Table 5.2 Effects of Adding Controls on the Partial Adjustment Coefficients

Controls	Northern Uplands	Red River Delta	North Central Coast	South Central Coast	Mekong Delta	Full sample
No controls	0.476	0.294	0.306	0.172	0.350	0.328
	(5.97)	(6.81)	(3.35)	(2.17)	(4.51)	(9.82)
Adding initial	0.170	0.094	0.129	0.025	0.221	0.218
land allocation	(1.61)	(2.67)	(1.24)	(0.37)	(3.06)	(7.09)
Adding commune	0.205	0.123	0.132	0.079	0.171	0.155
effects	(3.96)	(2.98)	(1.52)	(1.32)	(1.62)	(5.18)
Adding controls	0.255	0.150	0.175	0.074	0.215	0.182
for demographic shocks	(4.89)	(4.02)	(2.24)	(1.15)	(2.20)	(6.46)
Adding controls	0.268	0.071	0.173	0.069	0.074	0.131
for connections and assets	(4.54)	(1.39)	(1.68)	(1.16)	(0.73)	(4.09)
Number of observations	432	790	459	269	308	2,361

Sources: 1993 and 1998 VLSSs.

Note: The table gives regression coefficients of the change in log annual land allocation on the estimated proportionate deficit of the initial administrative allocation relative to the counterfactual market allocation. The regressions are cumulative in that as controls are added the previous controls are kept in.

while adding the rest of the control variables brings it down only slightly more, to 0.131 (table 5.2).

There are regional differences in the estimated adjustment coefficients, though the pattern of declining coefficients as controls are added is similar across regions. There is little sign of a difference between the North and the South; while the highest coefficient without controls is for the Northern Uplands, the South's Mekong Delta is the second highest. Although the speed of issuing formal titles (LUCs) was greater in the South, there is no sign that the pace of land reallocation in response to inefficiencies in the administrative allocation was any greater than in the North.

Our results suggest that any noncompetitive forces being picked up by our controls tended to be cooperant with competitive-market forces, as captured by our adjustment coefficient to initial deficits of the administrative allocation relative to the efficient solution. This is evident from the fact that, on balance, controls that raise (lower) land allocation tend to be positively (negatively) correlated with the initial land deficit. The only exception is for the controls for demographic shocks, which tended to work in the opposite direction (as is evident in table 5.2), though the effect on the partial adjustment coefficient is small.

In table 5.3, we give the complete results for the most comprehensive model we estimated. For this model, we added interaction

Table 5.3 Determinants of Changes in Allocated Annual Agricultural Land

Determinant	Northern Uplands	Red River Delta	North Central Coast	South Central Coast	Mekong Delta	Full sample
Proportional land deficit	0.433	0.197	0.501	0.230	1.494	0.700
	(2.65)	(0.52)	(1.09)	(0.67)	(2.90)	(4.51)
Log initial land allocation	−0.481	−0.434	−0.298	−0.495	−0.394	−0.405
	(−7.20)	(−6.32)	(−3.47)	(−10.04)	(−4.01)	(−11.78)
Interaction of loss with initial land allocation	−0.024	−0.017	−0.047	−0.022	−0.168	−0.077
	(−1.06)	(−0.34)	(−0.84)	(−0.52)	(−3.02)	(−3.87)
Adult household member died, 1993–98	0.096	0.110	0.043	−0.059	0.170	0.043
	(0.52)	(1.22)	(0.18)	(−0.53)	(1.07)	(0.53)
Elderly household member died, 1993–98	−0.150	−0.118	−0.034	−0.143	−0.162	−0.080
	(−0.67)	(−1.18)	(−0.14)	(−0.96)	(−0.99)	(−0.88)
Change in number of disabled household members, 1993–98	0.204	0.240	0.122	0.043	−0.008	0.119
	(2.15)	(1.66)	(1.77)	(0.43)	(−0.04)	(2.03)
Change in number of able-bodied household members	0.119	0.150	0.119	0.052	0.05	0.100
	(5.08)	(8.70)	(5.56)	(1.44)	(1.72)	(8.92)
New household member age 8–99, 1993–98	0.113	0.189	0.111	0.050	0.205	0.124
	(2.20)	(4.59)	(1.73)	(0.94)	(3.74)	(5.00)
Religion	0.151	−0.049	0.020	−0.054	0.126	0.005
	(2.13)	(−1.12)	(0.20)	(−0.45)	(2.61)	(0.16)
Ethnicity	0.254	−0.128	0.089	1.014	−0.288	0.096
	(2.06)	(−3.40)	(0.75)	(14.57)	(−1.44)	(0.93)

Locally born	0.159	0.018	0.160	0.178	−0.026	0.093
	(1.71)	(0.25)	(1.36)	(2.15)	(−0.22)	(2.13)
Gender of head of household: 1 if male	0.121	0.121	0.097	0.091	0.068	0.123
	(3.93)	(2.73)	(1.61)	(1.27)	(0.64)	(4.35)
Government job	−0.142	−0.060	−0.142	−0.171	0.124	−0.090
	(−1.01)	(−0.75)	(−1.58)	(−0.86)	(0.94)	(−1.56)
State-owned enterprise job	−0.462	0.104	−0.087	−0.216	0.174	0.036
	(−4.19)	(0.56)	(−0.37)	(−2.06)	(1.05)	(0.28)
Education of head of household	−0.006	0.011	−0.000	−0.001	0.028	0.006
	(−0.78)	(2.48)	(−0.05)	(−0.18)	(1.40)	(1.58)
Education of other adults	0.004	0.004	−0.001	0.007	0.009	0.004
	(1.52)	(1.60)	(−0.20)	(2.79)	(2.09)	(2.18)
Share of good-quality nonirrigated land	−0.032	−0.047	0.032	−0.058	0.005	−0.009
	(−0.38)	(−0.81)	(0.50)	(−0.63)	(0.06)	(−0.27)
Share of good-quality irrigated land	−0.256	−0.001	−0.088	0.118	0.271	−0.063
	(−2.21)	(−0.01)	(−0.84)	(1.59)	(1.94)	(−1.23)
Private irrigated land × 10³	0.051	0.249	0.275	−0.020	0.051	0.058
	(0.61)	(1.57)	(1.92)	(−0.18)	(2.56)	(2.44)
Private nonirrigated land × 10³	0.077	0.111	0.195	0.056	0.080	0.042
	(0.78)	(4.04)	(2.06)	(0.92)	(7.34)	(1.88)
Private perennial land × 10³	−0.031	0.015	−0.139	0.092	0.044	0.024
	(−0.063)	(0.016)	(−1.29)	(1.11)	(2.00)	(2.04)

(Continued on the following page)

Table 5.3 (Continued)

Determinant	Northern Uplands	Red River Delta	North Central Coast	South Central Coast	Mekong Delta	Full sample
Private water surface land $\times 10^3$	0.334	0.027	−0.043	n.a.	0.041	0.059
	(2.72)	(0.52)	(−0.31)		(5.45)	(3.86)
Cultivates swidden land	−0.149	0.266	0.242	0.122	0.171	0.064
	(−2.37)	(6.75)	(1.85)	(0.88)	(3.09)	(0.94)
Commune dummy variables	Yes	Yes	Yes	Yes	Yes	Yes
Constant	2.938	2.793	2.067	4.235	2.165	2.615
	(6.97)	(5.57)	(3.68)	(8.68)	(2.56)	(7.82)
R^2	0.631	0.461	0.435	0.548	0.438	0.490
Root mean square error	0.472	0.390	0.454	0.420	0.610	0.483
Number of observations	432	790	459	269	308	2,361

Sources: 1993 and 1998 VLSSs.

Note: n.a. = not applicable. The dependent variable is the change in log annual agricultural allocated land between 1993 and 1998. T-ratios in parentheses are based on standard errors corrected for heteroskedasticity and clustering. Unless otherwise noted, all variables are initial 1993 values.

effects between the initial land deficit and both the initial land allocation and the head of household's education, to allow the adjustment coefficient to vary within regions. The interaction effect with education was insignificant nationally and in most regions. However, we find a significant interaction effect between the initial land deficit relative to the efficient allocation and the initial land allocation. The speed of adjustment toward the efficient allocation was higher for those who started off with less land.

We find a number of other factors that influence land reallocation. There is a highly significant effect of an increase over the time period in the number of persons of working age and new people joining the household. (We also tried dropping the latter variable, given possible endogeneity concerns, but other results were affected little in the national model.) Households with male heads were also favored in the land reallocation process. Having higher amounts of other types of land resulted in significantly higher access to allocated land.

There are some regional differences in the model with controls. The significant negative interaction effect (such that there is a higher adjustment coefficient for households with less land) is found only in the Mekong Delta. Whether this is a market response is unclear; it could also reflect the efforts of local officials in the Mekong to avoid rising landlessness (chapter 2).

The impacts of demographic and labor force changes tend to be stronger in the northern provinces. This is also where local authorities were more likely to enforce periodic land reallocations. Being from an ethnic minority household helped increase annual landholdings in the North and (especially) in the South Central Coastal region. However, being from a minority household tended to reduce holdings in the Mekong Delta. (Note, however, that the ethnic groups are not the same in these two regions.) Ethnic effects also become significant and positive in the Northern Uplands and North Central Coast regions when we omit the number of new household members in 1998. Having a household member who works for a state-owned enterprise has a pronounced negative impact on annual land changes in the Northern Uplands and the South Central Coast, though it has no impact elsewhere. In both the Northern Uplands and the South Central Coast regions, a higher share of good-quality irrigated land reduced the land reallocation over time.[9] The tendency to favor male heads of household is strongest in the North.

We also tested for effects of the initial land deficit on the probability of becoming landless (in terms of allocated annual land). Table 5.4 gives the proportion of the 1998 sample that had no allocated land, classified by the estimated initial loss relative to the

Table 5.4 Disposal of Allocated Land

Quintiles of households ranked by the land deficit (efficient allocation − administrative allocation, 1993)	Percentage landless in 1998[a]
1 (gained land relative to the efficient allocation)	4.6
2	2.6
3	5.9
4	10.7
5 (lost land relative to the efficient allocation)	16.4
Overall mean	7.7

Sources: 1993 and 1998 VLSSs.
Note: Total number of sampled households is 2,559.
a. Percentage of households having no allocated annual agricultural land in 1998.

efficient allocation in 1993. The higher the land deficit relative to the efficient allocation, the higher was the probability of having disposed of all allocated land in 1998.

We also estimated probits for landlessness using the same regressors as in table 5.3.[10] We did this for both disposal of allocated annual land and disposal of all cultivated land. Virtually the only significant predictor in any of these regressions was the proportionate land deficit, which had a significant positive coefficient in most cases, and the geographic dummy variables. Becoming landless was more likely for households that had too little land relative to the efficient allocation, and it was more likely in the South than in the North.

These results suggest a "land polarization" process among those who started off with too little land relative to the efficient allocation. The bulk of these households "traded up," acquiring more land in the more market-oriented economy. However, a minority simply disposed of their allocated land. The results in table 5.4 suggest an interpretation in which a subset of those households that started out with too little land (relative to the efficient allocation) simply "cashed in," possibly to take up nonfarm activities or to pay off debts.

The difference in behavior of those households that disposed of their allocated land raises a concern about the possibility of sample selection bias in our main regressions for land reallocation.[11] In fact, there are two possible sources of such bias. The first stems from the fact that our preferred specification for the functional form required some observations to be dropped; the second is panel attrition, in that some households in the original sample could not be interviewed in the second survey for various reasons (they had left their original address or they chose not to participate again). Motivated by the approach to testing for panel attrition bias in Fitzgerald, Gottschalk, and Moffitt (1998), we tested for both sources of bias using initial land allocation as the auxiliary endogenous variable in a probit for whether a household dropped out of the sample (for either reason), with controls for all other observable exogenous characteristics in the baseline survey. (We used the same set of controls as in our model of land reallocation.) The initial land allocation variable was statistically insignificant (at the 10 percent level) nationally and for all regions, suggesting that there is little or no bias attributable to sample selection in our regressions for land reallocation.

Conclusions

We find signs that after legal reforms to introduce a market in land-use rights, land was reallocated in a way that helped redress the prior inefficiencies of the administrative assignment of land, as achieved at the time of decollectivization. Those households that started with an inefficiently low (high) amount of cropland under the administrative assignment tended to increase (decrease) their holdings over time. On average, about one-third of the initial proportionate gap between the actual allocation and the efficient allocation was eliminated within five years.

The adjustment process tended to favor the "land poor," in that households that started with the least cropland under the administrative assignment tended to see the largest increase in holdings during the transition (at a given land deficit or surplus relative to the efficient allocation). The process also favored households with long-term roots in the community, with male heads, with better education, and with more nonallocated land.

Local cadres undoubtedly played a continuing role in the process of land allocation, but our results do not suggest that this role was generally in opposition to market forces. We find that the other nonmarket factors influencing the adjustment process at local level tended to work in the same direction as the competitive forces. Thus, our results cast doubt on the view that strong noncompetitive forces in the local political economy worked against efficient land reallocation.

Next, we assess the implications of this adjustment process in land allocation for equity and (in particular) whether or not the rising land inequality in the wake of these reforms (as evidenced by rising landlessness) was a poverty-increasing force.

Notes

1. Marsh and MacAulay (2006) also note a number of conditions on rentals that apply to land sales as well. The family selling or renting out must be poor, be without sufficient labor, or have another occupation.

2. Deininger (2003) reviews the arguments and evidence on this claimed effect of land titling.

3. Do and Iyer (2007) address this problem by using administrative data on the issuance of LUCs, although this approach raises concerns about omitted geographic factors that influence productivity and are correlated with the geographic incidence of LUCs.

4. Deininger and Jin (2003) interpret the 1993 and 1998 VLSSs' "long-term-use (LTU) land" to be land that has an LUC. However, *LTU land* is simply the term used for land allocated by the commune after Resolution 10 under a particular type of contract common in the South, as described in chapter 3. The increase in the amount of LTU land between 1993 and 1998 reflects a change in the contractual basis of land whereby land identified in the 1993 VLSS as "allocated" land was converted to LTU land by 1998. There is no reason to assume that LTU land came with an LUC.

5. With an extra prereform survey round, one could correct for this problem by using an instrumental variables estimator, but that is not an option in our case, given that we have only two survey rounds.

6. Our usage reflects the fact that under this assumption and with $\eta = 0$, the relationship between L_i^R, L_i^A, and L_i^* is homogeneous of degree one.

7. All *t*-ratios are based on standard errors corrected for both heteroskedasticity and clustering.

8. We also tried defining the proportionate difference as the percentage change rather than the log difference, thus allowing us to keep these observations; the results were similar, though (again) the log difference specification gave a better fit.

9. We tested a dummy for being a social fund transfer recipient, one of the few ways to identify households that may be treated preferentially by local authorities. This was insignificant in the national model and in all regions except the North Central Coast, where it had a positive effect.

10. A *probit* is a nonlinear regression model where the observed dependent variable is binary (0, 1) but is generated by a latent continuous variable, which is itself a function of covariates, with a normally distributed error term. For a more detailed exposition, see, for example, Wooldridge (2002).

11. It might be conjectured that this explains why we get a better fit using the log difference specification; since the observations that households who disposed of their allocated land behaved very differently to differences in the initial inefficiency of their allocation, dropping these (because one cannot take the log of zero) improved the fit. However, we got a better fit with the log specification across the same (truncated) sample when compared to other values of η (tested at 0.1 interval over the [0, 1] interval).

6

Rising Landlessness: A Sign of Success or Failure?

The last chapter showed that in the wake of the legal reforms introducing a land market, the allocation of farmland responded such that those farmers with too little land (relative to the efficient allocation) tended to trade up by acquiring more land, while those with too much land traded down. However, we found in chapter 5 that this process was rather slow. We also saw that some of those with too little land abandoned farming entirely.

As discussed in chapter 2, there have been concerns in Vietnam about the rise in rural landlessness in the wake of these reforms. The arguments found in the literature and the policy debates suggest a number of reasons why there could be losers as well as gainers from reforms to introduce a market in land-use rights. There will undoubtedly be gains from specialization, whereby some farmers choose to cash in their holdings and take up more remunerative activities. More vulnerable farmers may be forced to sell their land following an unexpected shock and indebtedness. Others, better placed to specialize in farming, will aim to consolidate and augment their landholdings. Moreover, local cadres may use this reform as an opportunity to effectively force some farmers off their land, given that the existence of a land market creates opportunities for profit that were not available prior to the reform. A commonly identified instrument for encouraging poor farmers to quit their land is access to nonland inputs to production; some farmers may find that, side by side with this land-market reform, they lose their prior entitlements to these inputs (as discussed in chapter 2). Ironically, introducing the trappings of a free market in this setting might actually enhance the power of local authorities to obtain land for other, more profitable, purposes, and the poorest farmers may well be most vulnerable. There may also be general equilibrium effects on the labor market that generate welfare losses for those who were landless prior to the reform and for those who choose to become landless but do not anticipate the effects of many others doing so at the same time.

This chapter explores these hypotheses further, using both economic theory and empirical analysis of the four surveys spanning 1993–2004, as described in chapter 3.

Land Markets, Occupational Choice, and Welfare

The issues in this debate can be captured in a transparent way by using a relatively simple model of how the occupational choices of poor farm households are affected by a policy reform that removes restrictions on land markets. The model essentially pits the gains from expanded choice and specialization against the reform's "second-round" effects on other income sources, including through labor-market responses. The balance of these opposing effects determines the reform's impacts. In drawing out the implications of our model, we focus on three questions:

- Will landlessness rise among the poor as a result of this reform?
- Will the postreform landlessness rate be highest for the poorest?
- Who will gain and who will lose?

The Model

It can hardly be surprising that compulsory acquisitions of farmland by the state, such as for public works or nonfarm development projects, can increase poverty (depending on the terms of compensation). The more interesting issue is whether this can happen when a free market in land is introduced, allowing noncoercive, market-based land reallocation. We show here that one can interpret a number of the claims made in the debate reviewed in chapter 2 by using a model in which households with land are free to choose whether to stay farmers or become landless.[1] We show that one can expect to see rising landlessness among the poor once a market is introduced, but that this does not imply rising poverty. We provide an informal exposition in this section; annex 6A gives a formal treatment, including proofs of the claims made below.

Wealth can be held as land, human capital, or consumer durables (including housing).[2] We assume that there is no credit market prior to the reform, but liquidity-constrained borrowing is possible for those with land after the reform. The level of schooling is taken to be fixed postreform, and (given the credit constraint) schooling can be financed only by disposing of marketable assets.[3] Prior to the reform, land is equally allocated within the commune but cannot be traded or transferred. However, nonland assets vary across households. Postreform, the market value of assets rises to include the value of land. Once there is a market, land can be converted into housing subject to the wealth constraint.[4] Utility depends on consumption of a nondurable good—food—and on consumption of housing. Under the assumptions of our model, the optimal prereform levels of schooling and housing will be determined solely by initial wealth and will be strictly increasing in wealth. Thus, we can treat initial wealth as the relevant indicator of both schooling and prereform housing.

The household chooses between family farming and supplying labor to an outside activity (such as commercial farming or producing consumer durables). There is heterogeneity in ability at farming, and there is a positive return to wealth in farming. These assumptions can be interpreted in a number of ways: they can represent economic returns to schooling in farming;[5] costs of nonland inputs;[6] or some other contribution of wealth to output, such as through local tax transfers or (liquidity-constrained) access to credit to finance nonland inputs to farming, which we assume is only possible once land can be put up as collateral. We assume that the reform does not decrease farmers' marginal returns to nonland wealth. For the poorest, we also assume that the reform does not increase own food output from a given amount of land. Our assumption that the postreform return to wealth of the poorest is lower than the prereform return to wealth is motivated by the policy debate summarized in chapter 2. Suppose that, prior to the reform, the commune authorities in charge of land allocation provide certain benefits, such as help in acquiring complementary inputs to production or protection from idiosyncratic shocks. These benefits are curtailed once land markets are introduced, on the grounds that farmers can then be left to their own devices to obtain credit or to use land as a buffer against risk. Later we give an example of how this can happen.

The choice between supplying labor and working on one's own farm is constrained by the household's endowment of able-bodied labor and time (in short, its *labor constraint*). To simplify the analysis, we assume that the labor constraint entails that the household specialize in either farming or wage labor in a nonfarm activity.

The introduction of a land market can be expected to change labor-market outcomes. We assume competitive markets for labor of each skill or asset level. Labor demand is taken to be a stable, nonincreasing function of the wage rate and a nondecreasing function of schooling. An alternative model would allow for unemployment, with the available work rationed according to wealth as the key determinant of productivity (as in an efficiency-wage model). The following analysis allows either interpretation.

Implications for Landlessness and Poverty

Intuitively, the asset-rich will be able to acquire more land, giving larger output gains from their own farms. What about the asset-poor? In this model, there are two reasons we can expect to find rising landlessness among the asset-poor. The first is that the asset-poor will have a higher marginal utility of consumer durables (including housing), prompting them to sell their land and supply labor to other activities, driving down the unskilled wage rate. The second reason is that the asset-poor find that after the introduction of a land market, they are less well insured against shocks and have lower access to nonland inputs to farm production; these effects arise through the induced responses of local authorities to the introduction of land markets. Consistently with this intuition, we can state the following result, which is proved in annex 6A:

Proposition 6.1. On introducing a land market, the landlessness rate will rise for the asset-poor and fall for those who are sufficiently well off.

A rise in landlessness among the poor as a result of this reform, however, does not imply that the poor are more likely to be landless than the rich after the reform; instead, it may entail a flattening out of a positive wealth gradient in landlessness prereform. To assess to what extent class differentiation has emerged, we must study the *economic gradient* in landlessness—whether it is the poor who tend to be landless, while the nonpoor are not:

Proposition 6.2. The postreform wealth gradient in landlessness can go in either direction, depending on the structure of returns to wealth.

When the returns to schooling are low, farming will tend to be the more attractive option for the rich. On introducing a land market, a negative wealth gradient in landlessness will emerge, as demonstrated in annex 6A. By contrast, high labor-market returns to wealth naturally make the labor market more attractive to the rich and so foster a positive wealth gradient in landlessness.

Alternatively, we can characterize the different outcomes in terms of the wealth gradient in nonland inputs. Plainly, a sufficiently positive (negative) gradient in command over nonland inputs will tend to yield a negative (positive) gradient in the landlessness rate.

Turning finally to the incidence of the reform's welfare impacts, we cannot presume, even in this simple model, that this reform will help reduce poverty. Welfare gains stem from the economic gains from specialization, as those who have lower ability at farming or too little initial wealth take up more rewarding opportunities in the labor market. Welfare losses from introducing a land market arise from labor-market effects or diminished command over nonland inputs to production. This can be summarized in the following proposition, which is proved in annex 6A:

Proposition 6.3. There can be both gainers and losers from this reform, and the impact on aggregate poverty is ambiguous.

As discussed in chapter 2, welfare losses can occur because of unexpected general equilibrium outcomes in the presence of distortions in land markets. This can be the case when the decision to sell one's land is made *before* the new labor-market equilibrium is revealed, the outcomes of which are unanticipated, and when transaction costs make it very difficult to buy back one's land. The wage rate will fall because of the reform, and some farmers will end up worse off in the new equilibrium.

Incidence and Sources of Rising Landlessness

As shown in chapter 2, there have been two very different interpretations of rising landlessness in the wake of Vietnam's land-market reforms. The first says that starting from a relatively equitable allocation of land, a rural class structure emerged as rich farmers bought land from poor farmers, who then became the poor landless laborers found at the bottom of the new class structure. By this view, the main dynamic in the transition process that has led to rising landlessness is a structural shift in the relationship between landlessness and living standards, whereby, in the wake of the reforms, the probability of being landless rises among the poor.

The second interpretation assumes that rising living standards in a developing economy inevitably entail a partial shift out of farming. With sufficiently high returns to schooling, it is more likely to be the nonpoor who tend to be landless. By this view, there need not be any change over time in the relationship between the probability of being landless and one's standard of living. Rather, both rising landlessness and falling poverty happen in tandem, as some farmers choose to sell their land to take up new opportunities. Instead of a structural shift in the relationship between landlessness and poverty, rising landlessness and falling poverty jointly reflect a process of economic transition made possible by the introduction of land markets.

We now try to see which of these interpretations is more consistent with the data. First, we focus on the changing incidence of landlessness and labor-market participation across levels of living. Then we turn to the relationship between landlessness and poverty.

Incidence of Rising Landlessness and Land Transactions

While our theoretical model focuses on how the key variables of interest vary with initial wealth, we do not have data on wealth. Instead, we follow previous chapters in using consumption expenditure as the welfare indicator. This is the same consumption measure used in measuring poverty and inequality in chapter 3. We have no choice but to use current consumption, which will reflect impacts of the land reforms after 1993. (Ideally, we would have preintervention consumption, but this would require panel data.) We comment on likely biases arising from this feature of the data. Later in this chapter, we also examine the relationship using pseudo-panel data, formed from birth cohorts, to see if it confirms our findings.

Figure 6.1 gives the relationship between the mean landlessness rate and log consumption per person (in 1998 prices) for 1993 and 2004. (These are again nonparametric regressions, using locally smoothed scatter plots.) Rural landlessness in 2004 tends to have a positive consumption gradient; the poorest tend to be the least likely

Figure 6.1 Landlessness and Consumption per Person in Rural Vietnam, 1993 and 2004

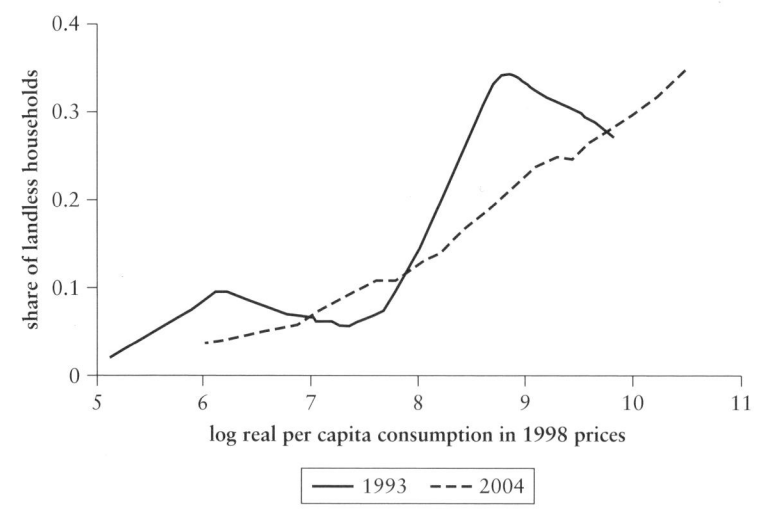

Sources: 1993 VLSS and 2004 VHLSS.

to be landless. In terms of our preceding theoretical analysis, this pattern is consistent with sufficiently high labor-market returns to schooling or other assets.[7] Note also that the landlessness rate for 2004 is nearly linear in log consumption, implying that it is concave in the level of consumption; thus, higher (lower) consumption inequality at a given mean will tend to lower (raise) the aggregate landlessness rate.

How will the fact that we are using 2004 consumption (which reflects gains from the reform as well as other changes since 1993) affect the estimated relationship with landlessness in 2004? That will depend on how the consumption gains since 1993 vary with landlessness. If the (proportionate) gains tend to be higher (lower) for those who become landless, and if landlessness rises with consumption, then we will overestimate (underestimate) the true economic gradient in landlessness. The fact that the proportionate gain in consumption over 1993–2004 was slightly lower for those with land suggests that we will be underestimating the economic gradient in landlessness measured against prereform consumption.

Over the period 1993–2004, there was a reduction in landlessness among the poorest (figure 6.1), though less than 3 percent of households in 2004 had consumption per person below the lower intersection point in the regression functions for 2004 and 1993. Note also that although we see only a relatively small interval of consumption for which there is rising landlessness, it is clear from figure 3.1 that a large share of the data is in this interval. In 1993, about 69 percent of the population lived in households with consumption per person in the interval for which landlessness rose; in 2004, the proportion fell to 42 percent. Thus, a large share of the population had consumption in the interval for which there was a rise in the mean landlessness rate conditional on consumption.

Note that there are landless households that still cultivate land by renting it in and there are households that are not landless by our definition but that do not cultivate—by renting out land. Figure 6.2 shows how the share of noncultivating households varies with log consumption for 1993 (panel a) and log consumption for 2004 (panel b). We find a marked change in rental behavior as a function of living standards. In 1993, the poorest rented in land on average, so the noncultivating rate was lower than the landlessness rate; at higher consumption levels, the two were roughly equal. This had changed by 2004, with the nonpoor renting out land, so the economic gradient of the share of noncultivating households was even steeper than that of landlessness (figure 6.2, panel b).

The ethnic minorities do not accord well with the predictions of our theoretical model. Landlessness is found to have fallen for poor

Figure 6.2 Noncultivating Households Compared with Landless Households, 1993 and 2004

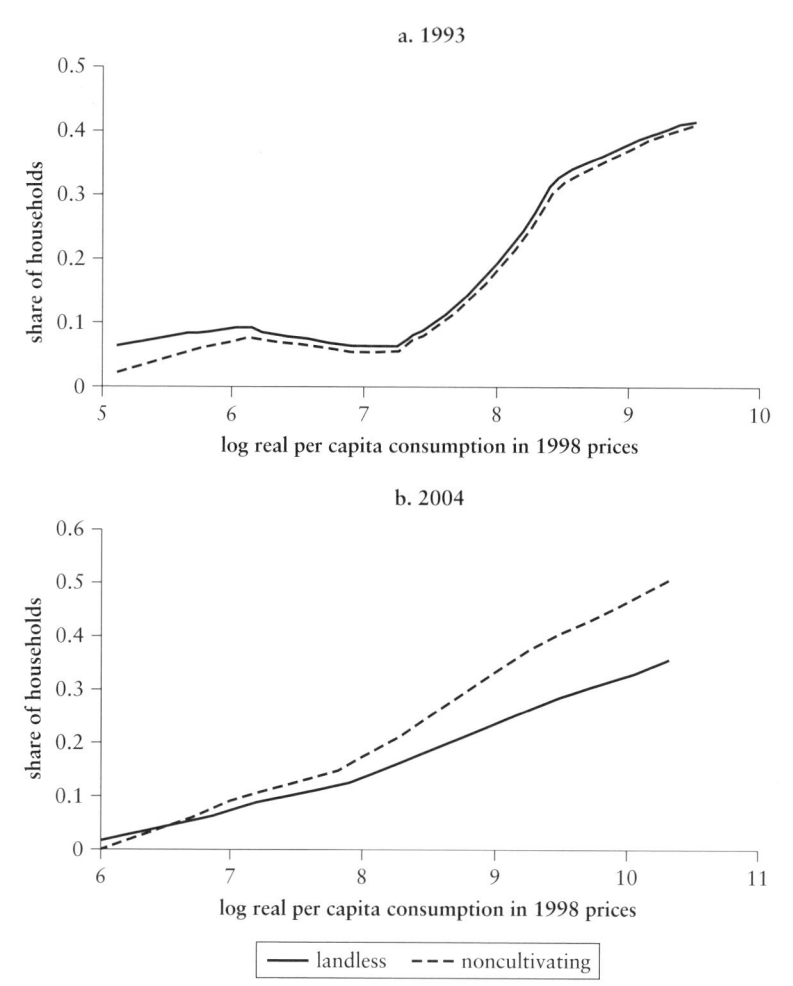

a. 1993

b. 2004

—— landless --- noncultivating

Sources: 1993 VLSS and 2004 VHLSS.

rural minority households and to have risen for higher-consumption groups (figure 6.3). The choices of the minorities may well be constrained by discriminatory features of labor markets that are not incorporated in our model; arguably land markets also work differently, given that the minorities tend to be concentrated in mountainous areas.[8] Among minorities, the overall correlation between landlessness and (log) consumption per person switches sign over the period, from being negative but not significant ($r = -0.04$) in 1993 to positive and significant ($r = 0.09$) in 2004. Thus, the

Figure 6.3 Landlessness and Consumption per Person for Ethnic Minorities, 1993 and 2004

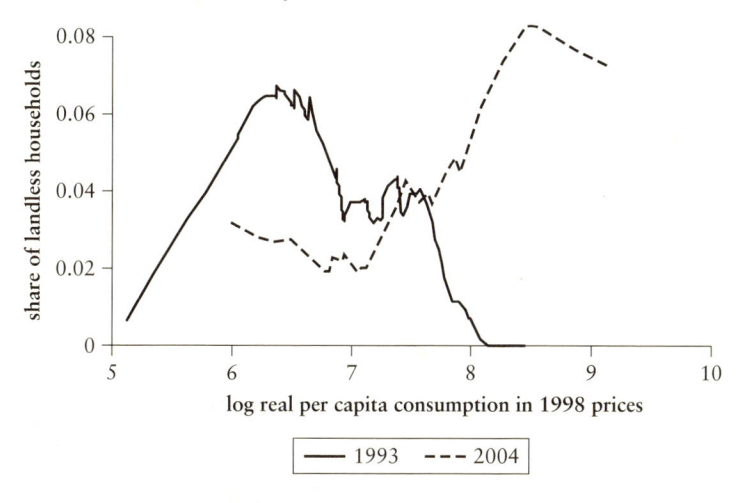

Sources: 1993 VLSS and 2004 VHLSS.

relationship for the minorities appears to have become more like that for the majority.

We find rising landlessness among the poor in the fertile northern and southern deltas (figure 6.4). Recall that the landlessness rate is much higher in the Mekong Delta—23 percent versus 6 percent in the Red River Delta in 2004 (table 3.2). The contrast is striking. In the Red River Delta, landlessness rises with consumption, while it is roughly the reverse in the Mekong Delta.[9] The pattern for the Red River Delta is consistent with a situation in which returns to schooling are relatively high, while the pattern for the Mekong Delta is more consistent with the opposite situation, in which returns to schooling are relatively low; these differences in the labor-market returns to schooling accord with the evidence cited in chapter 2. The historical differences noted in chapter 2 also make it more likely that access to nonland inputs was more wealth dependent in the Mekong Delta, creating pressure toward a negative wealth gradient in landlessness. Over time, we find rising landlessness among the poor in both regions, as predicted by our theoretical model. In the Mekong Delta, we also find a marked rise in landlessness among the highest-consumption households, as well as among the bulk of the poor. If we compare panels a and b of figure 6.4, it is evident that the big difference is in the incidence of landlessness among the poor. Among the poorest (log consumption around 7), the landlessness rate is about 5 percent in the Red River Delta versus 40 percent in the Mekong Delta.

Figure 6.4 Landlessness and Consumption in Rural Areas of the Two Deltas, 1993 and 2004

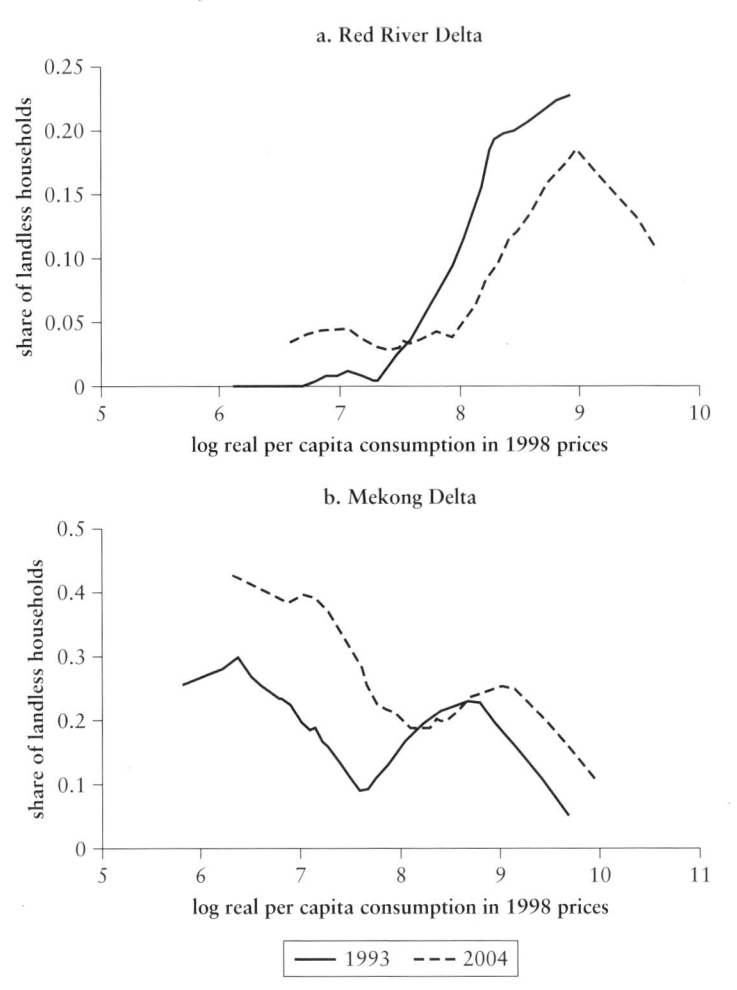

a. Red River Delta

b. Mekong Delta

—— 1993   - - - 2004

Sources: 1993 VLSS and 2004 VHLSS.

Before exploring the sources of rising landlessness more closely, we note that there were also changes in the relationship between the size of landholding and levels of living among those with land. Figure 6.5 plots (log) landholding (all types) against (log) consumption. We see that landholding conditional on consumption became more equal; the sharp positive gradient found in 1993 had largely vanished by 2004. Simultaneously with rising landlessness, the distribution of landholdings became more equal across levels of living.[10]

Figure 6.5 Land and Living Standards for Those with Land, 1993 and 2004

[Graph: x-axis "log real per capita consumption in 1998 prices" from 5 to 11; y-axis "log total land per capita" from 5.0 to 7.5; solid line 1993, dashed line 2004]

Sources: 1993 VLSS and 2004 VHLSS.

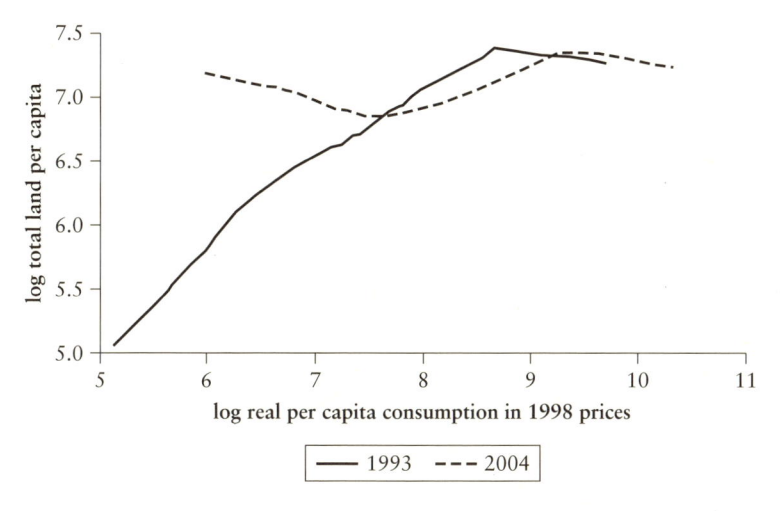

Figure 6.5 is not consistent with our model's prediction that postreform landholding should have a positive wealth gradient. However, our model ignored heterogeneity in land quality. On a closer inspection, we find that the poor have not seen gains in their land *quality*. This is evident from figure 6.6, which gives the share of annual cropland that is irrigated. There are marked gains over time at all levels *except* among the poorest. The same pattern was found when we looked at the distribution of the share of annual cropland that the commune authorities rated as high quality (see figure 6.7). A plausible explanation for these differences is the initial inequality in nonland wealth, given credit-market failures. Those with wealth were naturally in a better position to invest in their land.[11]

As we have noted, the 2004 survey allows us to study what land transactions households engaged in and how use rights to different land plots were acquired.[12] Figure 6.8 shows how the incidence of land transactions occurring during the 10 years prior to the survey varies with consumption. The totals include all means of acquiring or disposing of land that are allowed under the land laws (purchase, sale, inheritance, bequest, exchange). We also separately identify purchase and sale. We see that the upper consumption groups were more likely to take up the new opportunities for land-market transactions. These patterns are corroborated by the evidence from the Survey of Impacts of Rural Roads in Vietnam (SIRRV) panel, which allows us to track changes over time in whether households bought or sold

Figure 6.6 Share of Annual Cropland That Is Irrigated, 1998 and 2004

Sources: 1998 VLSS and 2004 VHLSS.

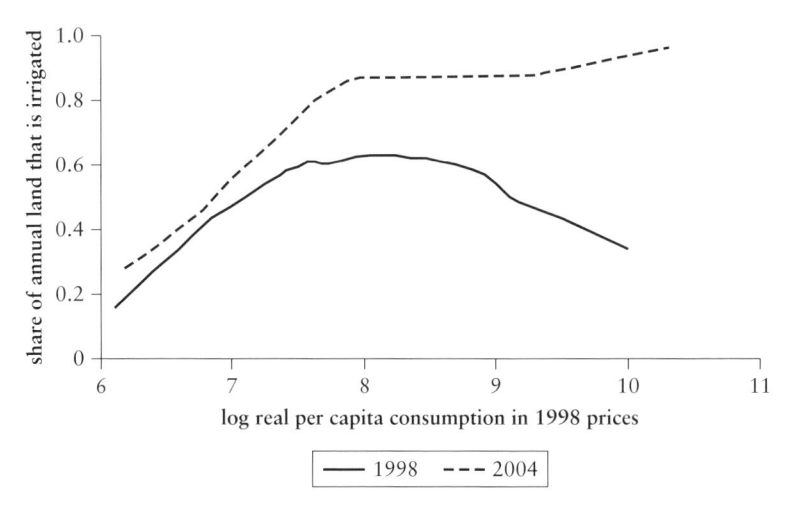

Figure 6.7 Land-Quality Gradients as Assessed by Commune Authorities, 1998 and 2004

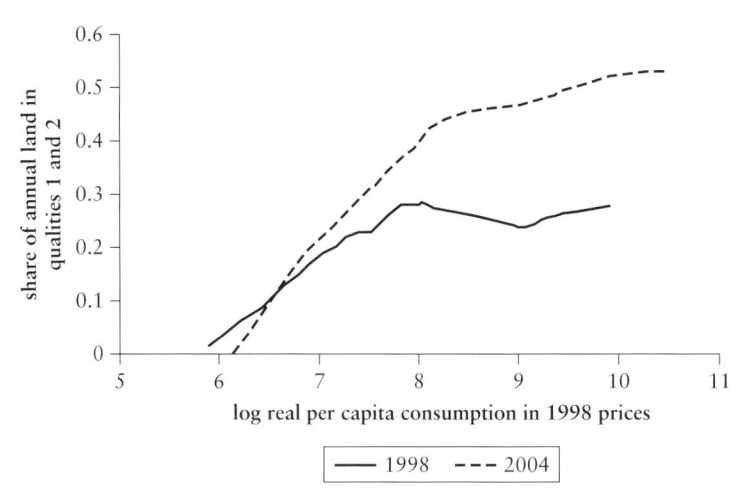

Sources: 1998 VLSS and 2004 VHLSS.
Note: Quality levels 1 and 2 are the highest land-quality levels.

Figure 6.8 Incidence of Market-Based Land Transactions, 1994–2004

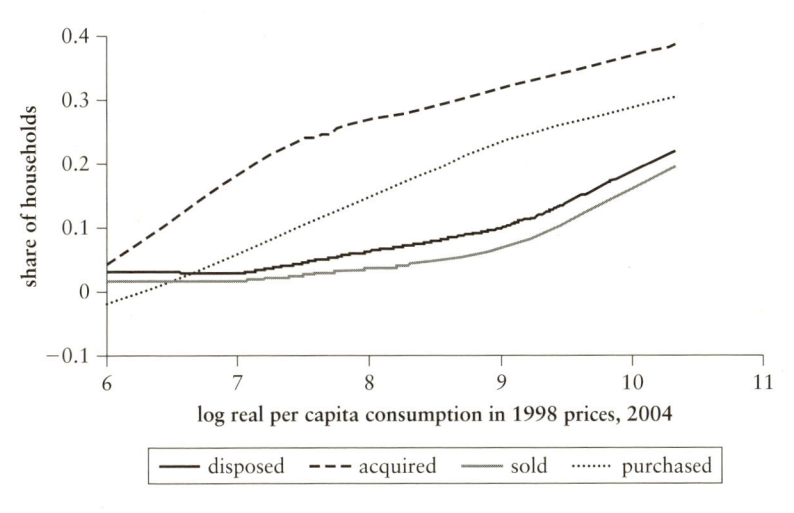

Source: 2004 VHLSS.

Note: Market-based transactions only: *disposed* consists of land sold, bequeathed, exchanged, or rent expired (excludes land taken back by government and other); *acquired* includes land inherited, bid for, purchased, or exchanged (excludes land reclaimed or commune allocated).

land (see chapter 3, "Data from the Survey of Impacts of Rural Roads in Vietnam," for a description of the SIRRV). Figure 6.9 shows how the incidence of rural households selling land in 1997 and 2003 varies by predicted 1997 consumption (as described in chapter 3, same section as above). Figure 6.10 does the same for whether or not households bought land. In 1997, few if any households in this sample sold land. By 2004, there was little change for the poorest households, while an increase is apparent for better-off households. The incidence of land buying does not show much change over time. At both dates, it has a positive consumption gradient. However, even for the richest, the share of households buying land is low, at less than 1 percent. These data are clearly not consistent with the view that the poor were selling their land to the rich *and* remaining poor. (It is likely that some of the transactions observed at middle consumption levels are for those who were previously poor.) This is further supported by figure 6.11, which shows how each household's landholdings in 2004 were initially acquired based on the 2004 Vietnam Household Living Standards Survey (VHLSS). We see that the poorest in 2004 had relied heavily on reclaiming land and hardly at all on market transactions for obtaining land; the purchase of land was more likely for the rich.

Figure 6.9 Incidence of Land Selling, 1997 and 2003

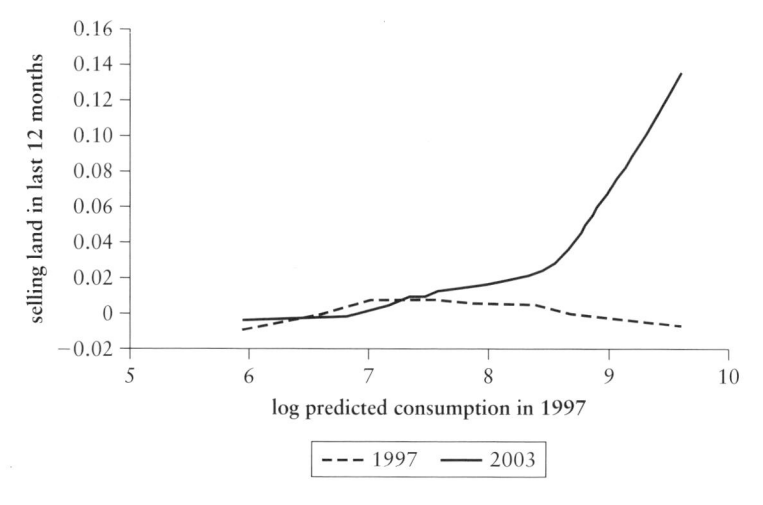

Sources: 1997 and 2003 SIRRVs.

Figure 6.10 Incidence of Land Buying

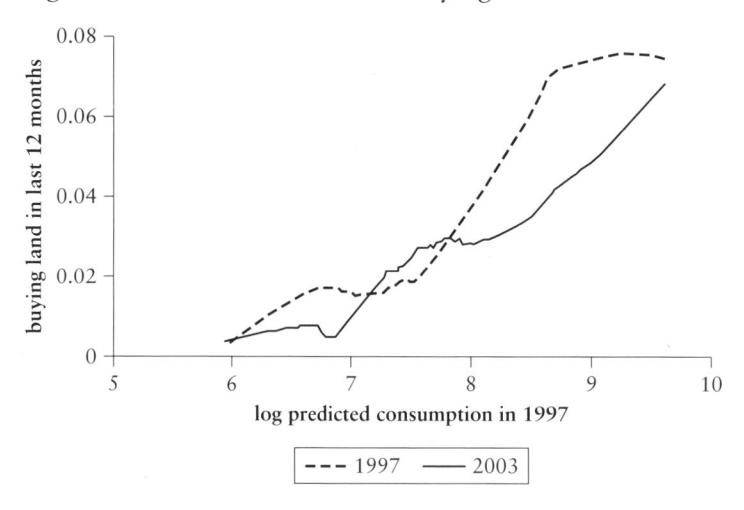

Sources: 1997 and 2003 SIRRVs.

Land titling, in the form of land-use certificates (LUCs), was another element of the 1993 Land Law. Figure 6.12 gives the proportion of land with an LUC according to the 2004 VHLSS, and figure 6.13 gives the share of households declaring that they have an LUC for their land according to the SIRRV panel data.[13] We see in figure 6.12 that LUCs are less common among the poor, though this

Figure 6.11 Sources of Land in Rural Vietnam, 2004

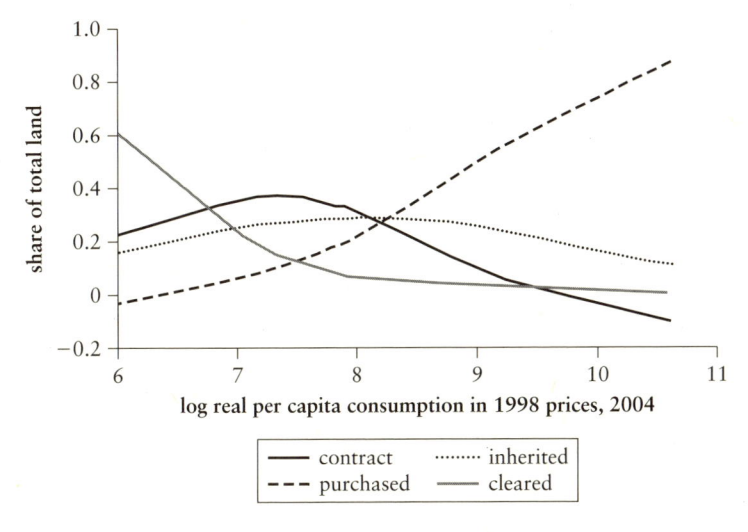

Source: 2004 VHLSS.
Note: Left out are the shares of land acquired through rental or auction, barter, borrowing, or other; these total 11 percent of currently cultivated land. *Contract land* refers to land obtained from local authorities through the allocation process as well as contracted from state farms and forest enterprises.

Figure 6.12 Incidence of Land Titles Based on the Vietnam Household Living Standards Survey, 2004

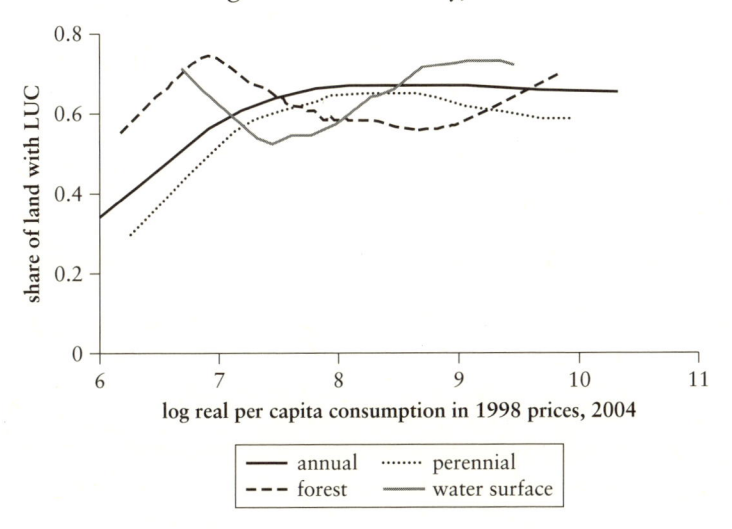

Source: 2004 VHLSS.

Figure 6.13 Incidence of Land Titles Based on the Survey of Impacts of Rural Roads in Vietnam, 1997 and 2003

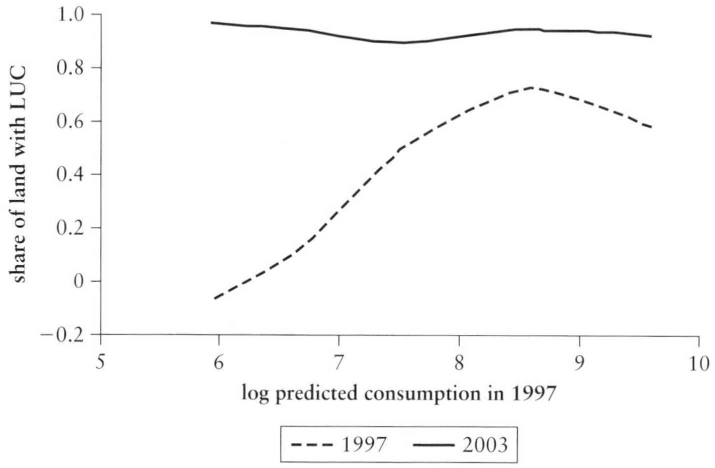

Sources: 1997 and 2003 SIRRVs.

varies somewhat according to the type of land. Figure 6.13 shows also that the poor were less likely to have an LUC in 1997, but by 2004, practically all households had LUCs in these data. Overall, we see again that it is the relatively well-off within rural society who appear to be benefiting most—or, at least, most rapidly—from the new land market.

The Changing Incidence of Wage Labor

The introduction of land markets is expected to bring changes in two other markets, namely, for wage labor and credit. Chapter 7 examines credit.

We find a striking change in the economic gradient of wage labor (figure 6.14). In 1993, there was no (monotonic) relationship between the number of adults (17 years of age and older) working for a wage and household consumption; the poor were just as likely to do wage work as the rich. This had changed by 2004, with a strong positive relationship emerging; the poorest were less likely to be working for wages in 2004 but were working more often in farming than in 1993. However, only 1.2 percent of households in 2004 have consumption less than the intersection point in figure 6.14; for the bulk of the 2004 population, there is a marked increase in wage-labor supply at given consumption.

Figure 6.14 Wage Earners by Household Consumption per Person, 1993 and 2004

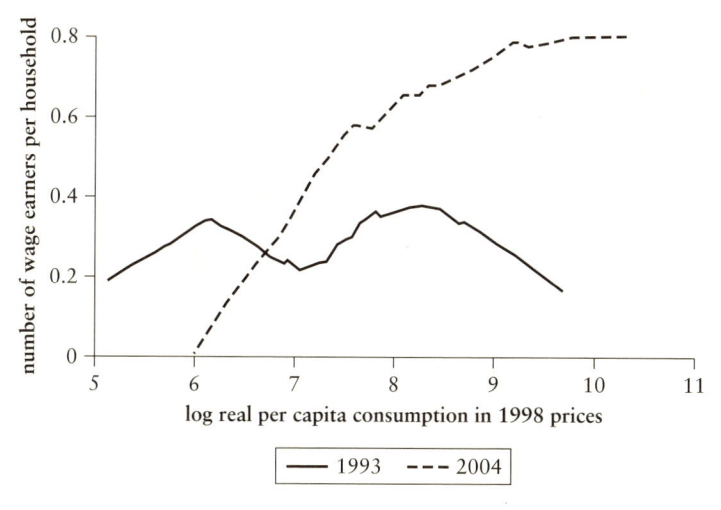

[Figure: line chart with y-axis "number of wage earners per household" from 0 to 0.8, and x-axis "log real per capita consumption in 1998 prices" from 5 to 11; two curves for 1993 (solid) and 2004 (dashed).]

Sources: 1993 VLSS and 2004 VHLSS.

There is a notable difference between the Red River Delta and the Mekong Delta in the incidence of wage workers, as is evident in figure 6.15.[14] In the Red River Delta, wage work has a positive economic gradient similar to that for the country as a whole in 2004 (but not in 1993). However, the direction of the relationship reverses in the Mekong Delta, with wage work more common among the poor. In the Mekong Delta, the rise in landlessness entailed a shift into wage labor.

Decomposition of the Change in Landlessness

The proportion of households that are landless could rise in either of two distinct ways. First, the landlessness rate rises at each level of wealth; both the rich and the poor switch out of farming. Second, the distribution of wealth changes, such that there are more people in the wealth strata with high landlessness rates; naturally this will increase the overall landlessness rate even if there is no change in the relationship between landlessness and wealth. Given that we find a positive economic gradient in landlessness (the landlessness rate tends to rise as consumption rises), we may expect to find a rise in the overall landlessness rate purely because there was a fall in overall poverty rates. It is thus of interest to know the relative strength of these two factors, given their rather different interpretations (as discussed at the outset of this section).

Figure 6.15 Wage Earners by Household Consumption per Person in the Two Deltas, 1993 and 2004

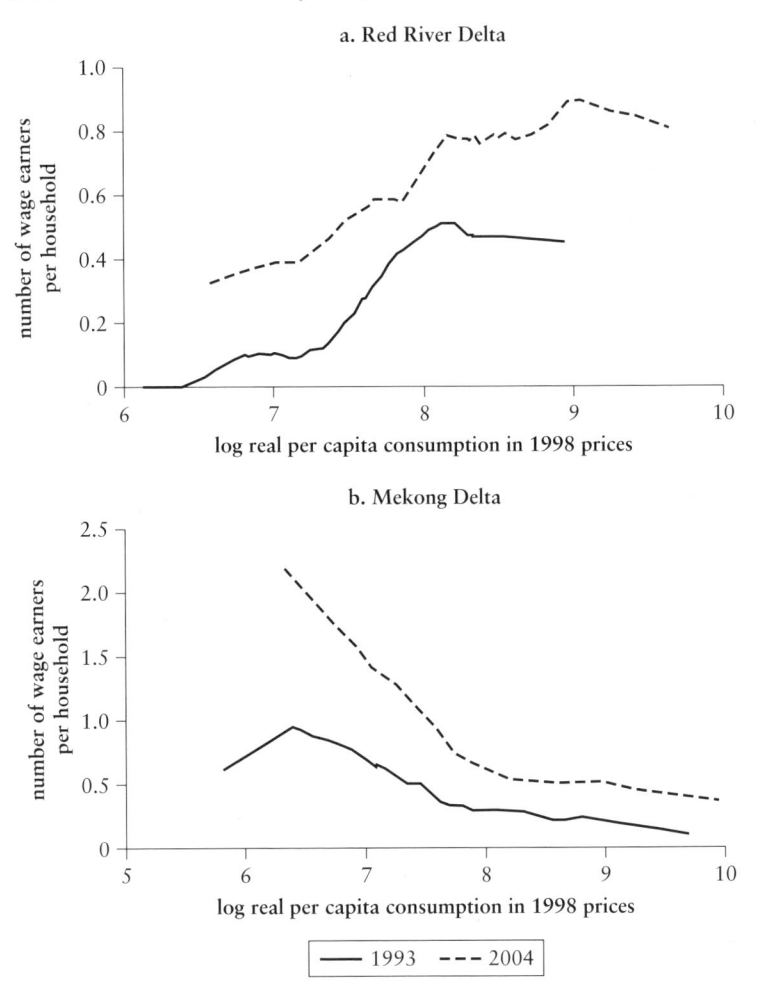

a. Red River Delta

b. Mekong Delta

— 1993 --- 2004

Sources: 1993 VLSS and 2004 VHLSS.

In more formal terms, the aggregate landlessness rate can be obtained by integrating the conditional landlessness rate (conditional on consumption) across the distribution of consumption. The overall rise in landlessness in rural areas thus reflects both a shift in the relationship between landholding and consumption—the economic gradient in landlessness—and a shift in the distribution of consumption. This can be seen if we divide the population into m

consumption groups and decompose the change in the proportion of the landless between 1993 and 2004 as follows:

$$(6.1) \quad LL_{04} - LL_{93} = \sum_{i=1}^{m}(LL_{04i} - LL_{93i})n_{93i} + \sum_{i=1}^{m} LL_{04i}(n_{04i} - n_{93i}).$$

Here LL_{ti} is the landlessness rate for consumption group $i = 1, \ldots, m$ at date t, while n_{ti} is the proportion of households in group i at date t. The first term on the right-hand side gives the contribution of the change in the relationship between landlessness and consumption, the *land reallocation component*, while the second term gives the contribution of changes in the distribution of consumption, the *consumption redistribution component*.

Table 6.1 gives the decompositions, based on fractiles of 1993 consumption per person.[15] We find that the change in the relationship between landlessness and consumption increased the overall landlessness rate by 2.3 percentage points, while the change in the distribution of consumption increased the landlessness rate by 2.9 percentage points, giving a total change of 5.1 percentage points (allowing for rounding off errors). Slightly more than half of the increase in landlessness is directly associated with falling poverty, as rural households that moved out of poverty also moved out of farming.

By contrast, in much of the South (Mekong Delta and Southeast), the rise in landlessness was caused by a land reallocation effect associated with the changing relationship between landlessness and living standards (table 6.1). This suggests that class differentiation is emerging in the South. However, it is nonetheless accompanying falling poverty. Indeed, figure 6.4, panel b, suggests that the shift in the relationship between landlessness and living standards in the

Table 6.1 Decomposition of the Change in Aggregate Landlessness, 1993–2004

			Decomposition		
	Landlessness rate (%)		Land reallocation (%)	Consumption redistribution (%)	Total change
Region	L_{93}	L_{04}	$\Sigma(L_{04i} - L_{93i})n_{93i}$	$\Sigma L_{04i}(n_{04i} - n_{93i})$	$L_{04} - L_{93}$
Rural Vietnam	8.42	13.55	2.27	2.85	5.13
Northern Uplands	2.15	3.48	−1.00	2.33	1.33
Red River Delta	2.54	6.73	1.19	3.01	4.20
North Central Coast	3.96	8.25	1.65	2.63	4.28
South Central Coast	12.24	14.76	−1.06	3.57	2.51
Central Highlands	9.38	3.84	−6.89	1.32	−5.54
Southeast	23.13	39.10	15.34	0.64	15.99
Mekong Delta	16.02	25.43	15.24	−5.84	9.40

Sources: 1993 VLSS and 2004 VHLSS.

Mekong Delta combined two factors: a vertical rise in landlessness at all levels of consumption and a horizontal shift, with rising consumption. (The Southeast showed a similar pattern.) The land reallocation effect in these southern regions can be interpreted as the combined effect of higher landlessness and rising living standards.

Rising Landlessness and Urbanization: Evidence from the Pseudo-Panel

In examining the changes in the incidence of landlessness, we have compared the static relationship with consumption at different points in time. We have seen that there has been a rising landlessness rate among households with the same relatively low level of consumption at each date. That is not the same as saying that there is rising landlessness among those who had a low level of consumption in the prereform situation, given that there is bound to be a certain amount of churning, whereby households swap places in the distribution. To address that question, we would ideally have a panel dataset that followed the same people over time, including after they moved from rural to urban areas when they became landless. This is rare even among (still relatively uncommon) panel datasets.

However, there is a way of examining this issue with repeated cross-sectional surveys. We can construct a synthetic panel spanning the cross-sectional surveys using birth cohorts based on the age of the household head. We can then see how the landlessness rate of a given age cohort evolves over time and how this might be related to other variables of interest. By using the national (urban plus rural) sample, we can ensure valid inferences from such a pseudo-panel, in that each cross-section gives a sample that is representative of the same population subgroup at each of two dates. In contrast, if we did the analysis for the rural sample only, then a bias could arise from selective migration to urban areas. Notice that in using pseudo-panel data in this way, we are not only making up for the lack of a true panel spanning the period; we are also addressing a data inadequacy of most such "true panels," given that movers are rarely traced after they move.

We can also use pseudo-panel data to study the incidence of urbanization. As chapter 2 noted, the implications for the pace of urbanization of reforms that encourage some farmers to leave their land have never been far from the concerns raised by both sides of the debates on Vietnam's agrarian transition.

We use the 1993 and 2004 surveys for this purpose. As described in chapter 3 (in the section "A Pseudo-Panel Based on Age Cohorts

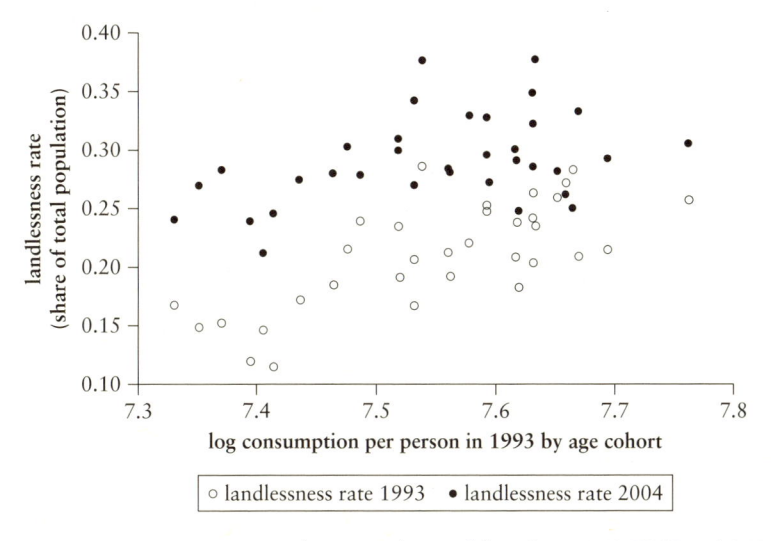

Figure 6.16 Landlessness Rates by National Age Cohorts, 1993 and 2004

[Scatter plot: x-axis "log consumption per person in 1993 by age cohort" from 7.3 to 7.8; y-axis "landlessness rate (share of total population)" from 0.10 to 0.40. Legend: ○ landlessness rate 1993, ● landlessness rate 2004.]

Sources: 1993–2004 age cohort pseudo-panel based on 1993 VLSS and 2004 VHLSS.

for 1993–2004"), we construct the means of all relevant variables based on the age of the household head in 1993 and do similarly for the corresponding groups in 2004. This gives us 34 age cohorts with minimum sample sizes of 100. (Annex 3B gives the means by age cohorts of the main variables we use here.)

In figure 6.16, we give the landlessness rates by age cohort for 2004 and 1993 plotted against the log of mean consumption per person in 1993. We again see patterns broadly consistent with our earlier results. Landlessness rates have risen more among the poor, but they still tend to be higher for the nonpoor. The correlation coefficient between the change in landlessness and 1993 log consumption is −0.38, which is significant at the 2 percent level ($t = -2.36$). Figure 6.16 shows the relationship found in the age-cohort data.

Since we need to focus on national cohorts, the national landlessness rate (as distinct from the landlessness rate in rural areas, as studied up to this point) is bound to be positively correlated with the changes in the urban population share.[16] When we compare the changes in the urban population share with the changes in the national landlessness rate across age cohorts, we find a correlation coefficient of 0.56, which is significant at the 1 percent level.

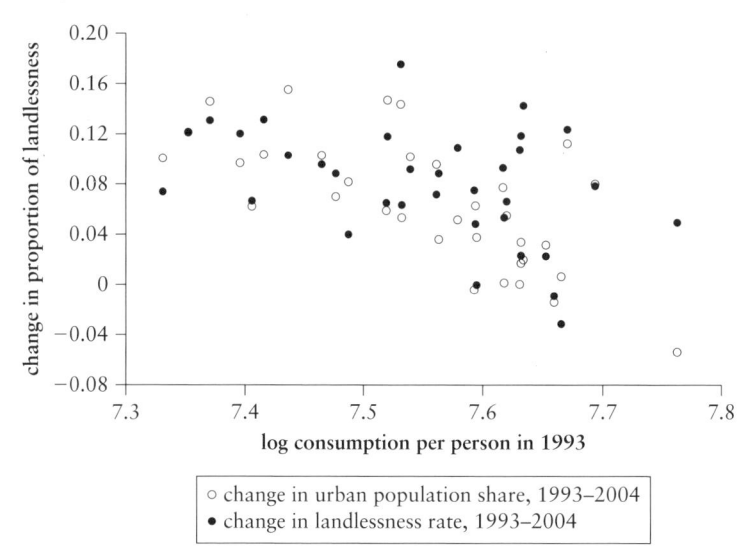

Figure 6.17 Changes in Landlessness Rate and Urbanization Rate, 1993–2004

[Scatter plot with x-axis "log consumption per person in 1993" ranging from 7.3 to 7.8, and y-axis "change in proportion of landlessness" ranging from −0.08 to 0.20. Legend: ○ change in urban population share, 1993–2004; • change in landlessness rate, 1993–2004.]

Sources: A 1993–2004 age cohort pseudo-panel based on 1993 VLSS and 2004 VHLSS.

It is not surprising, then, that we also find that poorer households in 1993 tend to have higher subsequent rates of urbanization, as is evident in figure 6.17. The correlation coefficient between the change in urban population share and 1993 log consumption per person is -0.68, which is significant at better than the 1 percent level ($t = -5.21$). This also holds when we add controls for ethnicity, schooling, and age of the head of household (table 6.2).[17]

So we find that both the rise in landlessness and the increase in the urban population share came in large part from those who were initially poor. Controlling for initial consumption, larger increases in landlessness and urbanization are found for ethnic minorities, those with higher schooling, and households with older heads.

But do we find any evidence consistent with the claim made by some observers that the poor became poorer in this process? We turn to that question next.

Poverty-Increasing Landlessness?

The hypothesis of a poverty-increasing landlessness effect (PILE) postulates that the forces generating rising landlessness are largely exogenous at the individual level and that the outcome is more poverty than one would have seen otherwise. There are a number of

Table 6.2 Pseudo-Panel Data Regressions for the Changes in Landlessness and Urbanization as Functions of 1993 Characteristics

Indicator	Change in landlessness rate (2004–1993)	Change in urbanization rate (2004–1993)
Constant	2.013	3.065
	(3.466)	(4.524)
Log consumption per person 1993	−0.234	−0.404
	(−2.712)	(−3.869)
Ethnicity 1993 (% in majority)	−0.567	−0.443
	(−2.802)	(−2.225)
Schooling of head of household 1993 (years)	0.021	0.033
	(1.667)	(2.291)
Age of head of household 1993 (years/100)	0.423	0.509
	(2.614)	(2.486)
R^2	0.414	0.577

Sources: 1993 VLSS and 2004 VHLSS.

Note: Thirty-four age cohorts; *t*-ratios based on heteroskedasticity-corrected standard errors in parentheses.

observations that lead us to question this hypothesis as a generalization of Vietnam's experience over this period. This section presents both analytic arguments and econometric tests on various datasets formed from the available surveys, at progressively higher levels of disaggregation as the section proceeds. The common element in all our tests is that we start with assumptions consistent with PILE and show that these imply things that we do not find in our data. Using various forms of this method of "proof by contradiction," we argue that the PILE hypothesis is hard to reconcile with the data for Vietnam as a whole, although it may contain an element of truth in some regions, notably the Mekong Delta.

Consider first a stylized version of PILE according to which initially nonpoor farmers become poor after abandoning their land. This would clearly put upward pressure on the poverty rate among both those without land and those with land. For rural Vietnam, the impact on the poverty rate among the landless will exceed that for the group with land. This is readily verified if we note that moving one nonpoor household out of the group of farmers will increase the poverty rate by $dH^{L>0} = H^{L>0}/N^{L>0}$ (where $H^{L>0}$ and $N^{L>0}$ denote the head-count index for those with land and their number, respectively), while adding one poor household to the group of landless will increase the poverty rate in that group by $dH^{L=0} = (1 − H^{L=0})/N^{L=0}$ (in obvious notation). We find that $(1 − H^{L=0})/H^{L=0} > N^{L=0}/N^{L>0}$ in all years, using the estimates from rural

Vietnam from table 3.3, implying that $dH^{L=0}/H^{L=0} > dH^{L>0}/H^{L>0}$. The proportionate increase in the poverty rate will be higher for the landless. On top of this effect of rising landlessness, we can allow for an independent trend attributable to other factors. For lack of a more plausible assumption, we assume that the proportionate rate of poverty reduction attributable to other factors is the same between the two groups. Under PILE, we would then expect that poverty will fall less rapidly among the landless, given that rising landlessness will put a brake on their rate of poverty reduction. That implication is not borne out by the data for Vietnam as a whole; indeed, the trend rate of poverty reduction between 1993 and 2004 is slightly higher for the landless (table 3.3). However, the preceding test cannot reject PILE for the Mekong Delta, where the rate of decline in poverty is lower for the landless.

Other aspects of the data cast further doubt on PILE, at least for Vietnam as a whole. We have seen that living standards tend to be higher for the landless. Suppose for the moment that a change in the share of the rural population that is landless comes about without any change in the distributions of consumption *within* each of the two groups. In other words, a representative household among farmers is transformed into a representative household among the landless. Rising landlessness must then cause a fall in the poverty rate. To see why, note that $H = H^{L>0} + (H^{L=0} - H^{L>0})LL$, where (as before) LL is the proportion of households that are landless. Then, under the within-group neutrality assumption, $\partial H/\partial LL = H^{L=0} - H^{L>0}$. This is negative for rural Vietnam in all years (table 3.1), but (again) the Mekong Delta is an exception; rising landlessness holding within-group distribution constant will be poverty increasing in the Mekong Delta.

The within-group neutrality assumption is questionable in the above test. We can use table 3.2 to construct a simple difference-in-difference (DD) test that does not require that assumption. The test entails regressing the log head-count index for each of the two groups (those with land and those without) for region i at date t on the landlessness rate, allowing for regional and time effects. For those with land:

(6.2) $$\ln H_{it}^{L>0} = \alpha + \beta LL_{it} + \pi_i + \delta_t + \varepsilon_{it}$$
$$(i = 1, \ldots, N; t = 1, \ldots, T),$$

where π_i is a regional effect, δ_t is a time effect (as could be attributable to macroeconomic or national agro-climatic conditions), and ε_{it} is a white noise error term. We estimate a similar regression for the landless, with dependent variable $\ln H_{it}^{L=0}$.[18] The specification in equation (6.2) allows landlessness to be endogenous, but only as long as this arises solely through the fixed effects—that is,

$Cov(LL_{it}, \pi_i) = Cov(LL_{it}, \delta_t) \neq 0$ but $Cov(LL_{it}, \varepsilon_{it}) = 0$. Then ordinary least squares estimates of the impact parameter β tell us the average causal impact of higher landlessness; if the PILE hypothesis were correct, then we would find that $\beta > 0$.[19]

It can be argued that the assumption that the changes in landlessness can be treated as exogenous ($Cov(LL_{it}, \varepsilon_{it}) = 0$) is consistent with the PILE hypothesis, so that assumption can be defended when testing the hypothesis. However, there are alternative hypotheses that would suggest that the changes over time in the landlessness rate may be correlated with changes in other factors influencing poverty. The direction of bias in $\hat{\beta}$ could go either way. For example, unusually good (regionally and temporally specific) agro-climatic conditions may simultaneously reduce poverty and encourage farmers to stay on the land; then $Cov(LL_{it}, \varepsilon_{it}) > 0$, implying that our estimate will be biased in favor of PILE, underestimating the poverty-reducing impact of landlessness. Region- and year-specific shocks to nonfarm output yield the opposite bias. Our expectation is that in a poor, rural economy such as Vietnam's, the bias arising from shocks to agriculture will be dominant, implying that the rise in landlessness is more pro-poor than our DD test suggests. Thus, if we find that $\beta > 0$, we will not be able to conclude that this is convincing support for the PILE hypothesis, given the likely bias in our DD test. However, if we find that $\beta < 0$, then we will be on safer ground in rejecting the hypothesis.

Pooling regions and dates from table 3.2 ($N.T = 28$), we obtained for the group with land $\hat{\beta} = -0.034$ with a t-ratio of -2.848 (based on a White standard error). The statistical precision improved when we dropped two regional effects that had very low t-ratios (North Central Coast and Mekong Delta); then we obtained $\hat{\beta} = -0.037$ with $t = -6.547$. This result suggests that rising landlessness has been poverty reducing among those with land and the effect is statistically significant. There is a poverty-increasing effect among the landless, but it is not statistically significant; the corresponding regression for the landless gave $\hat{\beta} = 0.020$ with $t = 0.561$.

These empirical findings point to a distributional effect in the impacts of rising landlessness, whereby poor farmers tend to become landless, echoing our theoretical model in annex 6A.[20] Thus, higher landlessness comes with a lower poverty rate among those with land, but we do not find a statistically significant impact on the poverty rate among the landless. This suggests that there are both gainers and losers in the group.

On balance, rising landlessness has been poverty reducing, and the effect is statistically significant. This is evident if instead we use the aggregate poverty rate (across both those without land and those with land) as the dependent variable. Then $\hat{\beta} = -0.042$ (*t*-ratio = -10.187).[21] When we use only the 1993 and 2004 surveys, we obtain $\hat{\beta} = -0.058$ (*t*-ratio = -8.658).[22]

These results are plainly inconsistent with the PILE hypothesis. However, the high level of aggregation in the preceding tests may be hiding important effects. Next, we consider two more disaggregated tests, one using a pseudo-panel dataset formed over 1993–2004 and one using a real (micro-level) panel formed over the shorter period, 1993–98.

Let us return to the synthetic panel spanning 1993–2004, as formed using birth cohorts. We can construct measures of poverty and landlessness for households classified by the age of the head in 1993 and similarly for the corresponding groups in 2004 (age in 1993 plus 11 years). Again, we can do this only for the national (urban plus rural) sample, given that valid inferences require that we can treat each cross-section as giving a sample that is representative of the same population subgroup at each date. (If we did this only for the rural sample, then a bias could arise from selective migration to urban areas by age cohort.)

Our test equation is

(6.3) $\quad \ln H_{it} = \alpha + \beta LL_{it} + X_i \gamma t + \pi_i + \delta_t + \varepsilon_{it}$
$\quad\quad\quad\quad (i = 1, \ldots, N; t = 1993, 2004),$

where X denotes the controls for initial conditions in 1993 that could influence the subsequent changes over time. As with the regional panel data model, this specification allows landlessness to be endogenous due to a correlation between landlessness and the fixed effects. Differencing over time, our estimable test equation is

(6.4) $\quad \ln H_{i04} - \ln H_{i93} = \delta + \beta(LL_{i04} - LL_{i93}) + X_i \gamma + \varepsilon_i$

(where $\delta = \delta_{04} - \delta_{93}$ and $\varepsilon_i = \varepsilon_{04} - \varepsilon_{93}$). Annex 3B gives the cohort means for the key variables.

On inspecting the data for the 34 age cohorts (in the previous section of this chapter), we found strong signs of a U-shaped relationship between the change in poverty rate and initial age, with the largest poverty reductions occurring for middle-age households (at an age of the head around 40 years). Including a quadratic function of age as controls, we found that $\hat{\beta} = -0.022$ (*t*-ratio = -2.103), which is lower (in absolute value) than the estimate based on our regional panel but still negative and significant (at the 5 percent level).[23] (The intercept implies an annual rate of poverty reduction—annualized change in the log head-count index—of about 10 percent, if the landlessness rate is held constant and the initial age is 30 years.) This result was robust to adding other controls (we used initial years of schooling of the head of household and initial mean consumption per person).

As a final test, we use the household panel data for 1993–98 to track what happened to the living standards of the farm households that became landless during this period. By tracking over this shorter period, we do not have the extent of the changes that we can exploit with the age-cohort analysis over 1993–2004. (Recall that the largest increase in landlessness was after 1998.) However, this data source has the advantage that it is a true panel, so we can eliminate individual effects. For this test, we use log consumption per person as the dependent variable, so the double-difference test entails regressing the change in log consumption on a dummy variable for whether the household became landless.[24]

For rural Vietnam as a whole, the panel gives us 3,211 households with agricultural land in 1993, of which 121 were landless in 1998. The subsequent change in log consumption over 1993–98 is uncorrelated with whether the household became landless over the period. The regression coefficient of the change in log consumption on the "becoming landless" dummy variable is 0.0609, with a standard error of 0.0412. When we divide the sample into North and South, we find that the regression coefficient is 0.2263 in the North (with a standard error of 0.0612) and 0.0357 in the South (with a standard error of 0.0420); 31 households became landless in the North versus 90 in the South. So we find significantly higher consumption growth among those farmers who became landless in the North, but no significant difference in the South.

This conclusion was found to be robust to adding controls for various 1993 characteristics of the household, including landholding, schooling, size, and demographic composition. Table 6.3 gives the results. With the controls, becoming landless added 0.1677 to log consumption in the North (with a standard error of 0.0560) versus −0.0093 (with a standard error of 0.0366) in the South. Among the controls, it is also notable that initial landholding has a negative (and statistically significant) coefficient in both regions; higher consumption gains occurred among those farm households with lower initial holdings.

Each of these tests makes assumptions that are consistent with PILE but imply things in the data that are inconsistent with that hypothesis. The exogeneity assumption for changes in landlessness is consistent with the arguments that have been made about the losses to poor farmers of a "push" process of essentially forced landlessness. Yet, under that assumption, we find that a higher landlessness rate implies lower—or at least not higher—poverty incidence. We have also argued that the likely direction of bias under alternative

Table 6.3 Panel Data Regressions for Change in Log Consumption per Person, 1993–98

Indicator	All rural farmers in 1993	North	South
Became landless	0.009	−0.009	0.168
	(0.23)	(−0.25)	(3.00)**
Log total land	−0.076	−0.075	−0.073
	(−5.43)**	(−3.76)**	(−3.52)**
Age of head of household	0.001	0.001	0.001
	(1.34)	(0.99)	(0.99)
Male head of household	−0.032	−0.023	−0.031
	(−1.51)	(−0.57)	(−1.34)
Years of education of household adults	0.002	0.002	0.003
	(1.46)	(1.23)	(1.62)
Ethnic majority	0.04	−0.044	0.121
	(0.82)	(−0.51)	(2.86)**
Share of 7- to 16-year-olds	0.227	0.342	0.243
	(2.76)**	(2.19)*	(2.47)*
Share of children 6 and younger	0.122	0.24	0.132
	(1.39)	(1.33)	(1.28)
Share of adults	−0.076	−0.013	−0.069
	(−1.55)	(−0.14)	(−1.24)
Log household size	0.124	0.083	0.099
	(3.16)**	(1.27)	(1.77)
Constant	0.833	0.614	0.546
	(6.77)**	(3.15)**	(2.97)**
Number of observations	3,208	1,267	1,941
R^2	0.11	0.05	0.08

Sources: 1993 and 1998 VLSSs.

Note: Robust *t*-statistics in parentheses. Regression for full sample included regional dummy variables. * = significant at 5 percent; ** = significant at 1 percent.

hypotheses would entail that we have underestimated how poverty reducing rising landlessness has been. So, taken as a whole, these observations cast doubt on the claims about the impoverishing effects of rising landlessness in Vietnam found in the literature and policy debates. The more plausible interpretation of the evidence we have assembled is that rising landlessness has been a positive factor in poverty reduction in Vietnam as a whole. The South's Mekong Delta region stands out as a possible exception.

Conclusions

Landlessness rose among Vietnam's poor in the aftermath of the agrarian reforms. However, this appears to have been a largely positive element of the process of aggregate poverty reduction as some farm households took up new economic opportunities, particularly wage labor. There is little to suggest that rising landlessness jeopardized the gains to the poor from the relatively equitable assignment of land-use rights that had been achieved at the time of decollectivization, as documented in chapter 4. Various tests and datasets lead us to reject the idea that rising landlessness has been increasing poverty in rural Vietnam as a whole; indeed, some of our test results clearly point in the opposite direction. There are signs of an emerging class differentiation in the South's Mekong Delta, though even there poverty has been falling among the landless.

However, as the next chapter shows, the rural landless are not being well served by Vietnam's antipoverty programs, including targeted credit, which appear to have not yet adapted to the changes we have documented in the country's rural economy.

Annex 6A: Model of Occupational Choice with and without a Land Market

To keep the analysis tractable, we make some simplifying assumptions, though we expect that similar results could be derived under weaker assumptions. Prior to the reform, land is equally allocated, giving $L_0 = \overline{L}$, but cannot be traded or transferred. Preform marketable assets, $A_0 \geq A_0^{min}$, can be devoted to consumer durables, which we denote "housing" (H) or schooling. Postreform, the market value of assets rises to $A_1 = A_0 + \overline{L}$ (the unit of land area is normalized so that the price of land is unity). (A subscript "0" denotes preform and "1" postreform.) Once there is a market, land can be converted into housing subject to $A_1 = H_1 + L_1$. It will be analytically convenient to make utility linear in the amount of food consumed, though we expect that the main results would hold under the more plausible assumption of diminishing marginal utility of food consumption.[25] Utility is $F + \phi(H)$, where F is consumption of food, and the subutility function $\phi(H)$ reflects the positive but diminishing marginal utility of housing ($\phi' > 0$, $\phi'' < 0$). Under the assumptions of our model, the optimal preform levels of schooling and housing will be determined solely by A_0 and will be strictly increasing in A_0.[26] Thus, we save notation by treating A_0 as the indicator of both schooling and preform housing.

The only relative price that will be allowed to vary is the wage rate. We can think of this as an open economy for the main food output; the fact that this is rice in Vietnam makes that assumption defensible in that context. In other (closed-economy) settings, however, there may also be welfare effects associated with a change in the relative price of food. (Land is treated as the numeraire, as already noted.)

The household chooses between family farming and supplying S of labor ($1 \geq S \geq 0$) to an outside activity (commercial farming or producing consumer durables). There is a return to wealth in farming, as represented by (twice-differentiable) functions of nonland wealth, $g_i(A_0)$, $i = 0,1$. Heterogeneity in ability at farming is represented by an i.i.d. random variable η. Own food output is $f(L_i) + g_i(A_0) + \eta$ ($i = 0,1$), where the nonnegative (twice-differentiable) function f is taken to be nondecreasing and at least weakly concave. (Any income from renting out land can be embedded in f.) Note that f is taken to be unaffected by the reform. Alternatively, one can allow for higher output from land because of greater security of land-use rights.[27] While one could readily introduce this feature, we interpret this effect as being picked up by the g_i functions.

The functions $g_i(A_0)$ can either represent economic returns to schooling in farming[28] or costs of nonland inputs—$g_i(A_0)$ can be negative for some A_0[29]—or some other contribution of wealth to output, such as through local tax transfers or (liquidity-constrained) access to credit to finance nonland inputs to farming, which we assume is only possible once land can be put up as collateral. We assume that the reform does not decrease farmers' marginal returns to nonland wealth. For the poorest, we also assume that the reform does not increase own food output at given land. More formally,

Assumption 6A.1. $g'_i(A_0) \geq 0$, $g''_i(A_0) \leq 0$, $g'_1(A_0) \geq g'_0(A_0)$ and $g_1(A_0^{\min}) \leq g_0(A_0^{\min})$.

The assumption that $g_1(A_0^{\min}) \leq g_0(A_0^{\min})$ is motivated by the policy debate summarized in chapter 2. Suppose that prior to the reform, the commune authorities in charge of land allocation provide certain benefits, such as help in acquiring complementary inputs to production or protection from idiosyncratic shocks. These benefits are curtailed once land markets are introduced, on the grounds that farmers can now use their land to obtain credit or as a buffer against risk. Then we may find that $g_1(A_0) < g_0(A_0)$ at low A_0.

The choice of S and L is constrained by the household's endowment of able-bodied labor and time (in short, its *labor constraint*). To simplify the analysis, we assume that the labor constraint entails that the household specialize in either farming or wage labor in a nonfarm activity; that is, it chooses between $\{L > 0, S = 0\}$ and $\{L = 0, S = 1\}$.[30] Food consumption is

(6A.1) $\qquad F_i = [f(L_i) + g_i(A_0) + \eta]I(L_i) + w_i(A_0)S_i[1 - I(L_i)]$

$(i = 0,1),$

where w_i is the wage rate (which varies with A_0 through returns to schooling) and $I(L_i)$ takes the value 1 when $L > 0$ and 0 when $L = 0$.

The maximum prereform utility for a farm household is $f(\overline{L}) + g_0(A_0) + \phi(A_0) + \eta$, and for a landless household it is $w_i + \phi(A_i)$ ($i = 0,1$). The postreform utility maximum in farming is $v(A_0) + \eta$, where

(6A.2) $\quad v(A_0) \equiv \max_{(L)} f(L) + g_1(A_0) + \phi(A_0 + \overline{L} - L).$

The optimal postreform landholding is $L_1^* = L(A_0)$. It is readily verified that $L'(A_0) > 0$. Farmers with $A_0 > A^* \equiv L^{-1}(\overline{L})$ acquire more land when the market is introduced ($L_1^* > \overline{L}$), while those with $A_0 < A^*$ acquire less. We also impose an upper bound on the land demand of the poorest (or an equivalent upper bound on the amount of food that can be produced with only $L(A_0^{\min})$ of land):

Assumption 6A.2. $L(A_0^{\min}) \leq f^{-1}\{\phi(A_0^{\min} + \overline{L})$
$\qquad\qquad\qquad\qquad - \phi[A_0^{\min} + \overline{L} - L(A_0^{\min})]\}.$

For example, this assumption would automatically hold if $f[L(A_0^{\min})] = 0$, that is, $L(A_0^{\min})$ is too small a holding to be a productive holding. However, we do not require that $f[L(A_0^{\min})] = 0$.

In the above model, the choice of whether to continue to hold land is deterministic for each household; that is, at given circumstances it can be known with certainty who is landless and who is not. However, the heterogeneity in ability at farming, as represented by the random variable η, is private knowledge. So, at given values of all publicly observable variables, there is a probability of becoming landless, which is the observed (conditional) "landlessness rate":

(6A.3.1) $\quad LL_1 = \Psi[w_1 + \phi(A_1) - v(A_0)]$

(6A.3.2) $\quad LL_0 = \Psi[w_0 - f(\overline{L}) - g_0(A_0)],$

where Ψ is the distribution function of η. Both LL_1 and LL_0 are strictly increasing in w and nonincreasing in A_0. Note that a landless class will emerge (with nonzero probability) postreform even if wealth is initially equal, given heterogeneous ability at farming.

We assume competitive markets for labor of each skill or asset level, A_0. Labor supplies are given by equations (6A.3.1) and (6A.3.2). Demand is taken to be a stable nonincreasing function of the wage rate and a nondecreasing function of A_0. Thus, wage rates equate (6A.3.1) and (6A.3.2) with aggregate demands $D(w_1, A_0)$ and $D(w_0, A_0)$, giving wages $w_1 = w_1(A_0)$ and $w_0 = w_0(A_0)$, which are both nondecreasing functions.[31] An alternative model would allow for unemployment, with the available work rationed according to wealth as the key determinant of productivity (as in an efficiency-wage model). The following analysis allows either interpretation of $w_i(A_0)$.

Proposition 6.1. On introducing a land market, the landlessness rate will rise for the asset-poor and fall for those who have sufficiently high assets.

Proof. Note first that, given stable downward-sloping demand functions, the equilibrium landlessness rate must be a decreasing function of the equilibrium wage rate; that is, the necessary and sufficient condition for $LL_1 > LL_0$ (at given A_0) is that $w_1(A_0) < w_0(A_0)$. Thus, a land market will increase landlessness if and only if $H(A_0) < f(\overline{L})$, where[32]

$$(6A.4) \quad H(A_0) \equiv f[L(A_0)] + \phi[A_0 + \overline{L} - L(A_0)] \\ - \phi(A_0 + \overline{L}) + g_1(A_0) - g_0(A_0).$$

It is readily verified that $H(A_0^{\min}) \leq 0$ under Assumptions 6A.1 and 6A.2. So the reform must increase the landlessness rate for the asset-poor. Differentiating equation (6A.4), we also find that

$$(6A.5) \quad H'(A_0) = \phi'(A_1 - L_1^*) - \phi'(A_1) + g_1'(A_0) - g_0'(A_0) > 0$$

(given that $\phi'' < 0$). Thus, there will be a rise in the landlessness rate for all those with $A_0 < H^{-1}[f(\overline{L})]$ and a fall for $A_0 > H^{-1}[f(\overline{L})]$ (figure 6A.1). (The switch point ($H^{-1}[f(\overline{L})]$) may be quite high; for example (as is evident below), if $g_1(A_0) = g_0(A_0)$, then $H^{-1}[f(\overline{L})] > A^*$,

Figure 6A.1 Functions Used in the Theoretical Analysis ($g_1(A_0) = g_0(A_0)$)

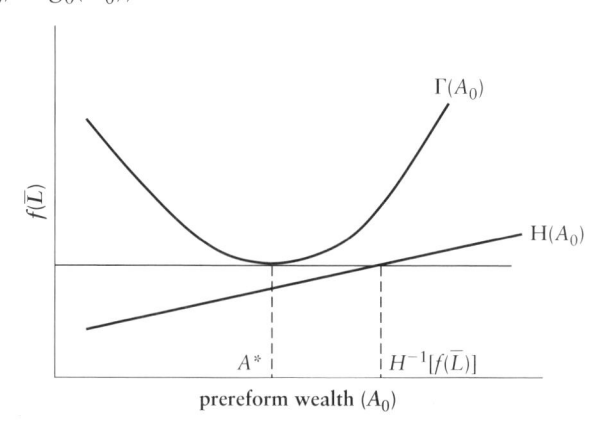

Source: Authors' representation.

the asset level below which land is sold once the market is introduced.) QED.

It is clear from the preceding analysis that the reform's implications for the aggregate rate of landlessness—obtained by integrating equations (6A.3.1) and (6A.3.2) over the distribution of wealth—depend on the initial distribution of wealth; if more than (less than) half of the population have $A_0 < H^{-1}[f(\bar{L})]$, then the aggregate landlessness rate will rise (fall). Intuitively, the greater the initial asset poverty, the more likely aggregate landlessness will rise because of the reform.

Proposition 6.2. The postreform wealth gradient in landlessness can go in either direction, depending on the structure of returns to wealth.

Proof. On substituting $w_1 = w_1(A_0)$ into equation (6A.3.1), the wealth gradient is given by

(6A.6) $dLL_1/dA_0 = \psi(\cdot)[w_1'(A_0) + \phi'(A_1) - \phi'(A_1 - L_1^*) - g_1'(A_0)]$

(where $\psi(\cdot) = \Psi'(\cdot) > 0$). The gradient could be positive or negative (unlike the partial derivative at a given wage rate, which is negative). It is instructive to consider two stylized cases:

Case 1: Low labor-market returns to wealth. When the returns to schooling are low, farming will tend to be the more attractive option for the rich. Suppose that only unskilled labor is available and there are no other returns to wealth in farming: that is, $w_i'(A_0) = g_i'(A_0) = 0$. Without a land market, the landlessness rate does not vary with wealth. On introducing a market, it is evident from equation (6A.6) that LL is nonincreasing in A; that is, the landlessness rate tends to fall with higher wealth. Allowing for positive returns to wealth in farming $g_i'(A_0) > 0$ (such as through access to credit when land can be used as collateral), LL will be decreasing in wealth both before and after the reform. In the special case of a uniform distribution of η (ψ constant) and $g_0' = g_1'$, the wealth gradient will be everywhere steeper after the reform.

Case 2: High labor-market returns to wealth. Naturally, this makes the labor market more attractive to the rich. A positive wealth gradient in landlessness is found if the returns to schooling are sufficiently high; that is, $w_0'(A_0) > g_0'(A_0)$ and $w_1'(A_0) > g_1'(A_0) + \phi'(A_1 - L_1^*) - \phi'(A_1)$. With a uniform distribution of η and a structure of returns to wealth that is unaffected by the reform, the wealth gradient will be everywhere flatter after the reform. QED.

Proposition 6.3. There can be both gainers and losers from this reform, and the impact on aggregate poverty is ambiguous.

Proof. Let us begin with the case of a farmer who stays a farmer. A welfare gain requires that $\Gamma(A_0) > f(\overline{L})$, where

(6A.7) $\quad \Gamma(A_0) \equiv f(L_1^*) + \phi(A_0 + \overline{L} - L_1^*) - \phi(A_0) + g_1(A_0) - g_0(A_0).$

We find that (using the envelope theorem):

(6A.8) $\quad \Gamma'(A_0) = \phi'(A_0 + \overline{L} - L_1^*) - \phi'(A_0) + g_1'(A_0) - g_0'(A_0).$

Consider first the special case in which $g_1(A_0) = g_0(A_0)$. Note that $\Gamma'(A_0) > (<)0$ as $L_1^* > (<)\overline{L}$, that is, as $A_0 > (<)A^*$. Thus, $\Gamma(A_0)$ has a U-shape, with a minimum at A^*, where $\Gamma(A_0) = f(\overline{L})$ and $\Gamma(A_0) \geq f(\overline{L})$, as in figure 6A.1.[33] There is a welfare gain (or at least no loss) for all farmers. Clearly, this result also holds if $g_1(A_0) > g_0(A_0)$ for all A_0.[34] However, farmers with $g_1(A_0) < g_0(A_0)$ could be worse off as a consequence of the reform. For a concrete example, suppose that $g_i(A_0)$ is the extra farm output that can be obtained with access to credit for acquiring nonland inputs, given A_0. Prior to the land-market reform, the same local authorities who allocate the land equally by administrative means also give everyone equal access to credit—that is, $g_0(A_0) = \overline{g}_0$. After the reform, farmers turn to an (imperfect) credit market in which lenders provide credit only on terms that ensure the farmer wants to stay a farmer. (We assume that this constraint holds in expectation only, in that the latent ability variable η is set to its mean of zero.) Then $g_1(A_0)$ equates $v(A_0)$ with utility when landless, giving

(6A.9) $\quad g_1(A_0) = w_1(A_0) + \phi(A_0 + \overline{L}) - \phi(A_0 + \overline{L} - L_1^*) - f(L_1^*).$

Now we find that a farmer gains (loses) from the reform according to whether $w_1(A_0) + \phi(A_0 + \overline{L}) - \phi(A_0)$ is greater than (less than) $f(\overline{L}) + \overline{g}_0$. The asset-poor will lose if the unskilled wage rate is sufficiently low ($w_1(A_0^{\min}) < \overline{g}_0 + f(\overline{L}) + \phi(A_0^{\min}) - \phi(A_0^{\min} + \overline{L})$), since they can attract little credit to finance nonland inputs to farm production. A clear separation into asset-poor losers and asset-rich gainers is also possible if the returns to schooling in the labor market are sufficiently high ($w_1'(A_0) > \phi'(A_0) - \phi'(A_0 + \overline{L})(>0)$).

Now consider a farmer who becomes landless as a result of the reform. Clearly, he or she cannot be worse off postreform than if he or she had stayed a farmer. Having established above that no farmer loses as a result of the reform for the case in which $g_1(A_0) \geq g_0(A_0)$, it cannot be the case that those farmers who choose to become landless lose as a result of the reform. However, when $g_1(A_0) < g_0(A_0)$, there can be losers among the newly landless.

Last, consider the prereform landless who stay landless. All that matters to the welfare impact for this group is what happens to the wage rate. For this group, a rise in landlessness signals a welfare loss, through the impact on the wage rate. Thus, we have verified Proposition 6.3. QED.

Annex 6B

Table 6B.1 Data for Decomposition of the Change in Aggregate Landlessness

1993 quintiles of households ranked by consumption per capita	Landlessness rate		Frequency	
	1993	2004	1993	2004
Rural Vietnam				
Quintile 1 (poorest)	0.0664	0.0646	0.2002	0.0481
Quintile 2	0.0652	0.0917	0.1999	0.0575
Quintile 3	0.0599	0.1116	0.2002	0.1020
Quintile 4	0.0704	0.1088	0.1999	0.1921
Quintile 5	0.1591	0.1578	0.1999	0.6002
Total	0.0842	0.1371	1.0000	1.0000
Northern Uplands				
Quintiles 1–3	0.0219	0.0035	0.6003	0.2275
Quintile 4	0.0000	0.0060	0.1990	0.1278
Decile 9	0.0164	0.0205	0.1003	0.1541
Decile 10	0.0667	0.0614	0.1003	0.4905
Total	0.0214	0.0375	1.0000	1.0000
Red River Delta				
Quintiles 1–3	0.0065	0.0310	0.6006	0.1030
Quintile 4	0.0293	0.0244	0.1992	0.1319
Decile 9	0.0392	0.0479	0.0996	0.1952
Decile 10	0.1176	0.0905	0.0996	0.5699
Total	0.0254	0.0678	1.0000	1.0000
North Central Coast				
Quintiles 1–3	0.0312	0.0433	0.6010	0.2132
Quintile 4	0.0434	0.0566	0.2003	0.1625
Decile 9	0.0526	0.0777	0.0993	0.1661
Decile 10	0.0702	0.1116	0.0993	0.4582
Total	0.0401	0.0821	1.0000	1.0000
South Central Coast				
Quintiles 1–3	0.0866	0.0882	0.6016	0.2391
Quintile 4	0.1039	0.1042	0.2005	0.2199
Decile 9	0.1316	0.1911	0.0990	0.2172
Decile 10	0.3684	0.1916	0.0990	0.3238
Total	0.1224	0.1479	1.0000	1.0000
Central Highlands				
Quintiles 1–3	0.0909	0.0078	0.6016	0.3075
Quintile 4	0.1154	0.0554	0.2031	0.2300
Decile 9	0.0000	0.0411	0.1016	0.1408
Decile 10	0.1667	0.0542	0.0938	0.3216
Total	0.0938	0.0386	1.0000	1.0000

(*Continued on the following page*)

Table 6B.1 *(Continued)*

1993 quintiles of households ranked by consumption per capita	Landlessness rate		Frequency	
	1993	2004	1993	2004
Southeast				
Quintiles 1–3	0.1927	0.3974	0.6000	0.1288
Quintile 4	0.2344	0.3187	0.2000	0.2235
Decile 9	0.250	0.4065	0.1000	0.1970
Decile 10	0.4375	0.4182	0.1000	0.4508
Total	0.2313	0.3920	1.0000	1.0000
Mekong Delta				
Quintiles 1 and 2	0.1938	0.3832	0.4005	0.0954
Quintile 3	0.1250	0.3438	0.2003	0.1445
Decile 7	0.0750	0.2468	0.1001	0.1028
Decile 8	0.1375	0.2183	0.1001	0.1270
Decile 9	0.1875	0.2281	0.1001	0.1747
Decile 10	0.1772	0.2110	0.0989	0.3555
Total	0.1602	0.2536	1.0000	1.0000

Sources: 1993 VLSS and 2004 VHLSS.

Notes

1. Note that there were some landless households before the reform, particularly in the South's Mekong Delta.

2. To simplify the analysis, we use *human capital* here to refer only to schooling. In actuality, however, it might also include health, demographic endowments, and farming ability, for example.

3. For evidence of a "wealth" effect on schooling in Vietnam, see Glewwe and Jacoby (2004).

4. Note that selling land to improve housing (or buy other consumer durables) does not require that agricultural land be converted into residential land, which would require changes in land-use laws.

5. T. M. Ngo (2004) and van de Walle (2003) provide evidence that schooling raises agricultural productivity in Vietnam.

6. Given our focus on the poor, we do not model the possibility that some farm households will employ agricultural wage laborers explicitly, but we note some implications along the way.

7. It is not clear that returns to schooling need to be high for a positive gradient in landlessness. In common with China (Fleisher and Wang 2004), wage compression in the more organized labor markets has kept returns to schooling relatively low in Vietnam; see Gallup (2004) and N. N. Nguyen (2004) for the 1990s, although it appears that returns to education have

increased substantially in recent years (World Bank 2005: chapter 7). Note also that the gradient could reflect a wealth effect on nonfarm earnings.

8. On the sources of inequality between the minority and majority ethnic groups in Vietnam, see van de Walle and Gunewardena (2001), whose results offer some support for our interpretation.

9. Recall that there will be a bias in using these regressions to infer the relationship with prereform consumption because we are using postreform consumption for 2004. Unlike for Vietnam as a whole (figure 6.1), when the true relationship is negative (as for the Mekong Delta), the sign of this bias is indeterminate.

10. The changes in the distribution of annual land show a very similar pattern.

11. This echoes Taylor's (2004) observations from fieldwork in the Mekong Delta.

12. The relevant questions were not asked in prior surveys.

13. To derive the share of land with an LUC from the 2004 VHLSS, we aggregated plot-specific responses, weighted by plot sizes.

14. The corresponding graphs for self-employment in farming were similar between the two regions and similar to the national pattern.

15. Given the large shift to the right in the distribution of consumption, we had to choose fractiles carefully to avoid small sample size in the 2004 fractiles. The precise fractiles by region are given in annex 6B.

16. Indeed, given that most urban residents are automatically "landless" in the sense of having no agricultural land, there is a virtual identity linking these two variables, whereby the national landlessness rate (LLN) is related to the rural landlessness rate (LL) and the urban population share (U) as $LLN = LL + U(1 - LL)$.

17. We also tried adding age squared, but this was (highly) insignificant.

18. We estimated this model using both the linear head-count index and its log, though the log specification gave a better fit for those with land.

19. Our standard errors also assume that the error term in equation (6.2) is serially independent. If this assumption fails to hold, then the standard errors on double-difference estimates can be biased downward (Bertrand, Duflo, and Mullainathan 2004). Testing this is problematic with only four observations over time (and unevenly spaced as well). However, all our results were robust to collapsing the panel to just two dates, 1993 and 2004.

20. This is confirmed by regressing the inequality index among those with land on LL (allowing for regional and year effects); we find a regression coefficient of -0.0016, which is significantly different from zero at the 5 percent level ($t = -2.14$); there is no such effect on inequality among the landless.

21. We dropped highly insignificant regions; with a complete set of regional effects, we obtained $\hat{\beta} = -0.032$ with a t-ratio of -2.778.

22. This suggests that serial correlation in the error is not a problem for inference in this case.

23. Sampling error is imparting some degree of attenuation bias. This can be corrected for using the method proposed by Deaton (1985). However, the results of Verbeek and Nijman (1992) suggest that the bias is likely to be small with the cohort sizes we have used here.

24. We switch to consumption rather than a poverty dummy variable (the micro analogue of our previous tests) given that it is inefficient to use qualitative econometric methods when the underlying continuous variable is observed.

25. A more general model would also allow leisure to have value.

26. This follows from our assumption that utility is separable between food and consumer durables.

27. For supportive evidence, see Deininger and Jin (2006) (using data for Ethiopia), who also refer to earlier literature, not all of which is supportive.

28. A more general model would allow for interaction effects with landholding.

29. At sufficiently high A_0, some farm households in the model will employ (presumably unskilled) wage labor in farming.

30. If the household chooses landlessness, then it will set $S = 1$, given that we do not attach a value to leisure. If we introduced unemployment, then S would be set at the maximum available work.

31. Prior to the land market, the supply of labor is independent of A, but the wage rate will still be nondecreasing in A via the demand side effect.

32. Note that (a) the labor-market clearing conditions can be written as $\Psi(w_i + x_i) = D(w_i)$ (for $i = 0,1$), implying that w is a strictly decreasing function of x, the supply shift, and (b) $H(A_0) - f(\overline{L})$ indicates the shift in the labor supply functions at a given wage rate, as in equations (6A.3.1) and (6A.3.2).

33. Note also that $\Gamma(A_0) \geq H(A_0)$ (given that $\Gamma(A_0) = H(A_0) + \phi(A_1) - \phi(A_0)$). It follows that $H^{-1}[f(\overline{L})] > A^*$ when $g_1(A_0) = g_0(A_0)$, as claimed in the example following Proposition 6.1 (figure 6A.1).

34. Introducing labor hiring by farmers with sufficiently large holdings would add further welfare gains to better-off farmers because of the reform's impact on the unskilled wage rate.

7

Access to Credit for the Landless Poor

Advocates of land-market reform have often argued that it will help in the development of credit markets by allowing farmers to use their land titles as collateral in obtaining finance. However, the rural landless may well be locked out of these opportunities, since (by definition) they lack this form of collateral. The landless poor may then have a particularly hard time taking up opportunities for investment (in both physical and human capital) that would help them escape poverty in the longer term.

Antipoverty programs in Vietnam have emphasized credit expansion for the poor. The aim is essentially to compensate for the credit-market imperfections that tend to inhibit opportunities for poor people to escape poverty; without intervention, it is believed that this lack of access to credit will both retard economic growth and perpetuate poverty and inequality. If, as we expect, the landless have fewer opportunities for private credit, given that they lack collateral, then the highest priority for public credit through the antipoverty programs should arguably be the landless poor. Whether Vietnam's policy makers have yet adapted to this need remains an open question.

This chapter addresses these issues for both untargeted credit sources (both formal and informal) and credit that is provided through Vietnam's antipoverty programs.

Land and Credit

Finance is often crucial to the prospects of escaping poverty, both for farm households and for (rural and urban) nonfarm households. Yet it is widely believed that credit markets perform poorly, or are nonexistent, in developing rural economies, which thus helps perpetuate

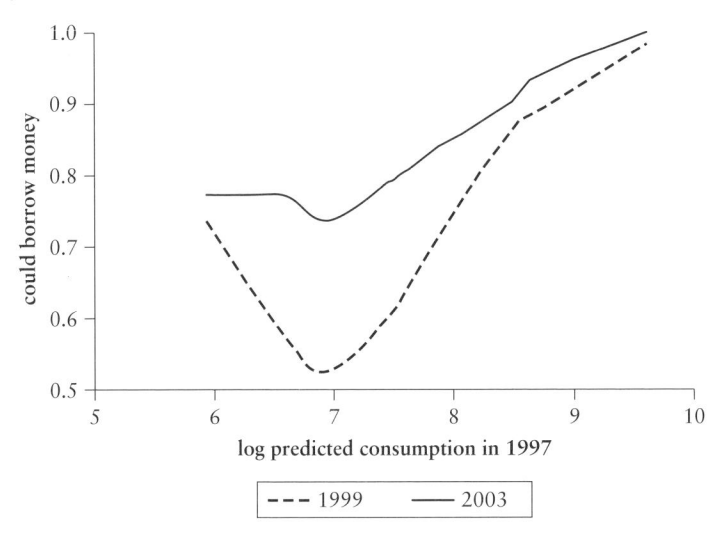

Figure 7.1 Perceived Credit Constraint, 1993 and 2003

[Figure: Line graph with x-axis "log predicted consumption in 1997" ranging from 5 to 10, and y-axis "could borrow money" ranging from 0.5 to 1.0. Two curves shown: dashed line for 1999 and solid line for 2003.]

Sources: 1999 and 2003 SIRRVs.
Note: Households were asked if they could borrow money if they wanted to. The figure shows the "yes" answers versus the "no" or "unsure" answers.

poverty and inequality.[1] Is that right? And does the answer depend on landholding status?

The Survey of Impacts of Rural Roads in Vietnam (SIRRV) asked about perceived credit constraints. (The SIRRV dataset is described in chapter 3.) Households were asked whether they thought that they would be able to borrow if they wanted to. Figure 7.1 shows how households' perceived credit constraint varies by consumption between 1999 and 2003, according to the SIRRV. Wealthier households are clearly more likely to say that they were able to borrow if they wanted to, but the proportion has increased over time for households along the entire distribution. In 2003, 80 percent or more of all households felt that they could borrow if they wanted to. This might suggest that credit constraints are not as widespread as the literature in development economics might lead one to suspect, although the constraints do appear to matter more to the poor. However, the fact that 80 percent of households believed that they have access to credit does not mean that such credit would in fact be forthcoming when they needed it or that it would be available on competitive terms; this statistic does not refute the view that credit-market imperfections are widespread in this setting.

Access to formal credit may well be more constrained. *Formal credit* is defined as credit from banks and various organizations, as distinct from *informal credit* from individuals. The sources of formal credit have increased over the period, as providing credit became a policy goal of the government. In 1993, the formal credit sources asked about in the Vietnam Living Standards Survey (VLSS) included private banks, other government banks, and cooperatives. In 2004, they also included "social policy banks," agricultural and rural development banks, the fund for employment promotion, credit organizations, and political or social mass organizations. At both dates, informal credit sources comprise private moneylenders, friends or relatives, and other individuals.

One of the expected gains from liberalizing land markets is to enhance access to formal credit. We see signs of this in figure 7.2, panel a, which gives the regression of the share of farm households that reported that they borrowed money from a formal credit source in the past 12 months against consumption for both 2004 and 1993; panel b gives the corresponding regressions for the landless only.

While landed households were more likely to use formal credit in both years than the landless, both groups experienced rising credit use over time. In 1993, the mean proportion using formal credit was 21.68 percent for farmers ($n = 3,514$) and 11.15 percent for the landless ($n = 323$), while in 2004, the corresponding proportions were 35.58 percent ($n = 6,035$) and 23.34 percent ($n = 904$), respectively. We also see a strong economic gradient in the expansion in formal credit for both landed and landless (figure 7.2); there was no gain for the poorest among the landless.

There are also signs in these data that formal credit displaced informal credit. The corresponding graphs for use of informal credit sources in figure 7.3 show a negative economic gradient with lower overall use in 2004 than in 1993. The mean proportion using informal credit in 1993 was 39.21 percent for farmers and 40.87 percent for the landless, while in 2004 the proportions were 20.36 percent and 21.13 percent ($n = 904$), respectively. The main change was a displacement of informal credit by formal credit (for both landed and landless).

While causality is very hard to establish given that other changes were going on in Vietnam's economy, these descriptive findings at least suggest that the liberalization of land markets and the expansion of land titling under these agrarian reforms came hand in hand with a formalization of credit sources, rather than an overall increase in credit use.

Figure 7.2 Formal Credit Use by Consumption, 1993 and 2004

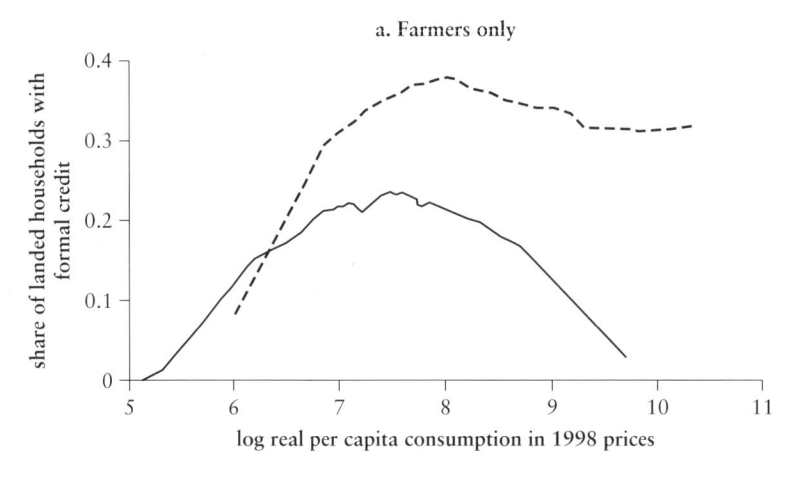

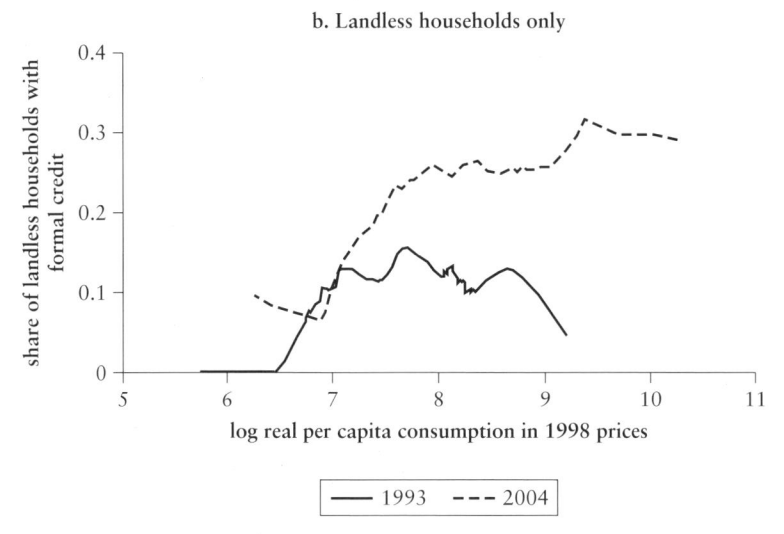

a. Farmers only

b. Landless households only

— 1993 --- 2004

Sources: 1993 VLSS and 2004 VHLSS.

Land and Participation in Antipoverty Programs

Possibly it is not surprising that the landless are less likely to get formal credit, since they lack the collateral provided by land. But, more surprisingly, we find that Vietnam's landless poor are also less likely to receive credit from the national antipoverty program. Credit subsidies are targeted to the poor through the Hunger Eradication and Poverty Reduction (HEPR) Program and Program 135. These two

Figure 7.3 Use of Informal Credit Sources, 1993 and 2004

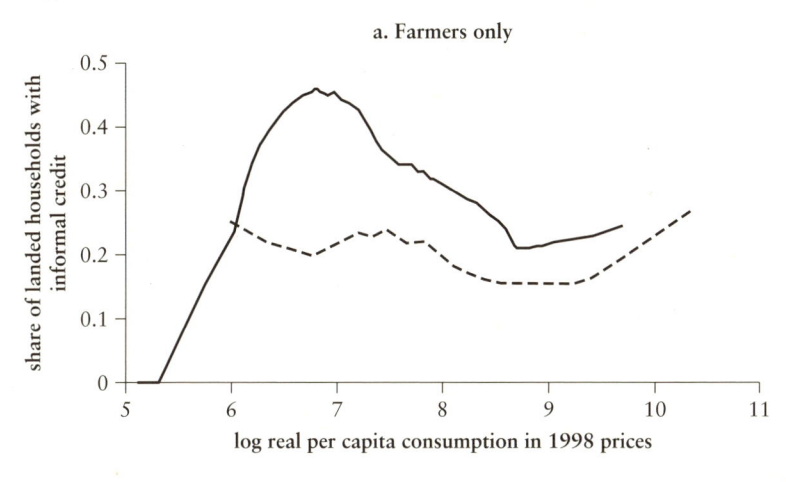

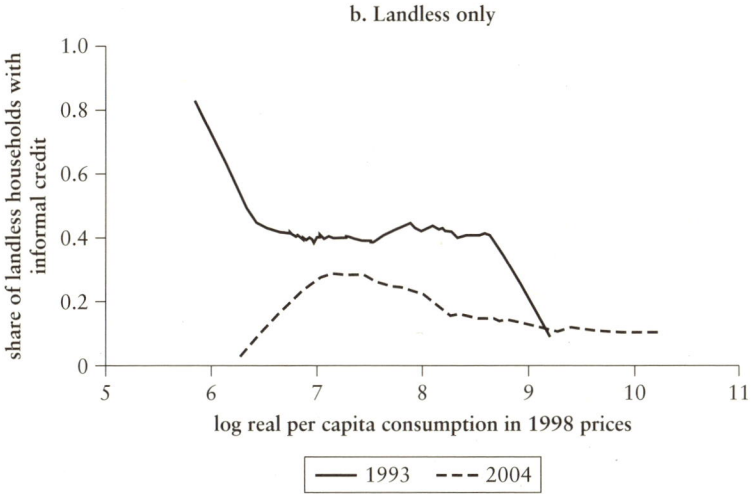

a. Farmers only

b. Landless only

—— 1993   --- 2004

Sources: 1993 VLSS and 2004 VHLSS.

programs also provide help with health care costs and local infrastructure, though microcredit is the main instrument.[2] Funds are provided primarily through the Vietnam Bank for Social Policies (previously the Bank for the Poor), which collaborates with the mass organizations to channel concessionary loans to poor households at the local level. Originally established in the 1930s to mobilize mass support for the Communist Party and the liberation struggle, the mass organizations have in recent years become closely involved in poverty reduction efforts. In 2004, almost 75 percent of all credit to the poor went through credit groups set up by the two largest mass organizations: the Women's Union and the Farmer's Union; a further 10 percent was directed through the Youth Union and the Veteran's Association (Sakata 2006). Access to these loans requires that one is classified as "poor" by the commune authorities with the assistance of the mass organizations, which focus on their members (the same poverty-status list as that described in chapter 3, p. 62). One must also join an officially recognized credit-borrowing group (CBG), usually set up with the help of the mass organizations for their members (Sakata 2006). A CBG is a group of people in the same village with its own management board. Members of the CBG must be long-term residents of the village, have someone who is able to work, and (of course) want credit. Relying on group memberships can serve an important role in reducing agency costs and sharing risks, as illustrated by Bangladesh's famous Grameen Bank. However, as we argue below, groups such as the landless poor may well be at a disadvantage.

The 2004 Vietnam Household Living Standards Survey (VHLSS) asked whether respondent households had participated in the antipoverty programs (since 1999). Figure 7.4 gives the conditional probabilities of receiving subsidized credit through these programs for both farm and landless households. Panel a shows the incidence of all programs, while panel b shows that of subsidized credit, and panel c shows participation in the noncredit components.

All three panels of figure 7.4 reveal a striking gap in participation between equally poor households according to whether or not they are landless. Households that are landless are much less likely to partake in the antipoverty programs: less than 20 percent of the poorest landless households participated, as compared with 60 percent among the poorest farming households (figure 7.4, panel a). The economic gradient is also much steeper for landed households, with participation falling as consumption rises. For the landless, the relationship is flatter and is actually concave for subsidized credit—rising from zero participation for the worst-off households to around 8 percent for those with consumption considerably above the rural mean, before falling and remaining higher than for the landed. Targeting is therefore much worse with respect to the landless.

It is of interest to compare these findings for Vietnam as a whole with those for the Mekong Delta. The situation in the Mekong Delta is for the most part similar to that of the rest of the country for antipoverty programs overall and the credit component (figure 7.5). Participation is very low for the poorest among the landless and much lower than for the landed poor. However, there are signs that better-off landless households do participate. The incidence of noncredit program participation in the Mekong Delta is rather different,

Figure 7.4 Participation in Targeted Antipoverty Programs, 2004

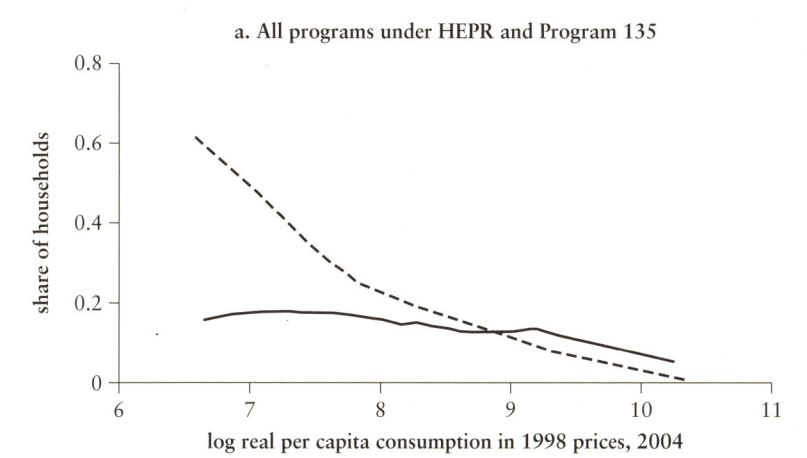

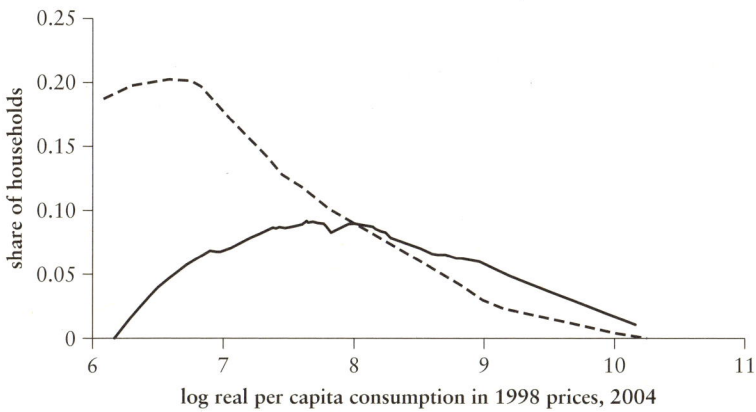

a. All programs under HEPR and Program 135

b. Subsidized credit only

c. Noncredit antipoverty programs

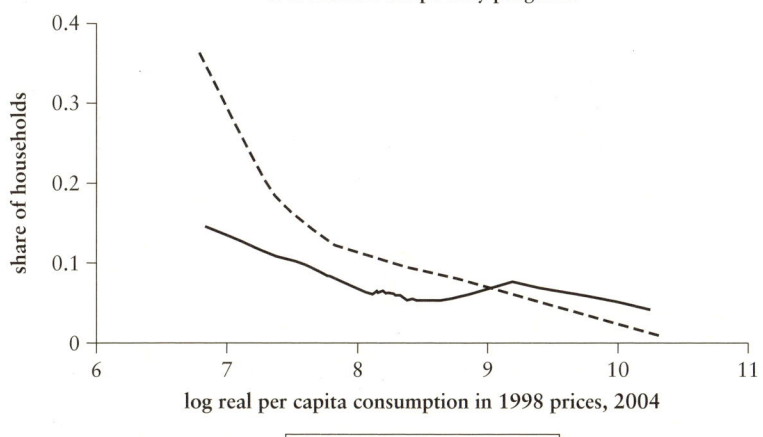

—— landless   --- landed

Source: 2004 VHLSS.

Figure 7.5 Incidence of Participation in Antipoverty Programs in Rural Mekong Delta, 2004

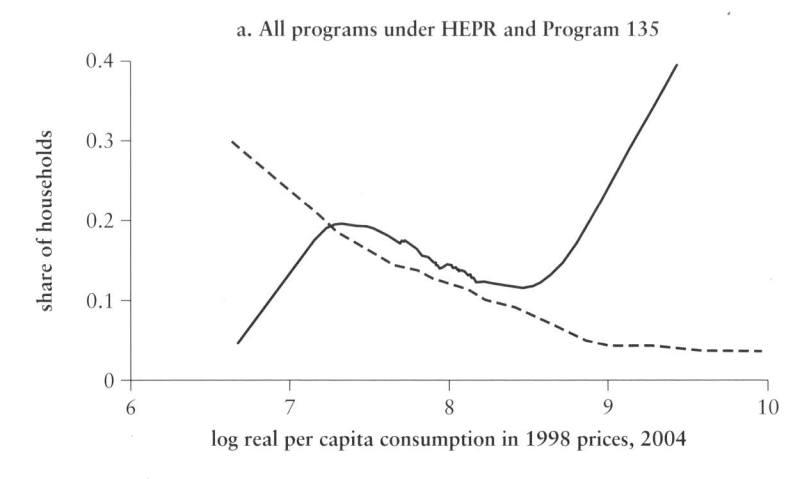

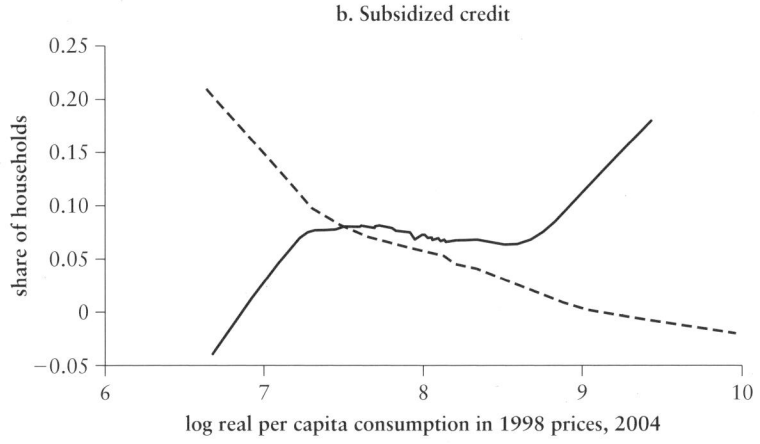

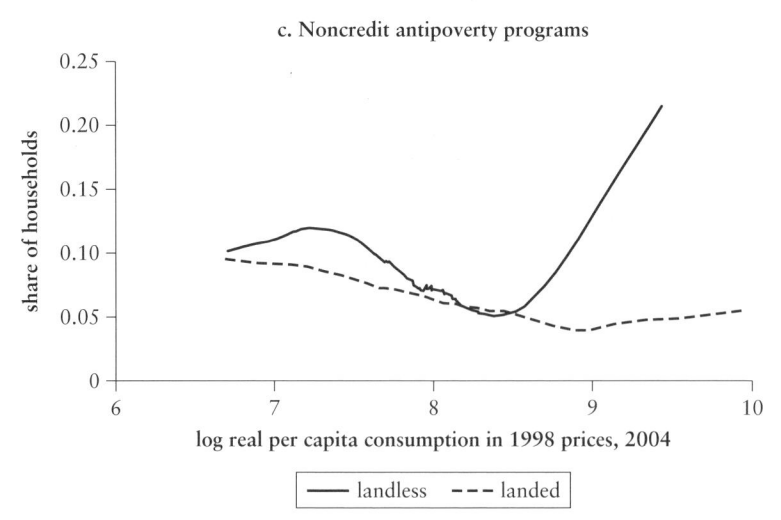

a. All programs under HEPR and Program 135

b. Subsidized credit

c. Noncredit antipoverty programs

—— landless   - - - landed

Source: 2004 VHLSS.

with the landless showing slightly higher participation at low levels of consumption than the landed.

Why Are the Landless Poor Being Missed for Targeted Credit?

There are a number of possible reasons why the landless poor have lower program participation rates than similarly poor farmers:

- *Indicator-targeting bias.* A belief that farmers are poorer may lead to what we can term *indicator-targeting bias* (ITB), whereby poor people who do not have the "poor characteristic" do not receive help. By this view, the authorities are assumed to have very little information to enable them to identify the poor among the landless.
- *Knowledge.* For various reasons, the landless may not know about the programs. Knowledge about such programs is to some extent endogenous to the selection process used by program administrators. Lack of knowledge about these programs among the landless could reflect efforts to target those with land; we consider this possibility below. There may be other factors at work. Being a relatively new phenomenon in many rural areas, poor landless households may be less well integrated into the community and its institutions, which means that they know less about how to access public programs.
- *Selection processes favoring farmers over the landless.* Officially, land is not required as collateral for access to credit through these antipoverty programs. Nonetheless, there are a number of ways that selection processes could favor those with land. Poor landless households may well have characteristics that make it less likely that they can be members of the local mass organizations that are instrumental in providing information on programs, guaranteeing loans, and channeling those loans to households. The mass organizations that play a considerable role in dispensing loans to the poor naturally focus on their members. Most communes have an active Farmer's Union, but it presumably does not cater to nonfarming landless households. On the basis of fieldwork in 71 villages in Ha Giang province in the Northern Uplands, Sakata (2006) notes that practically all loans there went to buying cows and buffalo, based on the strong preference of the Farmer's Union and Women's Union, which controlled the loans. This use of capital may not appeal to some credit-constrained households.

With respect to this last point, in fieldwork and interviews with observers of rural Vietnam, we have heard anecdotal comments to the effect that those with outstanding debts were not allowed to join a credit group and that one way to demonstrate that one did not have such debts was to show the land-use certificate (naturally precluding the landless, even those with no debts). We have also heard reports that commune authorities do not favor people who are less well known and well connected within the commune. The landless poor are often seen as having weaker roots in the community. Adult members of landless households are more likely to be migrants or are often traveling while looking for seasonal unskilled wage work. Being more mobile, the landless are seen as less worthy of assistance. In some provinces in the South, landlessness may overlap with other characteristics, such as ethnicity and lack of education—factors that may make such households less well integrated into commune structures and so less able to join local institutions.

It is notable that progressive efforts at land reform in the South prior to 1975, such as the Land-to-the-Tiller program (discussed in chapter 2), have also been criticized for largely bypassing the rural landless (Wiegersma 1988: chapter 9). There was certainly a historical precedent for the possible biases against the landless seen in the present period.

Favoring farmers over the landless is not necessarily discriminatory, however. It may well make economic sense to the commune authorities, if they can establish that the program's impacts tend to be lower for the landless. We return to this point.

We cannot say with confidence which of these explanations is closer to the truth, but there are some suggestive points to note from these data and other observations. It is plain enough that more information is available in practice to those implementing antipoverty policies than simply whether one has land, so the key assumption of the ITB explanation can be questioned on a priori grounds. The fact that the landless poor are also less likely to receive the antipoverty programs in the Mekong Delta casts doubt on ITB as the explanation, since the landless do have a higher incidence of poverty in this area. However, notice that the bias against the landless is not found in the Mekong Delta for the noncredit components. Possibly two factors are at work: (a) the landless face a handicap in access to credit through these programs, and (b) they face indicator-targeting bias in the North, notably for the noncredit components.

We saw that, among the poor, the landless are appreciably less likely to receive credit through these programs, which appear to be targeted instead to poor farmers (figure 7.4, panel a). Possibly the lack of land is seen to make the landless a credit risk. However, the bias appears to go deeper since we find a similar pattern in participation in

Figure 7.6 Knowledge about the Antipoverty Programs, 2004

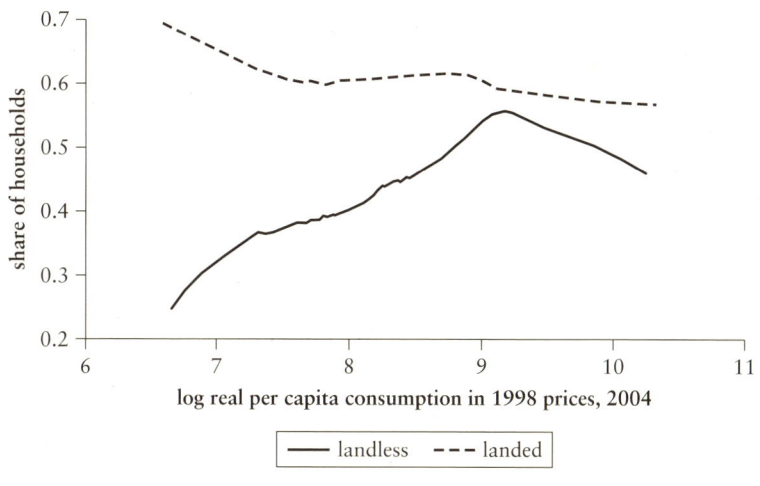

[Chart: x-axis "log real per capita consumption in 1998 prices, 2004" from 6 to 11; y-axis "share of households" from 0.2 to 0.7. Two curves: solid "landless" rising from about 0.25 at 6.7 to a peak near 0.56 around 9.2, then declining to about 0.46 at 10.3; dashed "landed" declining from about 0.68 at 6.7 to about 0.6 and leveling off.]

Source: 2004 VHLSS.

the *noncredit* components of the antipoverty programs, as can be seen in figure 7.4, panel c.

The 2004 survey also asked whether respondents knew about these programs. Figure 7.6 shows that this could be a factor, though it begs the question of why they do not know. Only around a quarter of poor landless households say they are aware of HEPR and its related programs, compared to 70 percent of the poor with land.

We now turn to the "mobile landless" explanation. While households that are only temporarily registered in the commune where their members live and work will face a handicap in accessing these public programs, such households are not easy to capture in a conventional household survey. To the extent that the survey underrepresents these types of households (chapter 3), the fact of being more mobile, without permanent registration in the commune of residence, does not explain why we find that the landless poor are underrepresented as participants in these programs.

Could it be that such programs are simply less effective for the landless? A clue to the welfare impacts of the antipoverty programs can be found in the community-based and subjective welfare data (chapter 3). Together with the survey information on whether the household has participated in antipoverty programs since 1999, we can create a simple difference-in-difference (DD) estimate of the impact of the programs. This estimate compares participants and nonparticipants in terms of the observed changes over time in measured outcomes, relative to a preintervention baseline.[3] DD will give an unbiased estimate of the impact of participation if the selection bias (the ex ante difference in outcomes between participants and nonparticipants) is constant over time.

For the community-based welfare assessment, the change between 1999 and 2003 takes one of three possible values: 1 for those who escaped poverty between 1999 and 2003, as indicated by the commune listings; 0 for those whose situation did not change; and −1 for those who fell into poverty according to the listings. For the self-assessed change in living standards, this can take four possible values: 2 (very much improved living standards), 1 (improved), 0 (no change), and −1 (worsened). In each case, we compare the value of this indicator for those who participated in the antipoverty programs and those who did not. We calculate conditional DD impact estimates by seeing how the estimate of DD varies with consumption per capita.

This impact estimate has clear limitations, and we think that the results can be seen at best as being suggestive of possible impacts. The most important limitation is that there may be initial conditions that simultaneously influenced selection into the antipoverty program and the subsequent changes in these welfare indicators.[4] If one has baseline data, one can address this problem by controlling for the observable differences preintervention, but that is not, of course, possible in this case, given that we are forced to rely on recall in postintervention survey data.

We graph the impact estimates for both subjective measures of welfare against log consumption per person in figure 7.7. We see a positive impact on both measures, which tends to be largest for the poorest households. But the impacts are small. Community-based welfare rises by about 0.05 for the poorest (on a scale of −1 to +1), while subjective welfare rises by 0.25 (on a scale of −1 to +2).

When we divide the sample according to landholding status, a similar picture emerges for both measures (figure 7.8). Program participation resulted in higher living standards for both the farmers and the landless. However, particularly large gains are evidenced for the landless when commune poverty status is used to denote welfare. For the landed, impacts tend to increase with consumption.

Although we caution against reading too much into these estimates, it is at least suggestive that we find signs of program impacts for the landless. The bias against the landless that we found does not appear to reflect lower impacts among the landless than among those with land.

Figure 7.7 Impacts of the Antipoverty Programs on Community-Assessed and Subjective Welfare, 2004

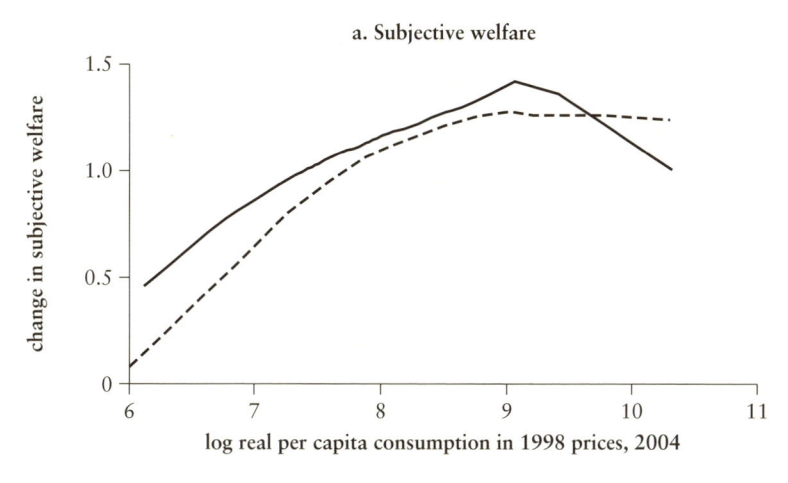

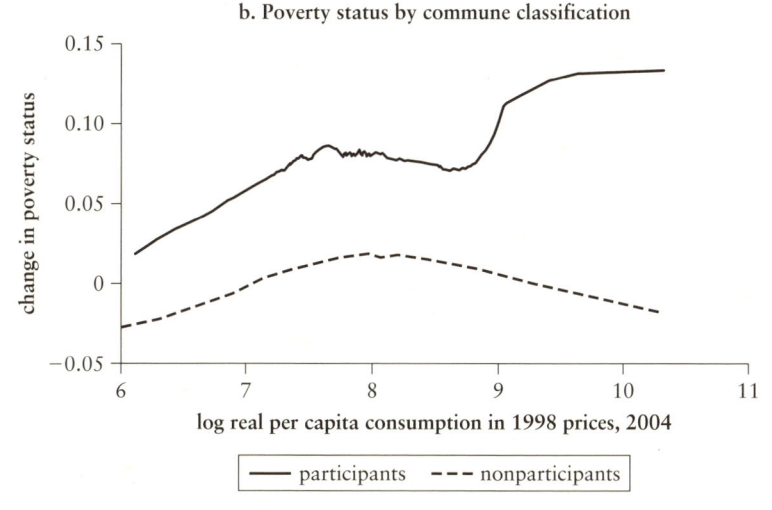

a. Subjective welfare

b. Poverty status by commune classification

——— participants   - - - nonparticipants

Source: 2004 VHLSS.

We are left with what would seem to be the most plausible explanation for the evident underrepresentation of the landless poor among participants in the antipoverty programs—namely, that the official selection processes favor farmers, even when the program would be just as effective for equally poor landless households. This bias is naturally reflected in the information available to potential participants.

Figure 7.8 Impacts of Antipoverty Programs, by Land Status

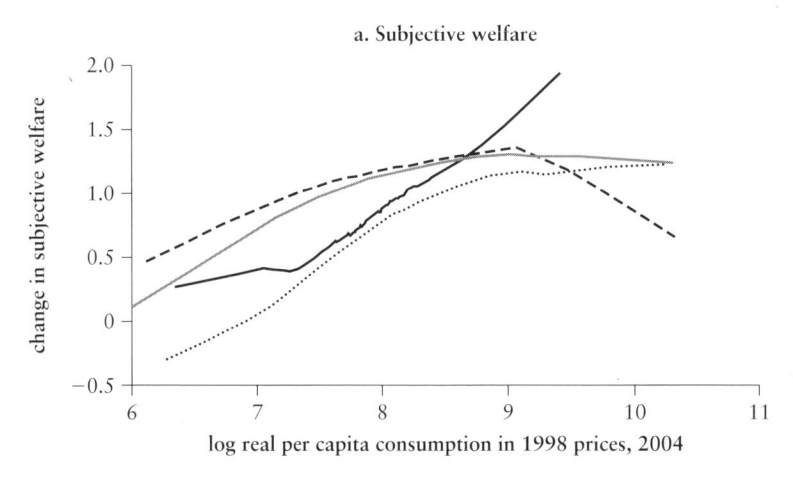

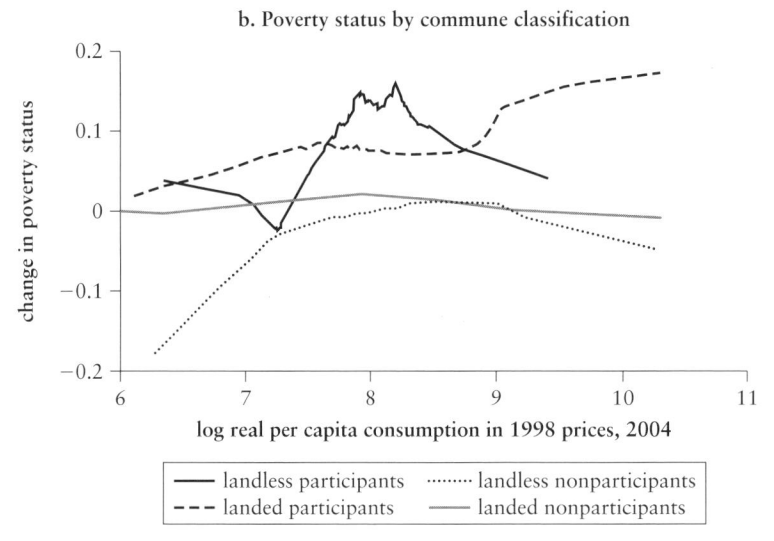

a. Subjective welfare

b. Poverty status by commune classification

——— landless participants ········ landless nonparticipants
- - - landed participants ——— landed nonparticipants

Source: 2004 VHLSS.

Conclusions

Although chapter 6 showed that rising landlessness has been, by and large, a positive factor in overall poverty reduction, it was also argued that there are likely to be some losers among the landless. This chapter indicates that the landless poor are not being well served by the market and the nonmarket institutions that have emerged in Vietnam's agrarian transition. Indeed, it is striking that the group that one would expect to be in greatest need for assisted credit, and for which the social benefits are likely to be largest, appears to be facing the greatest handicap in accessing that help. The weak coverage of the landless poor by these public programs is a concern for efficiency as well as equity, given that this is the group that is likely to be least well served by private credit.

Vietnam's antipoverty programs are not yet well adapted to the changes that have been going on in the rural economy, notably the rise in landlessness. Looking forward, policy makers will need to do better in adapting social policies to the new realities of Vietnam's postreform economy.

Notes

1. For a recent overview of this argument and the evidence, see World Bank (2006).

2. For fuller descriptions of these programs, see MOLISA and UNDP (2004) and V. C. Nguyen (2005).

3. *Difference-in-difference* refers to the fact that the estimator takes two differences, one between the participants and the comparison group at a given date and the other over time.

4. This source of bias in DD estimates of the impacts of antipoverty programs is discussed further with an example (using poor-area development programs in China) in Jalan and Ravallion (1998).

8

Conclusions

The standard policy prescription for transforming a socialist command economy into a market economy is first to privatize productive assets and then to change the law to permit free transactions in those assets. We have put this model to the test in the context of Vietnam's recent agrarian transition. Using the tools of counterfactual analysis, we have tried to assess the welfare impacts of Vietnam's major agrarian reforms. As in any poor country, efficiency implications must naturally have a high weight, since higher aggregate output makes it easier to escape poverty. But the implications for equity are no less important in such a setting. Deeply felt historical sensitivities to extreme inequality continue to resonate in the debates about Vietnam's agrarian transition. Highly inequitable agrarian reforms would have met popular resistance in the short term and potentially derailed future progress against poverty by stifling the economic opportunities of a large share of the population.

The way in which agricultural land was assigned to households in the first stage of the transition—in particular, the extent of inequality in access to land—was clearly crucial to both the equity and the efficiency of the subsequent performance of the economy. However, the heavy reliance on decentralized implementation of policy reforms in developing countries has raised concerns about capture by local elites whose interests are not well served by the central government's aims. We have first tried to see if such concerns are borne out by the evidence on how land-use rights were allocated in practice under the reforms to land laws introduced by Vietnam in 1988. This was arguably the most important step in the country's transition to a market-based agricultural economy after abandoning collective farming. Individual households had to be assigned the use rights for virtually the entire agricultural land area (about 4 million hectares) of a country in which three-quarters of the workforce depended directly on farming. We have used a model of household consumption to assess the distribution of the consumption impacts relative to counterfactual allocations, including the one that would have maximized aggregate consumption, which would have been the competitive-market allocation under our assumptions.

Our results are not consistent with the picture that some commentators have painted of an unjust land allocation stemming from the power of relatively well-off local cadres to capture the process. In terms of the impact on average consumption and consumption inequality, the observed allocation of land in our data was roughly equivalent to giving every household in the commune the same irrigated-land equivalent per person.

However, the observed allocation was significantly different from what one would have expected from an efficient allocation, as would have been achieved by a competitive privatization at market-clearing prices. The consumption-efficient allocation would have put greater weight on education (which raised the marginal utility of land) and given less weight to household size, labor force, minority groups, and male heads of household; with respect to the last aspect, the reform reinforced existing gender inequities at a cost to efficiency. However, we find no evidence that land allocation unduly favored households with government or semigovernment jobs. Indeed, the market allocation would have given higher weight to those attributes, because such households would have put a higher value on land, possibly because of better access to other farm inputs.

This decentralized reform achieved a more equitable outcome than one would have expected from a consumption-efficient allocation, as would have been achieved by free markets. Our results suggest an effort to protect the poorest and reduce overall inequality, at the expense of aggregate consumption. The solution that was arrived at entailed an equity-efficiency trade-off, indicating that both objectives were valued positively.

How then could the many reports of (seemingly widespread) abuse be so wrong? It is important to note that we do find some large individual deviations from the efficient allocation. Looking again at figure 4.1, we see that losses tend to be centered close to zero; however, there are sizable losses for many—particularly at middle- and upper-expenditure levels—and corresponding gains for others. There is ample scope in figure 4.1 for Vietnam's "hot spots" of the late 1980s and 1990s. But our results suggest that one should not generalize about how land-use rights were assigned at the time of decollectivization on the basis of these hot spots.

Combined with our reading of the history of Vietnam around this time, we can suggest two main reasons for the favorable overall welfare outcomes implied by our results. The first factor was the formation of a pro-reform coalition between farmers and reformers in the center. The latter were fully aware of the risks of local capture that were intrinsic to a decentralized administrative allocation of land and other farm inputs at the time of decollectivization. Also important was that the desire for reform was not just coming from the top but also reflected more deeply rooted concerns about the inefficiency of collective agriculture among those who were losing most, namely, the farmers. The reforms followed many years of farmer resistance. Nonetheless, the center was an active player. To help shift the balance of local power at the time of reform, the center (for a limited time) actively promoted farmers' organizations and used the press to channel complaints and expose corruption.

The second reason is that initial conditions at the time of the reform appear to have been favorable to achieving an equitable assignment of land-use rights at modest cost to total consumption. Vietnam's low inequality in the initial distribution of education—stemming from social policies under communism—meant a smaller trade-off than would have been faced otherwise (assuming that it would have been the poor who had relatively less education without those policies). The memory of past—but not too far past—redistributive land reforms prior to the introduction of socialist agriculture (such as the South's Land-to-the-Tiller program introduced in 1970) may have also helped in providing a relatively equitable fallback position in deciding how land should be allocated at the time of decollectivization. Nevertheless, the geographically uneven success of the earlier reforms undoubtedly meant that the fallback position was more equitable in some places than in others.

What happened to the allocation of land after decollectivization? We have compared the administrative allocation to counterfactual allocations calibrated to our 1993 survey data. The stickiness of the administrative allocation (whereby it had to be fixed ex ante) may mean that it became less efficient over time, relative to a market allocation with state-contingent recontracting. Against this conjecture, the new land law introduced in late 1993 attempted to foster free transactions in land-use rights. Some observers believed that this reform would allow a closer approximation to the efficient allocation, but at the expense of equity. The prospect of renewed class differentiation has fueled much debate about the wisdom of Vietnam's efforts at liberalizing land markets. A long-standing view (going back to the 1950s, when the collectives were created) was that even from an equal starting point, the market mechanism would generate excess inequality in the distribution of land and (hence) rural living standards. (This has been a concern in China, too.) Against that view, the same features of the setting that helped ensure an equitable allocation at the time of decollectivization may well have operated to moderate any unequalizing forces generated by the emerging market economy. And the fact that other policy reforms, including more open external policies, were creating new opportunities for diversification and growth is clearly relevant to the outcomes of the agrarian reforms.

What does the evidence we have presented suggest? We find signs that after legal reforms to introduce a market in land-use rights, land was reallocated in a way that attenuated the initial inefficiencies of the administrative assignment of land at the time of decollectivization. Households that started with an inefficiently low (high) amount of annual cropland under the administrative assignment tended to increase (decrease) their holdings over time. The adjustment was not rapid, however; in the aggregate, only one-third of the initial proportionate gap between the actual allocation and the efficient allocation was eliminated within five years.

The market mechanism worked more rapidly for some types of households than for others. At a given land deficit or surplus relative to the efficient allocation, households that started with the least annual cropland under the administrative assignment tended to see the largest increase in holdings during the transition. In other words, the transition process favored the land-poor. The speed of market adjustment was also affected by location and demographic shocks, and the new market-driven process favored households with long-term roots in the community, with male heads, with better education, and with more land in other (nonannual land) categories. We find that these factors were generally cooperant with competitive forces, in that they were jointly positively correlated with land reallocation and the initial land deficits relative to the efficient allocation.

It is of interest to put these findings in the context of the common observation that land markets tend to be thin or even nonexistent in developing rural economies. By this view, landlords derive substantial extra utility from large landholdings, beyond their productive value, and those with small holdings are locked out of the credit market and so cannot acquire extra land. Trades do not then occur. Yet there was clearly a land-market adjustment process going on, although hardly the rapid competitive adjustment process postulated in theories of the ideal market. There may well have been some resistance to selling land on the part of those with too much from an efficiency point of view, although the relatively equitable land allocation achieved at decollectivization did not leave many large landholders. Even in the 1990s, we suspect that the history of suppressing the landlord class back in the 1950s would have made most farmers wary of being seen to hold large, unproductive holdings. Also recall that we find that the speed of adjustment was higher for the land-poor. This does not sit easily with the standard arguments made for why the land market is thin. Credit markets probably did not work well, but even so, it seems that those with too little land could acquire extra land once the market was liberalized. The local state may well have helped make the market work better (or no worse) for the poor; local cadres (particularly in the North) continued to reallocate land in some communes and were undoubtedly reluctant to let a landless proletariat emerge in their villages, though that was still the outcome in a minority of cases. The sources of friction may well lie elsewhere.

Did these efficiency gains from introducing land markets come at a cost to the poor? We have argued that one should not be surprised to find a higher incidence of landlessness among the poor in a transition economy after breaking up the cooperatives and introducing a market in agricultural land. Many farmers will no doubt benefit from the new opportunities to use their limited wealth in other ways, including spending on consumer durables and housing. But there could also be losers from such a reform. Welfare losses can occur for those who were previously landless and receive lower wages than they would without the reform and for those farmers who find that other benefits provided by the cooperatives were retrenched once their role in land allocation was removed. It is an empirical question whether the process of rising landlessness in the wake of such a reform is poverty reducing on balance.

Our analysis of the survey data for Vietnam—spanning a decade after legal reforms to introduce markets in land-use rights—confirms the expected rise in the landlessness rate among the poor, who were responsible for the bulk of the rise in landlessness. Similarly, it was the initially poor who saw the highest pace of urbanization over this period. Even so, the postreform landlessness rate tends to be higher for the rural nonpoor in Vietnam as a whole. By and large, it is not the currently poor who took up the new opportunities for selling (or buying) land and acquiring land titles, but the relatively well off. Access to formal credit appears to have improved overall (and displaced informal credit), though more markedly for better-off households. Among equally poor households, the landless are less likely to receive credit from formal sources, including the targeted antipoverty programs.

We find little sign in these data that rising landlessness has undermined the gains to the poor from the relatively equitable assignment of land-use rights achieved at the time of decollectivization. Even in the South's Mekong Delta—where there are signs of class differentiation—poverty has been falling among the landless, albeit at a lower rate than for those with land. However, we find no sign that this pattern is emerging elsewhere in Vietnam; indeed, as a rule, the landless are enjoying similar (or even higher) rates of poverty reduction as those with land.

On the whole, rising rural landlessness appears to be a positive factor in the process of poverty reduction, as farm households take up new opportunities, notably in the labor market. This does not imply that any policy effort to encourage landlessness will be poverty reducing; it is one thing to give people the opportunity to sell their land to take up more rewarding opportunities but quite another to compel such changes by forcing farmers off their land. Policies should focus instead on making land markets work better for poor people and on complementary efforts to enhance nonfarm opportunities, notably for the landless rural poor, who tend to have less access to credit for financing investments in nonfarm enterprises.

Nonetheless, we find that Vietnam's direct interventions aiming to fight rural poverty through credit targeted to the poor have not yet adjusted to the realities of the economic transition, including rising rural landlessness. Our findings that the selection process for beneficiaries favors those with land among the poor suggest that public social protection is not helping as much as it might in either assisting poor and vulnerable households or underpinning the transition from a largely agriculture-based economy to a more diversified and growing economy. Better performance in reaching the landless poor through public programs must be central in the new challenges that lie ahead for Vietnam's policy makers.

Our final conclusions relate to some broader implications of this study. The first concerns neighboring China. At the start of this book, we noted both the similarities and the dissimilarities between Vietnam's agrarian reforms and those of China. Both countries collectivized their farming, and both came to realize that this system was not performing as expected, at least in peacetime. The cooperatives could ensure equity in rural areas, at least *within* communes, but they did so at too high a price in terms of efficiency. There can be little doubt that collectivized farming was, by and large, poverty increasing. After the breakup of the failed cooperatives and collectives, the pace of transition to a market economy has been greater in Vietnam than in China. In roughly a decade after decollectivization, Vietnam's agricultural output and factor markets had become roughly as free as found in most (long-standing) market economies. Key pro-market and pro-poor reforms, such as abandoning the quota system—whereby farmers had to sell a fixed quota of their output to the government, typically at below-market prices, so as to provide cheap food to typically better-off urban consumers—had happened at about the same time in both countries (in the mid-1990s), even though Vietnam had decollectivized 10 years after China. And China has still not taken Vietnam's radical, but controversial, step of abandoning administrative land allocation in favor of a market-driven process.

It would be naïve to see this difference between the two countries as simply a matter of how "market-friendly" their policy makers have been. There are important historical and contextual factors to consider in understanding the difference in agrarian reform policies. China had a more deeply rooted tradition of collectivized farming and (in contrast to Vietnam) had largely succeeded in displacing the peasant family economy. This alone made for a more rapid transition in Vietnam. There are other differences. Paradoxically, its longer period of collectivized farming probably left rural China with better prospects for successful rural nonfarm development after breaking up the cooperatives. In particular, China's rural industrialization process using township and village enterprises in the latter half of the 1980s and early 1990s would probably not have been possible without the strong farm cooperatives, whose leaders could switch from running farm enterprises to running nonfarm enterprises. With fewer options for localized rural industrialization, the pressure was greater for Vietnam to reform agriculture from within the sector.

While these differences between the two countries had an important influence on the policies chosen, China should not ignore the lessons from the experience of its neighbor. Vietnam's more radical approach of letting voluntary exchange among households play an important role in the evolution of land allocation did not have the dire consequences predicted by those who favored the Chinese model of nonmarket land allocation. The relatively equitable allocation of land achieved at decollectivization was clearly important to this outcome, though that is a feature China shares with Vietnam. Starting from a relatively equitable allocation of land, Vietnam found that introducing free exchange did not end in peril and poverty for the rural population, though (as in any major policy reform) there were both losers and gainers. Also, Vietnam's experience suggests that the efficiency gains do not happen overnight and may well take many years to be realized. But gains can be expected, including gains for the poor.

A second set of broader implications relates to the data and methods for assessing economywide reforms. When handled with care, a comparison group can provide important clues to the counterfactual—namely, the (unobservable) situation in the absence of the program under study. However, the classic tools of impact evaluation are not of much help in this case, given that we cannot observe a comparison group of nonparticipants in Vietnam's agrarian reforms; it is hard to imagine anyone in Vietnam who was not affected by these massive reforms. Yet an essential principle of impact evaluation remains as relevant as ever—namely, that impact should be assessed relative to explicit counterfactual outcomes. We have carried that principle to the task of assessing the equity and efficiency of Vietnam's rural land reforms.

Even when a comparison group is available, assumptions must be made for identifying impacts. (This is true even when the program is randomly assigned.) Without a comparison group, rather different assumptions are called for than are found in classic impact evaluations. We have pointed to the important role that economic theory can play in guiding those assumptions and in interpreting the empirical results. But we have also tried to illustrate how evidence from a wide range of sources can guide the analysis. Those sources include the historical record and qualitative observations from the field. However, we have relied most heavily on quantitative data from household and community surveys, often drawing on multiple surveys, each capturing somewhat different aspects of the reality. We have also emphasized the importance of being aware of the limitations of such data, including the problems of measurement error. The type of "policy evaluation" that emerges from this approach will never be as neat and tidy as the classic randomized experiment (though these are never as neat and tidy in practice as in theory). But it does offer some hope of throwing useful light on very important questions about development policy that might otherwise escape attention.

References

Akram-Lodhi, A. Haroon. 2004. "Are 'Landlords Taking Back the Land'? An Essay on the Agrarian Transition in Vietnam." *European Journal of Development Research* 16(4): 757–89.

———. 2005. "Vietnam's Agriculture: Processes of Rich Peasant Accumulation and Mechanisms of Social Differentiation." *Journal of Agrarian Change* 5(1): 73–116.

ANZDEC Limited. 2000. "Viet Nam Agricultural Sector Report ADB TA 3223-VIE: Phase I Technical Report." Asian Development Bank, Manila, Philippines.

Asian Development Bank. 2004. *The Impact of Land Market Processes on the Poor: Implementing de Soto: Project Report*. Hanoi: Asian Development Bank.

Atkinson, Anthony B. 1970. "On the Measurement of Inequality." *Journal of Economic Theory* 2(3): 244–63.

Axtell, Robert L., Joshua M. Epstein, and H. Peyton Young. 2001. "The Emergence of Classes in a Multi-agent Bargaining Model." In *Social Dynamics*, ed. Steven Durlauf and H. Peyton Young, 191–212. Cambridge, MA: MIT Press.

Bardhan, Pranab, Sam Bowles, and Herb Gintis. 2000. "Wealth Inequality, Wealth Constraints, and Economic Performance." In *Handbook of Income Distribution*, vol. 1, ed. A. B. Atkinson and F. Bourguignon, 541–604. Amsterdam: North-Holland.

Bardhan, Pranab, and Dilip Mookherjee. 2000. "Capture and Governance at Local and National Levels." *American Economic Review, Papers and Proceedings* 90(2): 135–39.

Bardhan, Pranab, and Christopher Udry. 1999. *Development Microeconomics*. Oxford, U.K.: Oxford University Press.

Benjamin, Dwayne, and Loren Brandt. 2002. "Property Rights, Labor Markets, and Efficiency in a Transition Economy: The Case of Rural China." *Canadian Journal of Economics* 35(4): 689–716.

———. 2004. "Agriculture and Income Distribution in Rural Vietnam under Economic Reforms: A Tale of Two Regions." In *Economic Growth, Poverty, and Household Welfare in Vietnam*, ed. Paul Glewwe, Nisha Agrawal, and David Dollar, 133–86. Washington, DC: World Bank.

Beresford, Melanie. 1985. "Household and Collective in Vietnamese Agriculture." *Journal of Contemporary Asia* 15(1): 5–36.

———. 1993. "The Political Economy of Dismantling the Bureaucratic Centralism and Subsidy System in Vietnam." In *Southeast Asia in the 1990s: Authoritarianism, Democracy, and Capitalism*, ed. K. Hewison, R. Robison, and G. Rodan, 213–36. Sydney, Australia: Allen & Unwin.

Bertrand, Marianne, Esther Duflo, and Sendhil Mullainathan. 2004. "How Much Should We Trust Differences-in-Differences Estimates?" *Quarterly Journal of Economics* 119(1): 249–75.

Binswanger, Hans, Klaus Deininger, and Gershon Feder. 1995. "Power, Distortions, Revolt, and Reform in Agricultural and Land Relations." In *Handbook of Development Economics*, vol. 3, ed. Jere Behrman and T. N. Srinivasan, 2659–772. Amsterdam: North-Holland.

Bloch, Peter, and Tommy Oesterberg. 1989. "Land Tenure and Allocation Situation and Policy in Viet Nam." Report to Swedish International Development Agency, Hanoi.

Brandt, Loren. 2006. "Land Access, Land Markets, and Their Distributive Implications in Rural Vietnam." University of Toronto, Toronto, ON.

Brümmer, Bernhard, Thomas Glauben, and Wencong Lu. 2006. "Policy Reform and Productivity Change in Chinese Agriculture: A Distance Function Approach." *Journal of Development Economics* 81(1): 61–79.

Byres, Terry J. 2004. "Neo-Classical Neo-Populism 25 Years On: Déjà Vu and Déjà Passé—Towards a Critique." *Journal of Agrarian Change* 4(1–2): 17–44.

Callison, Charles S. 1983. *Land-to-the-Tiller in the Mekong Delta*. Center for South and Southeast Asia Studies Monograph 23. Berkeley, CA: University of California.

Carter, Colin, and Andrew Estrin. 2001. "Market Reforms versus Structural Reforms in Rural China." *Journal of Comparative Economics* 29(3): 527–41.

Center for Rural Progress. 2005. "The Impact of Market Processes on the Poor: A Study of the Mekong River Delta." Research report for the Asian Development Bank project Making Markets Work Better for the Poor, Center for Rural Progress, Hanoi.

Childress, Malcolm. 2004. "Regional Study on Land Administration, Land Markets, and Collateralized Lending." Rural Development and Natural Resources, East Asia Region, World Bank, Washington, DC.

Cleveland, William S. 1979. "Robust Locally Weighted Regression and Smoothing Scatter Plots." *Journal of the American Statistical Association* 74(368): 829–36.

Dasgupta, Partha, and Debraj Ray. 1986. "Inequality as a Determinant of Malnutrition and Unemployment." *Economic Journal* 96(384): 1011–34.

De Brauw, Alan, and Tomoko Harigaya. 2007. "Seasonal Migration and Improving Living Standards in Vietnam." *American Journal of Agricultural Economics* 89(2): 430–47.

Deaton, Angus. 1985. "Panel Data from Time Series of Cross-Sections." *Journal of Econometrics* 30(1–2): 109–26.

Deininger, Klaus. 2003. *Land Policies for Growth and Poverty Reduction.* Oxford, U.K.: Oxford University Press.

Deininger, Klaus, and Songqing Jin. 2003. "Land Sales and Rental Markets in Transition: Evidence from Rural Vietnam." Policy Research Working Paper 3013, World Bank, Washington, DC.

———. 2006. "Tenure Security and Land-Related Investment: Evidence for Ethiopia." *European Economic Review* 50(5): 1245–77.

de Mauny, Alix, and Thu Hong Vu. 1998. "Landlessness in the Mekong Delta: The Situation in Duyen Hai District, Tra Vinh Province, Vietnam." Report prepared for Oxfam Great Britain, Hanoi.

Do, Quy-Toan, and Lakshmi Iyer. 2007. *Land Titling and Rural Transition in Vietnam.* Washington, DC: World Bank.

Dollar, David, and Paul Glewwe. 1998. "Poverty and Inequality in the Early Reform Period." In *Household Welfare and Vietnam's Transition*, ed. David Dollar, Paul Glewwe, and Jennie Litvack, 29–60. Washington, DC: World Bank.

Dong, Xiao-Yuan. 1996. "Two-Tier Land Tenure System and Sustained Economic Growth in Post-1978 Rural China." *World Development* 24(5): 916–28.

The Economist. 2006. "China: How the Other 800 Million Live." *The Economist*, March 11–17, p. 12.

Falaris, Evangelos. 2003. "The Effect of Survey Attrition in Longitudinal Surveys: Evidence from Peru, Côte d'Ivoire and Vietnam." *Journal of Development Economics* 70(1): 133–57.

Fan, Shenggen. 1991. "Effects of Technological Change and Institutional Reform on Production Growth in Chinese Agriculture." *American Journal of Agricultural Economics* 73(2): 266–75.

Fitzgerald, J., P. Gottschalk, and R. Moffitt. 1998. "An Analysis of Sample Attrition in Panel Data: The Michigan Study of Income Dynamics." *Journal of Human Resources* 33(2): 300–44.

Fleisher, Belton, and Xiaojun Wang. 2004. "Skill Differentials, Return to Schooling, and Market Segmentation in a Transition Economy: The Case of Mainland China." *Journal of Development Economics* 73(1): 315–28.

Foster, James, Joel Greer, and Erik Thorbecke. 1984. "A Class of Decomposable Poverty Measures." *Econometrica* 52(3): 761–65.

Galasso, Emanuela, and Martin Ravallion. 2005. "Decentralized Targeting of an Anti-poverty Program." *Journal of Public Economics* 85(4): 705–27.

Gallup, John Luke. 2004. "The Wage Labor Market and Inequality in Vietnam." In *Economic Growth, Poverty, and Household Welfare in Vietnam*, ed. Paul Glewwe, Nisha Agrawal, and David Dollar, 53–94. Washington, DC: World Bank.

Glewwe, Paul. 2003. "Procedure for Calculating Nominal and Real Expenditures, and Poverty Indicators, for the 2002 Vietnam Household Living Standards Survey (VHLSS)." University of Minnesota, Twin Cities, June 13.

———. 2005. "Mission Report for Trip to Vietnam October 17–25, 2005." University of Minnesota, Twin Cities, November 22.

Glewwe, Paul, Michele Gragnolati, and Hassan Zaman. 2002. "Who Gained from Vietnam's Boom in the 1990s?" *Economic Development and Cultural Change* 50(4): 773–92.

Glewwe, Paul, and Hanan Jacoby. 2004. "Economic Growth and the Demand for Education: Is There a Wealth Effect?" *Journal of Development Economics* 74(1): 33–51.

Griffin, Keith, Azizur Rahman Khan, and Amy Ickowitz. 2002. "Poverty and Distribution of Land." *Journal of Agrarian Change* 2(3): 279–330.

Guo, Xiaolin. 2001. "Land Expropriation and Rural Conflicts in China." *China Quarterly* 166: 422–39.

Hayami, Yujiro. 1994. "Strategies for the Reform of Land Policy Relations." In *Agricultural Policy Analysis for Transition to a Market-Oriented Economy*. FAO Economic and Social Development Paper 123, ed. Randolph Barker, 1–36. Rome: Food and Agriculture Organization.

Ho, Samuel, and George Lin. 2003. "Emerging Land Markets in Rural and Urban China: Policies and Practices." *China Quarterly* 175: 681–707.

Houghton, Jonathan. 2000. "Ten Puzzles and Surprises: Economic and Social Change in Vietnam, 1993–1998." *Comparative Economic Systems* 42(4): 67–88.

Jacoby, Hanan, Guo Li, and Scott Rozelle. 2002. "Hazards of Expropriation: Tenure Insecurity and Investment in Rural China." *American Economic Review* 92(5): 1420–47.

Jalan, Jyotsna, and Martin Ravallion. 1998. "Are There Dynamic Gains from a Poor-Area Development Program?" *Journal of Public Economics* 67(1): 65–86.

Kerkvliet, Benedict J. Tria. 1995. "Village-State Relations in Viet Nam: The Effect of Everyday Politics on De-collectivization." *Journal of Asian Studies* 54(2): 396–418.

———. 2006. "Agricultural Land in Vietnam: Markets Tempered by Family, Community, and Socialist Practices." *Journal of Agrarian Change* 6(3): 285–305.

Kerkvliet, Benedict J. Tria, and Mark Selden. 1998. "Agrarian Transformation in China and Vietnam." *China Journal* 40 (July): 37–58.

Kolko, Gabriel. 1997. *Vietnam: Anatomy of a Peace*. London: Routledge.

Lam, Thi Mai Lan. 2001a. "Land Fragmentation: A Constraint on Vietnamese Agriculture." *Vietnam's Socio-Economic Development* 26 (Summer): 73–80.

———. 2001b. "Landless Households in the Mekong River Delta: A Case Study in Soctrang Province." *Vietnam's Socio-Economic Development* 27 (Autumn): 56–66.

Li, Guo, Scott Rozelle, and Loren Brandt. 1998. "Tenure, Land Rights, and Farmer Investment Incentives in China." *Agricultural Economics* 19(1–2): 63–71.

Lin, Justin. 1992. "Rural Reforms and Agricultural Growth in China." *American Economic Review* 82(1): 34–51.

Luong, Hy V. 1992. *Revolution in the Village: Tradition and Transformation in North Vietnam, 1925–1988.* Honolulu: University of Hawaii Press.

Malarney, Shaun Kingsley. 1997. "Culture, Virtue, and Political Transformation in Contemporary Northern Viet Nam." *Journal of Asian Studies* 56(4): 899–920.

Marsh, Sally, and Gordon MacAulay. 2006. "Land Reform and the Development of Commercial Agriculture in Vietnam: Policy and Issues." University of Sydney, Sydney, Australia.

McGregor, Richard, and James Kynge. 2002. "China Promotes Protection of Private Property." *Financial Times,* November 9–10, p. 1.

Moene, Karl. 1992. "Poverty and Landownership." *American Economic Review* 82(1): 52–64.

MOLISA and UNDP (Ministry of Labour, Invalids, and Social Affairs and United Nations Development Programme). 2004. *Taking Stock, Planning Ahead.* Hanoi: MOLISA and UNDP.

Ngo, Thi Minh. 2004. "Education and Agricultural Productivity." London School of Economics, London.

———. 2005. "Establishing a Quasi-Private Property Rights System: Tenure Security and Investment Incentives in Vietnam." University of Wisconsin—Madison.

Ngo, Vinh Long. 1993. "Reform and Rural Development: Impact on Class, Sectoral, and Regional Inequalities." In *Reinventing Vietnamese Socialism: Doi Moi in Comparative Perspective*, ed. William Turley and Mark Selden, 165–207. Boulder, CO: Westview Press.

Nguyen, Nga Nguyet. 2004. "Trends in the Education Sector." In *Economic Growth, Poverty, and Household Welfare in Vietnam*, ed. Paul Glewwe, Nisha Agrawal, and David Dollar, 425–66. Washington, DC: World Bank.

Nguyen, Thu Sa. 1990. "Van De Ruong Dat o Dong Bang Song Cuu Long" [The land issue in the Mekong Delta]. In *Mien Nam trong Su Nghiep Doi Moi cua ca Nuoc*, 141–54. TP Ho Chi Minh, Vietnam: Nxb Khoa Hoc Xa Hoi.

Nguyen, Van Suu. 2004. "The Politics of Land: Inequality in Land Access and Local Conflicts in the Red River Delta since De-collectivization." In *Social Inequality in Vietnam and the Challenges to Reform*, ed. Philip Taylor, 270–96. Institute of Singapore: Southeast Asian Studies.

Nguyen, Van Tiem. 1992. "Agrarian Policy in Agriculture of Viet Nam since the August Revolution 1945." Ministry of Agriculture and Food Industry, Hanoi.

Nguyen, Viet Cuong. 2005. "Impact of Micro-Credit on the Poor and Vulnerable in Vietnam." National Economics University, Hanoi.

Pingali, Prabhu, and Vo-Tong Xuan. 1992. "Viet Nam: Decollectivization and Rice Productivity Growth." *Economic Development and Cultural Change* 40(4): 697–718.

Ravallion, Martin. 1994. *Poverty Comparisons*. Fundamentals of Pure and Applied Economics, vol. 56. Chur, Switzerland: Harwood Academic Publishers.

———. 1997. "Can High-Inequality Developing Countries Escape Absolute Poverty?" *Economics Letters* 56(1): 51–57.

———. 2008. "Evaluating Anti-Poverty Programs." In *Handbook of Development Economics*, vol. 4, ed. T. Paul Schultz and John Strauss. Amsterdam: North-Holland.

Ravallion, Martin, and Shaohua Chen. 2007. "China's (Uneven) Progress against Poverty." *Journal of Development Economics* 82(1): 1–42.

Ravallion, Martin, and Michael Lokshin. 2002. "Self-Rated Economic Welfare in Russia." *European Economic Review* 46(8): 1453–73.

Ravallion, Martin, and Dominique van de Walle. 2004. "Breaking up the Collective Farms: Welfare Outcomes of Vietnam's Massive Land Privatization." *Economics of Transition* 12(2): 201–36.

———. 2006. "Land Reallocation in an Agrarian Transition." *Economic Journal* 116(514): 924–42.

———. 2008. "Does Rising Landlessness Signal Success or Failure for Vietnam's Agrarian Transition." *Journal of Development Economics* 85.

Rozelle, Scott, and Johan Swinnen. 2004. "Success and Failure of Reform: Insights from the Transition of Agriculture." *Journal of Economic Literature* 42(2): 404–56.

Sakata, Shozo. 2006. "Changing Roles of Mass Organizations in Poverty Reduction in Vietnam." In *Actors for Poverty Reduction in Vietnam*, ed. Vu Tuan Anh and Shozo Sakata, 49–79. Chibe, Japan: Institute of Developing Economies, Japan External Trade Organization.

Scott, Steffanie. 1999. "Gender and Land in Policy and Practice: Analyzing Complexity in Inter- and Intra-Household Relations in Vietnam." In *Localized Poverty Reduction in Vietnam: Improving the Enabling Environment for Livelihood Enhancement in Rural Areas*, ed. Geoffrey B. Hainsworth, 155–77. Vancouver, BC: Center for South-East Asia Research, University of British Columbia.

Selden, Mark. 1993. "Agrarian Development Strategies in China and Vietnam." In *Reinventing Vietnamese Socialism: Doi Moi in Comparative Perspective*, ed. William Turley and Mark Selden, 209–53. Boulder, CO: Westview Press.

Sikor, Thomas, and Dao Minh Truong. 2000. "Sticky Rice, Collective Fields: Community-Based Development among the Black Thai." Center for National Resources and Environmental Studies, Agricultural Publishing House, Hanoi.

Smith, William. 1997. "Land and the Poor: A Survey of Land Use Rights in Ha Tinh and Son La Provinces." ActionAid, Hanoi.

Smith, William, and Tran Thanh Binh. 1994. "The Impact of the 1993 Land Law on Rural Households in the Mai Don District of Son La Province." ActionAid, Hanoi.

St John, Ronald B. 1980. "Marxist-Leninist Theory and Organization in South Vietnam." *Asian Survey* 20(8): 812–28.

Swinnen, Johan, and Scott Rozelle. 2006. *From Marx and Mao to the Market: The Economics and Politics of Agricultural Transition.* Oxford, U.K.: Oxford University Press.

Tanaka, Tomomi. 2001. "Evaluating the Land Distribution under the Renovation (Doi Moi) Policy in the Red River Delta, Vietnam." East-West Center, University of Hawaii, Manoa.

Taylor, Philip. 2004. "Redressing Disadvantage or Re-arranging Inequality? Development Interventions and Local Responses in the Mekong Delta." In *Social Inequality in Vietnam and the Challenges to Reform*, ed. Philip Taylor, 236–69. Singapore: Institute of Southeast Asian Studies.

Tran, Thi Que. 1997. *Agricultural Reform in Vietnam.* Singapore: Institute of Southeast Asian Studies.

———. 2001. "Land Reform and Women's Property Rights in Vietnam." Center for Gender, Environment and Sustainable Development, Hanoi, Vietnam.

———. 2005. "Annex: Land and Agricultural Land Management in Vietnam." In *Impact of Socio-economic Changes on the Livelihoods of People Living in Poverty in Vietnam*, ed. Ha Huy Thanh and Shozo Sakata, 175–96. Chibe, Japan: Japan External Trade Organization.

Tran, Thi Van Anh. 1999. "Women and Rural Land in Vietnam." In *Women's Rights to House and Land: China, Laos, and Vietnam*, ed. Irene Tinker and Gale Summerfield, 95–114. Boulder, CO: Lynne Rienner.

van de Walle, Dominique. 1998. "Infrastructure and Poverty in Vietnam." In *Household Welfare and Vietnam's Transition*, ed. David Dollar, Paul Glewwe, and Jennie Litvack, 99–136. Washington, DC: World Bank.

———. 2003. "Are Returns to Investment Lower for the Poor? Human and Physical Capital Interactions in Rural Vietnam." *Review of Development Economics* 7(4): 636–53.

———. 2004. "The Static and Dynamic Incidence of Vietnam's Public Safety Net." In *Economic Growth, Poverty, and Household Welfare in Vietnam*, ed. P. Glewwe, N. Agrawal, and D. Dollar, 189–228. Washington, DC: World Bank.

van de Walle, Dominique, and Dorothyjean Cratty. 2004. "Is the Emerging Non-Farm Market Economy the Route Out of Poverty in Vietnam?" *Economics of Transition* 12(2): 237–74.

van de Walle, Dominique, and Dileni Gunewardena. 2001. "Sources of Ethnic Inequality in Vietnam." *Journal of Development Economics* 65(1): 177–207.

Van Luong, Hy, and Jonathan Unger. 1998. "Wealth, Power, and Poverty in the Transition to Market Economies: The Process of Socio-Economic Differentiation in Rural China and Northern Vietnam." *China Journal* 40 (July): 61–93.

Verbeek, Marno, and Theo Nijman. 1992. "Can Cohort Data Be Treated as Genuine Panel Data?" *Empirical Economics* 17(1): 9–23.

Vietnam Communist Party. 1988. "Resolution of the Politburo: On Agricultural Economic Management Reforms." Vietnam Communist Party, Central Standing Committee, Hanoi, Vietnam.

Vu, Tuan Anh. 2005. "Implementation of Poverty Reduction Policies in Ethnic Minority Regions in Vietnam: Evidence from CBMS." Paper presented at the Fourth Poverty and Economic Policy Research Meeting, Colombo, Sri Lanka, June 13–17.

Vuong, Xuan Tinh. 2003. "Reviving Community Management of Land in Central Highland Villages of Vietnam: An Old Model in a New Context." Paper presented at the conference Politics of the Commons: Articulating Development and Strengthening Local Practices, Chiang Mai, Thailand, July 11–14.

Wiegersma, Nancy. 1988. *Vietnam: Peasant Land, Peasant Revolution*. London: Macmillan.

Wiens, Thomas B. 1998. "Agriculture and Rural Poverty in Vietnam." In *Household Welfare and Vietnam's Transition*, ed. David Dollar, Paul Glewwe, and Jennie Litvack, 61–98. Washington, DC: World Bank.

Wooldridge, Jeffrey. 2002. *Econometric Analysis of Cross-Section and Panel Data*. Cambridge, MA: MIT Press.

World Bank. 1995. "Viet Nam Living Standards Survey (VLSS), 1992–93: Basic Information." Research Development Group, World Bank, Washington, DC.

———. 2000. "Viet Nam Living Standards Survey (VLSS), 1997–98: Basic Information." Development Research Group, World Bank, Washington, DC.

———. 2002. "Land Use Rights and Gender Equality in Vietnam." Promising Approaches to Engendering Development Note 1, World Bank, Washington, DC.

———. 2004. "Vietnam Development Report 2004: Poverty." Joint Donor Report to the Vietnam Consultative Group Meeting, December 2–3, 2003, Vietnam Development Information Center, Hanoi.

———. 2005. *Vietnam Development Report 2006: Business*. Hanoi: World Bank.

———. 2006. *World Development Report: Equity and Development*. New York: Oxford University Press for the World Bank.

Wurfel, David. 1993. "Doi Moi in Comparative Perspective." In *Reinventing Vietnamese Socialism: Doi Moi in Comparative Perspective*, ed. William Turley and Mark Selden, 19–52. Boulder, CO: Westview Press.

Yardley, Jim. 2006. "China Rules Out Revaluing in 2006: Wen Addresses Illegal Land Seizures, Rural Poverty, and Internet Censorship." *International Herald Tribune*, March 15, p. 1.

Yeh, Anthony Gar-On, and Xia Li. 1999. "Economic Development and Agricultural Land Loss in the Pearl River Delta, China." *Habitat International* 23(3): 373–90.

Zhou, Jian-Ming. 1998. "Is Nominal Public but De Facto Private Land Ownership Appropriate? A Comparative Study among Cambodia, Laos, Vietnam, Japan, Taiwan Province of China, South Korea, China, Myanmar, and North Korea." Working Paper ECO 98/12, European University Institute, San Domenico, Italy. http://www.iue.it/ECO/WP-Texts/98_12.html.

———. 2001. *Sustainable Development in Asia, America, and Europe with Global Applications: A New Approach to Land Ownership*. Cheltenham, U.K.: Edward Elgar.

Index

Information presented in boxes, figures, notes, and tables is indicated by b, f, n, and t, respectively.

absolute poverty, 7, 10, 12n13
administrative reallocations by communes, 102
age cohorts, pseudo-panel based on, 59–60, 70–71t, 140–42, 141f, 143f
agricultural productivity
  decollectivization leading to increase in, 3–5
  education and, 89, 156n5
  land-use certificates (LUCs) and, 103
  quotas for, 3, 16
  size of holdings and, 21
  wealth and, 124, 152
Akram-Lodhi, A. Haroon, 4, 11n5, 27, 32–33
allocated land
  defined, 72n3
  irrigated land equivalents, calculating, 66–67, 68–69t
  as land type, 41, 42, 52
allocation of land. *See* land reform in Vietnam
antipoverty programs
  conclusions regarding, 172–73, 180
  DD estimates of effectiveness of programs, 169–70, 173n3–4
  ethnic minorities, 29
  ITB affecting, 167, 168
  knowledge about programs affecting, 167, 169f
  landless poor less likely to receive credit, 162–67, 165–66f
  mechanics of, 162–64
  mobility of landless, 168, 169
  noncredit, 164–65, 168
  participation in, 10, 159
  reasons for low participation rate of landless poor, 167–71, 169f, 171–72f
  regional differences in, 164–67, 166f
  selection processes favoring farmers, 167–69, 171
Asian Development Bank, 36n12
Atkinson, Anthony B., 55
attrition of households between surveys, 48, 118–19
auctioned land, as land type, 42, 102

bald hill land. *See* swidden land
Bangladesh, 164
Bank for the Poor (now Vietnam Bank for Social Policies), 163
Bardhan, Pranab, 11n9, 21, 36
Benjamin, Dwayne, 11n12, 31, 33, 35n9
Beresford, Melanie, 18–19
Binh Thuan province, 64
Brandt, Loren, 5, 11n12, 31, 33, 34, 35n9, 61–62, 101–02
Byres, Terry, 12n15

193

cadres, local. *See* local cadres
Cambodia, 15, 27, 36*n*11
capital response to land
  reallocation, 102–03
CBGs (credit-borrowing
  groups), 164
Center for Rural Progress, 25, 33
Central Highlands, 38
  ethnic conflicts in, 28
  landlessness in, 57*t*, 139*t*
  lowlands, marked differences
    from, 36*n*15
  in VLSS 1992/93, 41
China
  dissatisfaction with
    collectivization, 14, 15
  family farming in, 11*n*6
  food aid to Vietnam, end of, 15
  household responsibility
    system, 3
  implications of Vietnamese
    situation for, 180–81
  inequality in, 36*n*16, 156*n*7, 177
  land allocation and reallocation
    policies in, 5
  land market, absence of, 5, 6
  land policy debates in, 27, 181
  land-use rights, 6
  market economy, effects of
    transition to, 1–4
  poor-area development programs
    in, 173*n*4
Chinese ethnic minority in
  Vietnam, 36*n*11, 43, 52
Cleveland, William S., 64
collectivization of land, 5,
  13–16
communes, administrative
  reallocations by, 102
Communist Party members,
  surveys not identifying, 44
community-assessed welfare in
  2004 VHLSS survey, 62–64, 63*f*,
  169–70, 171–72*f*
consumption
  frequency distributions of,
    39, 40*f*
  incidence of land transactions
    and levels of, 131–33,
    133–35*f*
  landlessness and
    incidence of land transactions,
      131–33, 133–35*f*
    incidence of landlessness,
      126–27, 126*f*
  welfare impact of initial land
    reform
    consumption-efficient
      allocation, 77–78, 87–88*t*,
      90, 92, 97
    levels of consumption relative
      to land allocation, 90–97,
      91*t*, 93–94*f*, 96*t*
    regressions for consumption
      and allocated land, 81–90,
      82–85*t*, 87–88*t*
consumption-efficient allocation
  reallocation of land after
    introduction of land market,
    104, 107
  welfare impact of initial land
    reform, 77–78, 87–88*t*, 90,
    92, 97
Contract 100, 16, 61
contract farming, 11*n*5, 15
contract land, as land type, 52
counterfactual, 5, 7, 8, 75–78, 91*t*,
  96*t*, 97–99, 113*t*, 175–77,
  181–82
credit for landless poor, 10,
  159–73. *See also* antipoverty
  programs
  formal vs. informal credit,
    161, 162*f*
  perceived credit constraints,
    159–61, 160*f*
  SIRRV data, 160
credit-borrowing groups
  (CBGs), 164
credit constraints, 159–61, 160*f*

Dasgupta, Partha, 30
data and summary statistics,
  2–3, 37–74

INDEX

age cohorts, pseudo-panel based on, 59–60, 70–71t, 140–42, 141f, 143f
consumption, frequency distributions of, 39, 40f
detailed land module in 2004 survey, use of, 60–62
household surveys, 37–39
  attrition of households between, 48, 118–19
  benefits of careful analysis of, ix
  SIRRV (1997–2003), 64–66
  VHLSS, 2002 and 2004. *See* Vietnam Household Living Standards Survey
  VLSS, 1992/93 and 1997/98. *See* Vietnam Living Standards Survey
implications of study regarding, 181–82
initial allocation, 39–44, 45–47t
irrigated land equivalents, calculating, 66–67, 68–69t
landlessness. *See under* landlessness in Vietnam
local cadres, identification of, 44
poverty, measures of, 39
for reallocation of land after introduction of land market, 48–52, 49–51t
types of land, 41–42, 52, 53
for welfare impacts of initial land reform, 39–44
DD (difference-in-difference) estimates of impact of antipoverty programs, 169–70, 173n3–4
De Brauw, Alan, 48
Deaton, Angus, 158
decollectivization and privatization process, 2–5, 16–20
decomposition, of change in landlessness, 137–40, 139t, 155–56t

Deininger, Klaus, x, 11n8, 36n10, 120n2, 120n4, 158n27
difference-in-difference (DD) estimates of impact of antipoverty programs, 169–70, 173n3–4
disabled persons and veterans, social protection of, 17–18, 20, 43–44, 89
Doi Moi (renovation) program, 2, 16
Dong, Xiao-Yuan, 27, 30

education, effects of, 33
  agricultural productivity and, 89, 156n5
  landlessness and education levels, 125, 156–57n7
  reallocation of land and, 117, 119
  welfare impacts of initial land reform and, 86
equity/inequity in land allocation
  extremes in, 3
  issues regarding, 4–5, 9–10, 175–76
  landlessness. *See* landlessness in Vietnam
  levels of consumption, inequality, and poverty relative to land allocation, 90–97, 91t, 93–94f, 96t
  policy debates regarding, 23–30
  reallocation addressing inefficiencies. *See* reallocation of land after introduction of land market
  trade-offs, 19–20
ethnic minorities
  landlessness and poverty amongst, 55, 127–29, 129f
  policy concerns regarding, 28–29
  reallocation of land, 117
evaluation, impact, 99n1, 182

Falaris, Evangelos, 48
Fan, Shenggen, 3
Farmer's Union, 164
farming productivity
   decollectivization leading to increase in, 4–5
   quotas for, 3, 16
French War of Independence, 2, 13–14

gainers and losers, from reform, 10, 103–04, 125, 145, 153–54
gender issues, 28, 29, 117, 119
Glewwe, Paul, x, 39, 92, 156n3
government service
   persons in. *See* local cadres
   surveys identifying, 44
Grameen Bank, 164
Griffin, Keith, 11n6, 12n14
Guo, Xiaolin, 27

Ha Giang province, 167
Ha Tinh province, 22
Harigaya, Tomoko, 48
Hayami, Yujiro, 25, 31, 36n13, 43, 72n6
head-count index as poverty measure, 39
HEPR (Hunger Eradication and Poverty Reduction) Program, 62, 162–63, 165–66f
historical process of land reform, 2–5, 13–36
   cooperatives in North, 13–15
   decollectivization and privatization process, 2–5, 16–20
   French War of Independence and Viet Minh, 2, 13–14
   land market, creation of, 5–6, 20–23
   local cadres
      decollectivization, role in, 4, 16–19
      land market, control of, 21–22
   LTT program, 14, 31, 35n1, 168
   NLF, 13–14, 61
   policy debates, 23–30
   post-war attempts to collectivize South, 14
   precollectivization allocations, effect of, 19
   regional differences, 30–34
   unpopularity of collectives by 1980s, 14–16
   U.S. in Vietnam, 13–14
Ho Chi Minh City, 16, 18, 31
Houghton, Jonathan, 26, 31, 55
household surveys. *See under* data and summary statistics
Hunger Eradication and Poverty Reduction (HEPR) Program, 62, 162–63, 165–66f

Ickowitz, Amy, 11n6, 12n14
indicator-targeting bias (ITB), 167, 168
Indonesia, 36n11
inefficiencies in initial allocation. *See under* reallocation of land after introduction of land market
inequity. *See* equity/inequity in land allocation
initial land allocation, welfare impacts of. *See* welfare impacts of initial land reform
investment response to land reallocation, 102–03
irrigated land equivalents, calculating, 66–67, 68–69t
ITB (indicator-targeting bias), 167, 168

Jacoby, Hanan, 5, 156n3

Kerkvliet, Benedict J. Tria, 11n4, 11n6, 14, 19, 23, 25, 28
Khan, Azizur, 11n6, 12n14
Kinh ethnic majority, 28, 43, 52
Kolko, Gabriel, 17
Kon Tum province, 64

labor market, 33, 102–03, 123, 136–37, 137–38f, 151–54
Lam, Thi Mai Lan, 19, 26, 81

Land Law (1988), 2, 8, 9
  data and summary statistics, 43, 62
  historical context, 16–20, 22, 25
Land Law (1993), 5, 9
  data and summary statistics, 38, 43, 52
  historical context, 20, 22, 25, 29, 35*n*5
  landlessness and, 134
  reallocation of land and, 101, 102
land market
  China, absence in, 5, 6
  creation of, 5–6, 9, 10, 20–23
  landlessness resulting from. *See* landlessness in Vietnam
  occupational choice and, 122–24, 149–54
  policy debates regarding, 25–30
  reallocation of land following. *See* reallocation of land after introduction of land market
  reform, 26, 29, 121, 125, 159
  rentals, 101–02, 120*n*1
  transaction costs, 22–23
land quality. *See* quality of land
land reform in Vietnam, ix, 1–7
  analyzing effects of, ix, 7
  antipoverty programs. *See* antipoverty programs
  conclusions regarding, 175–82
  data and statistics on. *See* data and summary statistics
  historical process of. *See* historical process of land reform
  landlessness. *See* landlessness in Vietnam
  overall favorable outcomes of, 176–77
  policy issues and debates, 16, 23–30
  regional differences in, 30–34, 38, 147. *See also* Central Highlands; Mekong Delta; North; North Central Coast; Northern Uplands; Red River Delta; South; South Central Coast; Southeast
  welfare impacts of. *See* welfare impacts of initial land reform
Land-to-the-Tiller (LTT) program, 14, 31, 35*n*1, 168, 177
land-use certificates (LUCs)
  agricultural productivity and, 103
  data and summary statistics, 60
  historical context, 20, 22, 29
  landlessness and, 134–36, 135–36*f*
  reallocation of land and, 103
landlessness in Vietnam, 10, 121–58
  age cohorts, pseudo-panel based on, 59–60, 70–71*t*, 140–42, 141*f*, 143*f*
  consumption levels
    incidence of land transactions and, 131–33, 133–35*f*
    incidence of landlessness and, 126–27, 126*f*
  credit access and. *See* credit for landless poor
  data and summary statistics
    age cohorts, pseudo-panel based on, 59–60, 70–71*t*
    consumption, frequency distributions of, 39, 40*f*
    detailed land module in 2004 survey, use of, 60–62
    poverty and, 53–59, 54*t*, 56–57*t*, 58*f*
    SIRRV data, 131–34, 146*f*
  decomposition of change in, 137–40, 139*t*, 155–56*t*
  definition of, 53
  education levels and, 125, 156–57*n*7
  ethnic minorities, 127–29, 129*f*
  initial land deficit, relationship to, 117–18, 118*t*
  labor market and, 123, 136–37, 137*f*

landlessness in Vietnam (*Continued*)
  Lorenz curves for annual and perennial cropland showing increase in inequality of landholding, 55, 58*f*
  LUCs, evidence of, 134–36, 135–36*f*
  mobile landless, 38–39, 168, 169
  model for, 122–24, 149–55, 152*f*
  noncultivating households compared, 127, 128*f*
  policy debates regarding, 26–28
  poverty, relationship to, 29–30
    antipoverty programs. *See* antipoverty programs
    community- and self-assessed welfare segments of 2004 survey, 62–64, 63*f*, 65*f*, 169–70, 171–72*f*
    conclusions regarding, 148–49, 179–80
    credit access. *See* credit for landless poor
    data and summary statistics, 53–59, 54*t*, 56–57*t*, 58*f*
    different interpretations of, 125–26
    model-based propositions, 124–25
    PILE hypothesis, doubtfulness of, 142–48, 148*t*
    regional differences in, 129, 130*f*, 137, 138*f*, 139–40, 139*t*, 144, 148. *See also under* specific regions
    size of landholding and living standards, relationship between, 120–31, 131*f*
    types of land, 53
    unemployment and, 55–58
    urbanization and, 140–42, 142–43*f*
Lao Cai province, 64
Lao People's Democratic Republic, 27, 36*n*11
Li, Guo, 5
Li, Xia, 27
Lin, Justin, 3

living standards, impact on. *See* welfare impacts of initial land reform
Living Standards Measurement Study (LSMS), household surveys sponsored by, 38
local cadres
  decollectivization, role in, 4, 16–19
  farm capital stock, distribution of, 44
  identification in household surveys, 44
  land market, control of, 21–22
  reallocation of land and, 117, 119
  welfare impacts of initial land reform and status as, 86, 89
Lokshin, Michael, 63
long-term-use land, as land type, 41, 42, 52
Lorenz curves for agricultural landholdings, 55, 58*f*
LSMS (Living Standards Measurement Study), household surveys sponsored by, 38
LTT (Land-to-the-Tiller) program, 14, 31, 35*n*1, 168, 177
LUCs. *See* land-use certificates

Malarney, Shaun Kingsley, 4
market economy
  effects of transition to, ix, 1–7
  redistributive land reforms in. *See* land reform in Vietnam
mass organizations, credit provided by, 163–64
Mekong Delta, 38
  antipoverty program participation in, 164–67, 166*f*, 168
  collectivization, early resistance to, 31
  detailed land module in 2004 survey, interpretation of, 61–62
  education in, 33
  heterogeneity of land reform impacts in, 33

INDEX 199

irrigated land equivalents,
  calculating, 67, 68–69t
land inequality in, 36n17
land market in, 25
landlessness in, 26, 55, 57t,
  63–64, 64t, 65f, 129, 130f,
  137, 138f, 139t, 140, 144,
  148, 149
reallocation of land in, 102,
  113t, 114–16t, 117
safety nets, absence of, 32
unemployment in, 58
in VLSS 1992/93, 41, 44, 45–47t
in VLSS 1997/98, 49–51t
wage labor market in, 137, 138f
welfare impacts of initial land
  reform in, 82–85t, 86, 87–88t,
  89, 90, 91t, 92, 94f, 95, 96t
military veterans and disabled,
  social protection of, 17–18, 20,
  43–44, 89
mobile landless, 38–39, 168, 169
Moene, Karl, 30

National Liberation Front (NLF),
  13–14, 61
newly cleared land. See swidden
  land
Nghe An province, 64
Ngo, Thi Minh, 21, 35, 156n5
Ngo, Vinh Long, 16, 17, 31, 43,
  44, 99n3
NLF (National Liberation Front),
  13–14, 61
noncultivating households compared
  to landless households, 127, 128f
nongovernmental organizations
  (NGOs), 22, 32, 62
North
  cooperatives introduced into,
    13–15
  differences between South and,
    30–34, 147
  landlessness and poverty in, 147
North Central Coast, 38
  irrigated land equivalents,
    calculating, 67, 68–69t
  landlessness in, 56t, 139t

reallocation of land in, 113t,
  114–16t, 117, 120n9
in VLSS 1992/93, 41, 45–47t
welfare impacts of initial land
  reform in, 82–85t, 86, 87–88t,
  90, 91t, 94f, 96t
Northern Uplands, 38
antipoverty program
  participation in, 167
irrigated land equivalents,
  calculating, 67, 68–69t
landlessness in, 56t, 139t
local cadres in, 22
lowlands, marked differences
  from, 36n15
reallocation of land in, 113t,
  114–16t, 117
in VLSS 1992/93, 45–47t, 41
welfare impacts of initial land
  reform in, 82–85t, 86, 87–88t,
  89, 90, 91t, 93f, 96t

occupational choice, 122–24,
  149–54
Oxfam, 32

Philippines, 36n11
PILE (poverty-increasing
  landlessness effect) hypothesis,
  142–48, 148t
Pingali, Prabhu, 14, 17, 19, 31,
  99n3
policy issues and debates, 16, 23–30
poverty
  antipoverty programs. See
    antipoverty programs
  community- and self-assessed
    welfare segments of 2004
    VHLSS, 62–64, 63f, 65f,
    169–70, 171–72f
  credit. See credit for landless
    poor
  equity issues. See equity/inequity
    in land allocation
  gap, 39, 91t, 92, 95, 96t
  landlessness, relationship to.
    See under landlessness in
    Vietnam

poverty (*Continued*)
   levels of consumption, inequality, and poverty relative to land allocation, 90–97, 91*t*, 93–94*f*, 96*t*
   measures of, 39
   quality of land and, 131, 132*f*
   urbanization and, 142
   wage labor and, 123, 136–37, 137–38*f*
   welfare issues. *See* welfare impacts of initial land reform
private land, as land type, 42–43
privatization and decollectivization process, 2–5
productivity of farming. *See* agricultural productivity
Program 135, 62, 162–63, 165–66*f*

quality of land
   fragmentation of holdings to ensure equitable distribution in, 20
   poverty and, 131, 132*f*
   problems in assessing, 42
   VHLSS 2004 detailed land module on, 60
   welfare impacts of initial land reform and, 80–81, 90

Ravallion, Martin, ix, x, 1, 11n3, 11*n*7, 12*n*13, 63, 99, 173
Ray, Debraj, 30
reallocation of land after introduction of land market, 9, 101–20
   administrative reallocations by communes, 102
   capital and labor market responses to, 102–03
   conclusions regarding, 178–79
   consumption-efficient allocation, 104, 107
   data and summary statistics used for (VLSS 1997/98), 48–52, 49–51*t*, 102, 103
   education, effects of, 117, 119
   to ethnic minorities, 9, 101–20
   gender issues in, 117, 119
   inefficiencies in initial allocation
      characterization of, 103–05
      landlessness and, 117–18, 118*t*
      as offset to, 103, 119
      proportionate changes relative to, 109–11*f*, 109–12, 112*t*
   local cadres in family, effect of, 117, 119
   model for assessing, 105–08
   regional differences in. *See under* specific regions
   rentals, 101–02
   results obtained, 108–19
      bias, sources of, 118–19
      controls to partial adjustment coefficients, adding, 112–13, 113*t*
      for most comprehensive model, 113–17, 114–16*t*
      proportionate changes relative to initial inefficiencies, 109–11*f*, 109–12, 112*t*
   types of land, 52
Red River Delta, 38
   education in, 36*n*22
   irrigated land equivalents, calculating, 67, 68–69*t*
   land ceilings in, 35*n*6
   land inequality in, 36*n*17
   landlessness in, 26, 56*t*, 129, 130*f*, 137, 138*f*, 139*t*
   reallocation of land in, 113*t*, 114–16*t*
   in VLSS 1992/93, 41, 45–47*t*
   wage labor market in, 137, 138*f*
   welfare impacts of initial land reform in, 82–85*t*, 86, 87–88*t*, 89, 90, 91*t*, 93*f*, 96*t*
redistributive land reforms. *See* land reform in Vietnam
regional differences, 30–34, 38, 147. *See also* Central Highlands; Mekong Delta; North; North Central Coast; Northern Uplands; Red River Delta; South; South Central Coast; Southeast
   antipoverty program participation, 164–67, 166*f*

in landlessness, 129, 130f, 137, 138f, 139–40, 139t, 144, 148
rental market, 101–02, 127
Resolution 10, 16, 31, 35n5, 43
Rozelle, Scott, 5, 11n1, 15

safety nets for crisis management, presence or absence of, 32
Sakata, Shozo, 167
schooling. *See* education, effects of
Scott, Steffanie, 89
Selden, Mark, 11n6, 17, 18, 25, 28
self-assessed welfare, 62–64, 65f, 169–70, 171–72f
sharecropped or rented land, as land type, 42
Sikor, Thomas, 17, 22
SIRRV (Survey of Impacts of Rural Roads in Vietnam, 1997–2003), 64–66, 131–34, 146f, 160
size of landholding and living standards, relationship between, 120–31, 131f
slash and burn agriculture. *See* swidden land
Smith, William, x, 22–23, 27, 29, 32, 35n7
sneaky contracts, 15
social protection of veterans and disabled, 17–18, 20, 43–44, 89
SOEs (state-owned enterprises), persons working in. *See* local cadres
Son La province, 22, 32
South
differences between North and, 30–34, 147
landlessness and poverty in, 147
LTT program in, 14, 31, 35n1, 168, 177
post-war attempts to collectivize, 14
South Central Coast, 38
irrigated land equivalents, calculating, 67, 68–69t
landlessness in, 56t, 139t
reallocation of land in, 113t, 114–16t, 117
in VLSS 1992/93, 41, 45–47t
welfare impacts of initial land reform in, 82–85t, 86, 87–88t, 89, 90, 91t, 92, 94f, 95, 96t, 99n33
Southeast, 38
landlessness in, 55, 56–57t, 57t, 139t, 140
market economy, openness to, 31
in VLSS 1992/93, 41
squared poverty gap index, 39
state-owned enterprises (SOEs), persons working in. *See* local cadres
subjective (self-assessed) welfare, 62–64, 65f, 169–70, 171–72f
summary statistics. *See* data and summary statistics
Survey of Impacts of Rural Roads in Vietnam, 1997–2003 (SIRRV), 64–66, 131–34, 146f, 160
swidden land
in data and summary statistics, 41, 43, 47t, 51t, 52, 53, 67
defined, 72n2
reallocation of land after establishment of land market and cultivation of, 116t
welfare impacts of initial land reform and cultivation of, 83t, 85t, 88t, 89
Swinnen, Johann, x, 11n1, 15

Tanaka, Tomomi, x, 18, 81
targeted antipoverty programs. *See under* credit for landless poor
targeting bias, 167, 168
Thai Nguyen province, 64
Thailand, 36n11
Tra Vinh province, 32, 64
trade-offs in allocation of land, 19–20
Tran, Thi Que, 15, 17, 18, 20, 29, 32, 35n4, 35n7, 72n6
Truong, Dao Minh, 22

Udry, Christopher, x, 21, 36n10
unemployment and landlessness in Vietnam, 55–58

United States in Vietnam, 5, 13–14
urbanization
  impact of land reforms on, 26
  poverty and, 142, 179
  rising landlessness and, 60, 140–42, 142–43f

van de Walle, Dominique, ix, x, 28, 32, 48, 66, 80, 156n5, 157n8
veterans and disabled, social protection of, 17–18, 20, 43–44, 89
Veteran's Association, 164
VHLSS. *See* Vietnam Household Living Standards Survey
Viet Minh, 13–14
Vietnam. *See* land reform in Vietnam
Vietnam Bank for Social Policies (previously Bank for the Poor), 163
Vietnam Household Living Standards Survey (VHLSS), 38
  2002 survey, 38, 53–59, 54t, 56–57t
  2004 survey, 38
    age cohorts, pseudo-panel based on, 59–60, 70–71t
    antipoverty program participation, 164
    community- and self-assessed welfare, 62–64, 63f, 65f, 169–70, 171–72f
    detailed land module, 60–62
    landlessness and poverty, overall comparisons of, 53–59, 54t, 56–57t
    reallocations in, 102
    rental market, 101, 102
    sources of land, 133, 135f
Vietnam Living Standards Survey (VLSS), 38
  1992/93 survey, 38
    access to credit, 161
    age cohorts, pseudo-panel based on, 59–60, 70–71t
    irrigated land equivalents, calculating, 66–67, 68–69t
    landlessness and poverty, overall comparisons of, 53–59, 54t, 56–57t
    rental market, 101, 102
    welfare impacts of initial land reform, 39–44, 45–47t, 79
  1997/98 survey
    landlessness and poverty, overall comparisons of, 53–59, 54t, 56–57t
    reallocation of land after establishment of land market, 48–52, 49–51t, 102, 103
    rental market, 101
  attrition of households between surveys, 48, 118–19
Vietnam Peasant Union (VPU), 18–19
Vinh Long Ngo, 17, 44
VLSS. *See* Vietnam Living Standards Survey
Vo Van Kiet, 16
VPU (Vietnam Peasant Union), 18–19

wage labor market, 33, 102–03, 123, 136–37, 137–38f
war veterans and disabled, social protection of, 17–18, 20, 43–44, 89
wealth gradient, in landlessness, 124, 129, 131, 153
welfare, community- and self-assessed, in 2004 VHLSS survey, 62–64, 63f, 65f, 169–70, 171–72f
welfare impacts of initial land reform, 4–5, 75–99
  conclusions regarding, 97, 177–78
  consumption-efficient allocation, 77–78, 87–88t, 90, 92, 97
  data and summary statistics used for (VLSS 1992/93), 39–44, 45–47t, 79
  definition of "impact," 75
  definition of welfare/living standards, 2

education, effect of, 86
empirical implementation
  of model, 78–81
levels of consumption,
  inequality, and poverty relative
  to land allocation, 90–97, 91t,
  93–94f, 96t
local cadre member in
  household, effect of, 86, 89
model used in assessing, 76–78,
  97–99
policy concerns regarding, 29
quality of land, model's
  robustness regarding,
  80–81, 90
regional differences in. *See
  specific regions*
regressions for consumption and
  allocated land, 81–90, 82–85t,
  87–88t
size of landholding and living
  standards, relationship
  between, 120–31, 131f
types of land, 41–42
Wiegersma, Nancy, 11n6, 13–15,
  17, 19, 29–31, 33, 35n1–3, 168
women's land rights, 28, 29,
  117, 119
Women's Union, 164
World Bank, x, 1, 11n3, 29, 38,
  39, 157n7, 173n1
Wurfel, David, 18–19

Xuan, Vo-Tong, 14, 17, 19, 31,
  99n3

Yeh, Anthony Gar-On, 27
Youth Union, 164

Zhou, Jian-Ming, 27, 36

ECO-AUDIT
Environmental Benefits Statement

The World Bank is committed to preserving endangered forests and natural resources. The Office of the Publisher has chosen to print *Land in Transition* on recycled paper with 30 percent postconsumer fiber in accordance with the recommended standards for paper usage set by the Green Press Initiative, a nonprofit program supporting publishers in using fiber that is not sourced from endangered forests. For more information, visit www.greenpressinitiative.org.

Saved:
- 7 trees
- 5 million Btu of total energy
- 651 lb. of net greenhouse gases
- 2,701 gal. of waste water
- 347 lb. of solid waste

green press INITIATIVE